Joshua

THE CHALLENGE OF THE PROMISED LAND

Pardes | פרדס
Institute of Jewish Studies

מגיד
MAGGID

Michael Hattin

JOSHUA
THE CHALLENGE OF
THE PROMISED LAND

Pardes Institute of Jewish Studies
Yeshivat Har Etzion
Maggid Books

Joshua
The Challenge of the Promised Land

Maggid Studies in Tanakh – The Stone Edition

First Edition, 2014

Maggid Books
An imprint of Koren Publishers Jerusalem Ltd.

POB 8531, New Milford, CT 06776-8531, USA
& POB 4044, Jerusalem 9104001, Israel
www.korenpub.com

The publication of this book was made possible
through the generous support of *Torah Education in Israel.*

ISBN 978 159 264 304 2, *hardcover*

A CIP catalogue record for this title is
available from the British Library

Printed and bound in the United States

In loving memory of Irving and Beatrice Stone,
who dedicated their lives to the
advancement of Jewish education.
We are proud and honored to continue their legacy.

Their Children, Grandchildren and Great-Grandchildren
Cleveland, Ohio USA

לעילוי נשמת יהושע בן הלל ע״ה

Dedicated in loving memory of
Richard J. Silvera ע״ה

by his children
Hillel, Albert and Michelle

Contents

Preface

The Book of Joshua seamlessly continues the Torah's narrative that ended with the death of Moses. The people of Israel were encamped on the outskirts of Canaan when Moses died at the end of Deuteronomy, finally preparing to enter the Promised Land after a lengthy and lethal delay. As much as the book is a concise record of the trials and triumphs of the people of Israel as they take their first tentative steps to settle the new land, it is also a personal account of Joshua's challenge to succeed his storied mentor as their leader. These two dimensions of the national and the individual, also at play in many other books of the Tanakh, unfold in the Book of Joshua simultaneously.

The basic outline of the Book of Joshua is probably known to many readers from their grade school education, but not all have studied the book from beginning to end. Fewer still have studied it in Hebrew while paying careful attention to vocabulary, grammar and syntax, literary structure, intertextuality, or historical context. Yet all of these form the basis for the fruitful work of the commentaries, ancient as well as modern, and all are critical tools for exploring the book. To neglect any of them is to compromise the potential for a more comprehensive understanding.

Our tradition of text study has been honed over thousands of years and has produced a prodigious and diverse body of secondary and tertiary material that continues to expand to the present day. But all of it is predicated upon one methodological foundation principle that also forms the bedrock for the following study: It is through careful reading and review of the original biblical text that one acquires more profound appreciation of the book and its timeless themes.

The Hebrew text of the Bible is concise, compact and sometimes cryptic, omitting descriptive material that is not directly relevant to the matter at hand. When detail is present, it is not intended as literary artifice for the enjoyment or entertainment of the reader but rather to provide essential meaning-bearing content. Furthermore, interpreting the intent of a biblical passage sometimes hinges upon a few critical words, whose meaning in the original Hebrew may be obscure.

For all of these reasons, a cursory reading of the material can never be sufficient.

ACKNOWLEDGEMENTS

I have had the opportunity of studying and teaching the Book of Joshua a number of times at the Pardes Institute of Jewish Studies in Jerusalem, where I have been privileged to teach for over a decade. I am thankful to my students and to my colleagues who have raised so many thoughtful questions and provided so many meaningful insights, challenging me to sharpen my own ideas, to frame them more precisely, and to revise them in order to yield a more coherent and consistent reading.

I would also like to acknowledge the generosity of spirit of Yeshivat Har Etzion and its innovative Israel Koschitzky Virtual Beit Midrash. Much of the material in this book was first committed to writing as a series of articles for the online learning of the Book of Joshua, and the Yeshiva has kindly allowed me to make use of it for the purposes of the present study. During my time at the Yeshiva, where a rigorous and thoughtful approach to Torah study was applied not only to Talmud and Halakha but also to Tanakh, I had the honor of hearing lectures from some of Israel's most brilliant teachers. I am indebted to all of them.

A special thanks is due to the dedicated team of Maggid Books, led by Rabbi Reuven Ziegler, for their professionalism, attention to detail, and consummate skill. In this regard, I am indebted to Matthew

Miller for his initial backing for the project and his ongoing support until its completion.

At this time I would like to express my profoundest gratitude to those who were most instrumental in inspiring me to turn ideas into text. My wife Rivka and our five children – Elchanan, Akiva, Hillel, Leeba, and Miriam – are an endless source of encouragement and strength.

Michael Hattin
Alon Shevut
Kislev 5775/November 2014

ෆෆෆ

The author gratefully acknowledges the following people, who gener-
ously dedicated their support for this project:

In loving memory of our dear parents:

שמואל יצחק בן מנחם מנדל	אריה לייב בן חיים
הכהן בינהקר ז"ל	ספקטור ז"ל
ורעייתו	ורעייתו
שרה בת פנחס הכהן מבית	שיינדל בת זנוועל מבית
ברכר ז"ל	קאופמן ז"ל

Dr. Leo Lyon and Janet Spector   *Dr. Samuel Israel and Sadie Beinhaker*

ת.נ.צ.ב.ה.

Philip Howard and Constance Kaufman Beinhaker

פנחס צבי בן שמואל יצחק הכהן ורעייתו חנה בת אריה לייב

*"Appoint a teacher for yourself; acquire a friend for yourself;
and judge everyone favorably" (Pirke Avot 1:6).
Throughout the years, you have had a major impact on our lives
as our valued mentor, our caring friend, and as an important role
model of derekh Hashem.
May you go from strength to strength.
Michael and Carol Dean and Family*

*In memory of our beloved grandparents
Aharon & Sarah Feiga Hattin and
Louis (Shmuel Leib) & Phoebe (Leeba) Markowitz
and in memory of our dear cousin Virginia (Tamara) Schlifer.
The Hattin Siblings:
Lisa, Adrienne, Simone, Alan, Michael, and families*

Introduction

The Book of Joshua is the first book in the division of Tanakh known as *Nevi'im*, and its contents describe the entry into Canaan and the settlement of the land by the Israelite tribes. "Tanakh" is a Hebrew acronym for Torah (Pentateuch), *Nevi'im* (Prophets), and *Ketuvim* (Writings), the three components of the Hebrew Bible.

The Book of Joshua is named after its protagonist, the loyal disciple of Moses, who eventually succeeds his esteemed mentor as leader of the tribes of Israel. Although the book provides very few details about Joshua's personal life, its events are tightly bound up with the span of his lifetime and it is Joshua's death that constitutes the book's conclusion. Chronologically, the book succeeds the last verses of the Book of Deuteronomy, beginning its account in the immediate aftermath of Moses' death with the tribes of Israel poised to enter the Promised Land.

The contents of the book can be conveniently broken down into several units:

Chapters 1–5: This section introduces us to Joshua, familiarizes us with the enormity of the challenges faced by him and by the people of Israel on the eve of entering the land, and consciously evokes the national failures of the past in order to highlight the triumphs of the present.

Chapters 6–12: In these chapters, the people of Israel embark on the wars of conquest, first capturing Jericho and then defeating two coalitions of Canaanite kings from the southern and northern hill country respectively. The section concludes with a list of the conquered tyrants.

Chapters 13–21: In this unit, the conquered territories are distributed by lot among the tribes, with the boundaries demarcated according to topographical features and place names. The cities of refuge and the Levitical cities are carefully enumerated at the end of this section.

Chapters 22–24: The book's last unit opens with the return of the tribes of Reuben, Gad, and half Menashe to the Transjordan. It ends with two parting addresses by Joshua to the people of Israel in which he exhorts them to follow in God's ways so that they might succeed in the new land.

Any serious study of the Book of Joshua involves not only grappling with textual difficulties and the intricacies of exegesis, but also reflecting upon the many foundational issues that are introduced by its narratives. These include defining the confluence of divine intervention and human initiative, understanding the physical geography as well as the metaphysical sanctity of the land of Israel, attempting to delineate the parameters of just warfare, contrasting individual choices with communal responsibilities, and recognizing the awesome struggle of forging disparate tribes into the united people of Israel. Before considering any of these issues, however, a number of preliminary remarks and observations are in order.

TRANSLATIONS

The biblical Book of Joshua is available in many different translations. There are a number of good English translations of the text available, but it is critical to bear in mind that a translation of any sort cannot take the place of the original Hebrew text. Biblical Hebrew is a rich and layered language, full of subtle nuances and multiple gradations of meaning. A translation cannot but convey only one out of a large number of possible readings of the text, and perhaps not the best reading at that. A translation is itself an interpretation that offers the reader a window into the text, but it can never replace a study of the text in its original language. Critical literary and interpretive elements such as alliteration, word play, and meter are difficult to reproduce in translation, and most translations can therefore convey only an incomplete reading.

Additionally, the Hebrew Bible chooses its words with extreme care. Recurring expressions and phrases, both within a book as well as with reference to the larger context of the other books of the Tanakh, often carry the possibility of additional interpretation. This is a possibility that simply does not exist in most translations, where no attempt is made to link remote references by utilizing a vocabulary of equivalent terms.

To offer a striking example, the ark of Noah is described in the biblical text by the word *teva* (Gen. 6:14). The only other usage of this term in the entire Hebrew Scriptures occurs in the context of Yokheved's poignant attempt to save the life of her infant son Moses by placing him in a box of reeds, a *teva*, and then positioning it among the reeds on the Nile River's edge (Ex. 2:3). Studying the text in translation (in this case, that of the *New JPS Translation*, Philadelphia, 1988) indicates that Noah built an "ark," and that Yokheved prepared a "basket," and suggests that there is absolutely no connection between the two episodes. Reading the text in the original Hebrew, however, in which the same word *teva* is used in both passages, raises the possibility that there is in fact a fundamental link between them.

In biblical Hebrew, a sea-going vessel is often called an *oniya* (for example, see Gen. 49:13, Deut. 28:68, and Jonah 1:3), or rarely a *sefina* (as in Jonah 1:5), but never, barring the context of Noah and Yokheved, a *teva*. What is the structural difference between a *teva* and the vessels described by these other terms? Rabbi Abraham Ibn Ezra (twelfth century, Spain) remarks that with respect to Noah, the Torah uses this choice of words for the following reason: "*Teva* rather than *sefina*, because this craft does not have the form of an *oniya*, and has no oars or rudder" (Ibn Ezra on Gen. 6:14).

The significance of this unusual maritime deficiency is quite obvious. The lack of oars or a rudder for the ark effectively renders it incapable of being steered. The rising flood waters will bear the craft, but Noah will play no role in piloting it or in directing it to land. Only God's merciful providence will ensure that the ark successfully weathers the torrential flood waters and is set down intact on safe shores. God alone is the guiding power who drives the ark through the churning deep and steers it clear of mishap.

In a similar vein, when Yokheved places her infant son into his *teva* and releases him to the unknown, she is not simply attempting to save his life by aiding his escape down river. Her seemingly hopeless gesture, after all other possibilities of concealing Moses have been exhausted, actually represents an act of great faith. By constructing this craft for him and deliberately locating it among the reeds at water's edge, she is actually entrusting the life of her child to the merciful God. It is He who will care for Moses and lovingly guide him into the unexpectedly tender arms of Pharaoh's own daughter. Here again, the *teva* represents God's role in shaping human destiny, and by entering the realm of the *teva* we entrust our survival to a transcendent Being who cares, preserves, sustains, and saves.

Of course, a reading such as that offered above is not possible in translation except as a fanciful literary leap of imagination, since there is no reason to textually link "arks" with "baskets." It is only in the original Hebrew that a meaningful connection emerges. In our study of the Book of Joshua we will come across further examples of this critically important interpretive tool.

CHAPTER AND VERSE

The conventional numbering of the biblical text into chapters and verses is not the product of Jewish tradition. In the handwritten Torah scroll, for example, the content is divided into paragraphs and sections according to visual breaks in the text. These breaks consist in the main of two types: a minor division signified by a space between two paragraphs on the same line, and a major division signified by a blank space that concludes a line. Verses may be regarded as separate sentences, but are not numbered.

It was Jerome, a prominent fourth-century Church father responsible for translating the Hebrew Bible, Apocrypha, and New Testament into Latin, who first introduced the basis for the system of chapters that is now universally accepted. His translation, undertaken for the benefit of the common people, was known as the Vulgate (from the Latin "vulgata," meaning "popular"), and became the official Scriptures of the Roman

Catholic Church. Stephen Langton, a thirteenth-century English cardinal and later the Archbishop of Canterbury, refined Jerome's work by dividing the Old Testament books of the Vulgate into the chapters and verses as we now know them. Ironically, the impetus for his work was the desire to facilitate disputations of the Scriptures with the Jews, by introducing a more uniform method for citing references. In any case, these divisions into chapter and verse were accepted by all subsequent translations and, with the invention of the printing press, became an indispensable feature of the printed Hebrew editions as well.

Often, Jerome's divisions are at odds with the traditional Jewish separations of the biblical text. Thus, for example, chapter seven of the Book of Joshua begins with Akhan's trespass and theft of booty from the conquest of Jericho. There is no such division in the Hebrew text, where the verse describing Akhan's indiscretion is connected to the previous one describing Joshua's spreading fame in the aftermath of the victory over Jericho. Some of the modern Jewish translations of the Hebrew Bible (such as the *Jerusalem Bible* by Koren Publishers, Jerusalem, 1992) have attempted to remedy the situation by incorporating the traditional divisions into their translated text.

It is important to realize that sometimes, the text's internal divisions may be critical tools in helping us evaluate its intent. After all, a verse does not stand on its own but must be understood as part of the larger context. The interpretation of a passage may hinge upon how it is connected to the verses that precede and follow it. Thus, it will be necessary for us to bear in mind that the chapter/verse divisions are not immutable, and are in fact unsubstantiated from the point of view of Jewish tradition. We should also not be surprised if occasionally interpretations are offered that seem to conflict with the chapter divisions themselves.

MODERN CONTRIBUTIONS

The modern age has witnessed an explosion of knowledge concerning the world of the Bible. Archaeology has unearthed and revived ancient and forgotten civilizations that had been known only from the biblical text, paleography has deciphered ancient Near Eastern languages long ago extinct, stratigraphy has provided the possibility of correlating far-flung discoveries to provide a more solid historical framework, and intense study of cognate languages has provided much assistance (and conjecture) for interpreting unusual biblical terms and references otherwise inexplicable. Modern literary analysis has searched for underlying structure, characterization and plot, tonal qualities, and cadence. All of this information and analysis sheds much light on the biblical text, and to ignore it is to overlook an important dimension of biblical exegesis that was, sadly, unavailable to the classic commentaries.

At the same time, these modern tools have often been used for quite a different purpose, to bolster arguments both for and against the authenticity of the biblical accounts. Some archaeologists have enthusiastically donned the mantle of polemicists, using the conclusions of their work to undermine the biblical account. More significantly, they have thrust aside the God silent and steadfast behind the text, with all of His moral, ethical, and spiritual demands. Proponents of various critical schools with a focus on historicity and textual origins have deconstructed the apparently cohesive narratives to reveal a multiplicity of faceless authors and unskilled editors. Biblical scholars introduced emendations into the text ostensibly to reconcile what they perceived to be divergences and inconsistencies, but their approach frequently hinges upon charging the text with a literary superficiality that is ludicrous. In the process, they have often relegated the underlying message of the narrative, its profound pith, to the proverbial dustbin.

The Tanakh is, at its core, a sacred document that describes the ongoing interaction between God and humanity, between God and the people of Israel. It is a document that continuously challenges us to ask penetrating questions that relate to the essence of human nature and to the purpose and meaning of existence. Its ancient but timeless words kindle the spiritual yearning that glows in every human heart, the longing for God, for goodness and a better world. No assault on the text can ever rob it of this transcendent quality. To approach the Tanakh as a secular historical account or else as a fanciful mythology, only to then reject it on the grounds of inaccuracy or else absurdity, divests it of its fundamental character and does a grave disservice to both text and reader.

In short, this book does not look towards archeology or other modern disciplines to substantiate the account of the Book of Joshua. The divine element that animates the text requires no external proof for its validation. However, where archeology or literary analysis can shed light on properly understanding a biblical text or event, those contributions are cautiously embraced, bearing in mind the limitations stated above. In the end, the veracity of the text and the "objective truths" provided by modern scholarship must be reconciled, but tentative facts based upon inconclusive findings (or lack thereof) can be calmly ignored.

TERMS, TRANSLITERATIONS, AND READING AHEAD

In general, this study will adopt English translations for place names and personal names. Thus, Yehoshua will be referred to as Joshua, Moshe as Moses, Yericho as Jericho and Yarden as the Jordan River. Additionally, biblical books will be referred to by their English names, such as Genesis, Exodus, and Leviticus. With respect to grammatical syntax, English conventions will be adopted. Thus, for example, the "Emorim" (Hebrew plural for "Emori") will be referred to as the Amorites, utilizing English language plural endings.

This study is not meant to stand alone as a substitute for a close and careful reading of the biblical Book of Joshua. It is highly recommended that those who are not familiar at all with that book's contents avail themselves of the opportunity to read it alongside this study. It will not be possible to recount at length every episode occurring in the primary text. No such assumptions, however, will be made concerning readers' familiarity with external sources.

COMMENTARIES

The Hebrew Bible is one of the most studied books in human history. It has been intensively learned for millennia and has inspired innumerable commentaries. The earliest rabbinic interpretations that have survived as authorized texts are from the late Second Temple period (first century, CE) and there has been a continuum of exegesis until the present day. The medieval period constitutes one of the most fruitful epochs insofar as commentary is concerned, and our study will focus on some of the luminaries of this age.

While many readers have heard of Rashi, who lived in France in the eleventh century, fewer are familiar with Rabbi David Kimḥi, who lived in Provence in the thirteenth century. Known by the acronym

Radak, he wrote extensively on the Hebrew Bible and laid the ground-work for Hebrew grammar as we now know it. These two commentaries will receive particular attention, though not in a comprehensive way. There will be no attempt made to lay out their respective methodologies in a systematic fashion, but only to give the reader an indication of how they, and other commentaries like them, were careful readers of the text. The basis of any true understanding of the work of the commentaries in our tradition begins with a thorough and thoughtful reading of the biblical text. To read the Tanakh carefully is to be sensitive to issues of a linguistic, grammatical, or thematic nature and to anticipate the sorts of questions that the commentaries raise. To read the medieval commentaries carefully is to appreciate that they rarely provide us with a complete thesis on any given issue. Instead, they extend to us an invitation to explore matters further.

Joshua 1:1–9

Transitions

The Book of Joshua may be said to commence where the Torah, or the Five Books of Moses, concludes:

> It came to pass after the death of Moses the servant of God, that God said to Joshua son of Nun, Moses' loyal disciple: "Moses My servant has died. Now, arise and traverse the Jordan River, you and this entire people, to the land that I am giving to them, to the people of Israel. Every place wherein you will tread I will give to you, just as I said to Moses. From the wilderness and this Lebanon until the great river [Euphrates], all of the land of the Hittites up to the Great Sea where the sun sets [the Mediterranean] shall be your borders." (Josh. 1:1–4)

These introductory verses of the book are transitional, narrating the succession in leadership that has recently taken place. Moses is dead, and God has chosen Joshua to bring the people into the land. But it has been some time since Joshua was formally selected to eventually succeed his master Moses (Num. 27:12–23), and we have known almost from the beginning of Moses' leadership that Joshua was his close disciple. Who exactly is this Joshua, the protagonist of our book? In order to address this question, we must briefly turn our attention to the Torah texts that serve as the necessary background to the Book of Joshua.

A BRIEF HISTORY OF JOSHUA'S EXPLOITS

Joshua was introduced for the first time at the clash with the marauding tribe of Amalek, who had mercilessly attacked the weary and worn-out people of Israel soon after they had left the land of Egypt some forty years earlier (Ex. 17:8–16). There, he had been appointed by Moses and bidden to "arise and select men to go out and give battle against Amalek," a contest that Joshua waged successfully. He appeared again as Moses' faithful student at the sin of the Golden Calf, when he waited expectantly, at a distance from the people's encampment, for the return of his master from the encounter with God at Sinai (32:17). In the aftermath of that debacle, when Moses relocated his tent to the outside of the Israelite encampment, Joshua was for the first time referred to as Moses' protégé or *mesharet*, who "never leaves his master's tent" (33:11). We met him next at the incident of Eldad and Medad, vociferously defending Moses' honor (Num. 11:28–29). Finally, we anxiously followed his appointment as one of the twelve spies, and later marveled at his steadfast refusal, along with Caleb son of Yefuneh, to adopt the self-defeating report of the other ten (13:8, 14:6–10). It was in the aftermath of this event that Joshua's place in biblical history was assured, for God indicated at that time that he and Caleb would be spared from the decree that condemned the generation of the Exodus to perish in the wilderness. Towards the end of the wilderness wanderings Joshua again emerged, this time at Moses' side, as the latter conveyed his poignant song of farewell to the people of Israel (Deut. 32:44).

Taken together, the above catalogue of references indicates that Joshua had been present, involved, and active in every single formative event that the people experienced during the course of the previous forty years. He never strayed from Moses' side and was always a source of support to him, as well as an exemplar to the people of steadfast trust in God. He demonstrated devotion but also showed independence, initiative, and leadership. Taking our cue from this background material, we would have to conclude that there was no one more worthy than

The Land of Canaan

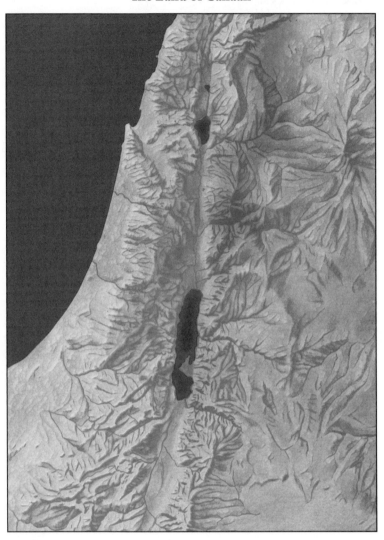

he to become Moses' successor as leader of Israel and no one more capable of transmitting Moses' teachings. It is therefore no wonder that when aged Moses asked God to choose a worthy successor in his stead to lead the people into the land, that Joshua was immediately selected (Num. 27:12-23).

WHAT'S IN A NAME?

Significantly, Joshua's name indicates salvation or deliverance, from the root יש״ע, and it was Moses himself who altered the original name of Hosea to Joshua (Num. 13:16). This second form, abruptly introduced on the eve of the aborted mission of the spies, includes an added emphasis on God, and can be literally translated as "God will save." The subtle modification was not only an expression of Moses' wish that his loyal student achieve success on the mission, but also an indication that Moses saw in him great promise, that Joshua would be the instrument by which God would deliver His people. Presumably, though, Hosea's name change took place much earlier, when he first became the disciple of Moses.[1] If so, introducing the name change on the eve of the mission of the spies may constitute an ironic subtext to the story. When Moses renamed his loyal disciple Joshua, meaning "God will save through him," did he already realize that as an indirect result of the episode of the spies that was about to transpire, he would be denied entry into the land and his leadership would be prematurely terminated? Might Moses have already intuited that Joshua would indeed succeed him and that under Joshua's command God would deliver the people of Israel?

Nahmanides, the great thirteenth-century Spanish commentator, contributes another layer to the matter of Joshua's name, by directing our attention to his unusual surname. Strictly speaking, we may have expected Joshua son of Nun to be referred to in the original Hebrew as "Yehoshua *ben* Nun," where "ben" means "son" or "son of." Instead, the text invariably refers to him as Yehoshua *bin* Nun, vowelized with the *ḥirik* or "long e" instead of the *segol* or "short e." Nahmanides suggests that the variation is grammatically sound, and then adduces a small number of other scriptural examples such as Proverbs 30:1, which reads, "The words of Agur bin Yakke." Nevertheless, he adds an important insight:

---

1. Compare Joshua's name change to that of Abraham and Sarah in Genesis 17 or to Joseph's in Genesis 41:45. The former indicates a divinely-mandated change in destiny; the latter, the forging of a special relationship between the sovereign and his subject. Joshua's name change by Moses contains elements of both.

The people would refer to him in this way out of respect, for he was the most illustrious of Moses' disciples. Thus, they would call him "Binun," meaning "the wise one," for there was none as wise as he. (Nahmanides on Ex. 33:11)

Nahmanides perceptively connects "bin Nun" to "binun," construing "son of Nun" into a single word from the Hebrew root בי"ן that signifies comprehension, understanding, and wisdom. By this he means that the people of Israel intentionally pronounced Joshua's surname in a way that could be interpreted not only as "son of Nun" but, more importantly, as "the wise."

To sum up thus far, the biblical texts that serve as the background to the Book of Joshua make it quite clear that Joshua was for a long time the most suitable candidate to one day take Moses' place at the helm of the people of Israel. Although we might have expected him to have been waiting impatiently in the wings for his master's demise, Joshua never demonstrated anything other than absolute fidelity to Moses, complete devotion to the people, and utter subservience to God. During the long buildup to his assumption of leadership, he exhibited none of the pretentious, arching ambition and engaged in none of the degrading, devious machinations that characterize many aspirants to leadership until this very day.

JOSHUA'S ROLE IN COMPLETING THE TORAH

A measure of the esteem that the early sources accorded to Joshua may be gauged by the well-known and remarkable tradition that ascribes to him the completion of the final eight verses of the Torah. It will be recalled that the Book of Deuteronomy draws to a close with Moses' eloquent blessing of Israel and then God's inexorable invitation to Moses to ascend Mount Nevo in order to die:

Moses ascended from the plains of Moav to the peak of Mount Nevo opposite Jericho, and God showed him the whole land … God said to him: "This is the land that I swore to Abraham, Isaac, and Jacob … I have shown it to you with your own eyes, but you shall not cross over to it." There Moses the servant of

God died in the land of Moav, by God's decree...the people of
Israel cried for Moses at the plains of Moav for thirty days, until
the days of mourning for Moses were completed. Joshua son
of Nun was full of the spirit of wisdom, for Moses had placed
his hands upon him. The people of Israel hearkened to him,
just as God had commanded Moses. There arose no another
prophet in Israel like Moses, whom God had known face to
face. (Deut. 34:1–10)

The Talmud relates:

The verse states that, "there Moses the servant of God died." Is
it possible that Moses had died and yet he wrote the verses that
follow? Rather, Moses composed up to this point, and Joshua
completed the Torah. So says R. Judah. Said to him R. Simeon:
Is it possible that the Torah lacked even a single letter when
Moses commanded the Levites to "take this book of the Torah
and place it next to the Ark of the Covenant of the Lord your
God" (Deut. 31:26)? Rather, up until this point [describing Moses'
death] God dictated the text and Moses repeated it and wrote.
After this point, God dictated the text and Moses wrote it while
in tears. (Bava Batra 15a)

According to the opinion of R. Judah, it is Joshua who is responsible
for completing the text of the Torah. This is the view that the Talmud
adopts earlier in its discussion as definitive (Bava Batra 14b). The doc-
trinal ramifications of R. Judah's opinion are staggering, for the Mosaic
transcription of the five books in their entirety is regarded by traditional
sources as the touchstone of the text's divinity and authority. Moses
talked with God, and God in turn dictated His eternal message to Moses,
as a master speaks to his loyal and exacting scribe. To include Joshua in
this unparalleled process, statistically minor though his contribution may
have been, speaks worlds about the man's stature and standing. Indeed,
it is obvious from R. Judah's reading that Joshua had God's conviction
that he would succeed, for the lengthy, winding path of his leadership
career was still before him, and much could have happened along the

way to compromise and to discredit the divine selection of Joshua to complete the Torah's transcription.

R. Judah's opinion also casts the transitional nature of the beginning of the Book of Joshua in an entirely different light, for it now emerges that the texts of the Book of Deuteronomy and our book are actually regarded as a single overlapping unit, with Joshua's authorship bridging both. The implication of this tradition is that Moses' leadership and that of Joshua his successor are to be regarded as a seamless continuum. In essence, Joshua does not simply come to replace Moses as leader of Israel, but somehow to embody the spirit of Moses' mission. Joshua is not simply Moses' authority continued; he is also the bearer of Moses' legacy as lawgiver and servant of God.[2]

BE STRONG AND COURAGEOUS

The above analysis may be helpful in explaining a recurring phrase that emphasizes the great challenge facing Joshua at this critical juncture:

> No man shall stand before you all of the days of your life. I will be with you just as I was with Moses; I will neither let you go nor leave you. *Be strong and courageous,* for you will cause this people to settle the land that I swore to their ancestors to give them. Only *be very strong and courageous* to observe and fulfill in accordance with all of the teaching commanded to you by Moses My servant, do not stray from it neither to the right nor to the left, in order that you will be successful in all of your endeavors. The words of this Torah will not depart out of your mouth, for you shall meditate upon it day and night so that you will observe to do all that is recorded in it, for only then will you be successful and triumphant. Did I not command you to *be strong and courageous*? Do not be afraid or terrified, for the Lord your God is with you wherever you go. (Josh. 1:5–9)

---

2. Compare to the view of some nineteenth-century critical scholars that the Book of Joshua was originally joined to the Torah to form a Hexateuch or "Six Books."

The expression "be strong and courageous" is mentioned in this short passage three times. By carefully considering the context of each of the expressions, Rashi detects three discrete components to Joshua's mission that will require special perseverance: (1) settling the people in the new land, (2) carefully observing the commands of the Torah, (3) engaging in warfare to conquer the Canaanites. Obviously, these three elements are all intertwined, for Joshua's failure in one will hamper if not preclude his success in the others.

This emphatic phrase of reassurance and encouragement occurs only fourteen times in all of the Tanakh, and of those, seven are addressed to Joshua. Of the additional four mentioned outside our immediate context, two are spoken by Moses and God respectively (Deut. 31:7, 23), as Joshua is formally invested with leadership, and another is spoken by the tribes of Israel in response to his first directives as their chief (Josh. 1:18). It therefore seems that Joshua must be encouraged in his task from all sides: Moses his mentor, God his benefactor, and Israel his constituents.

Later in biblical history, the same phrase is employed by David to reassure his young and inexperienced son Solomon, as the latter prepares to ascend the throne and to undertake the awesome task of building the Temple (I Chron. 22:13, I Chron. 28:20). Later still, Hezekiah, the eighth-century BCE King of Judea, uses these words to raise the flagging spirits of the inhabitants of Jerusalem when the menacing Assyrian hordes threaten to overwhelm their weakened state (II Chron. 32:7). It should therefore be clear that the expression "be strong and courageous" is invoked when there is every reason to feel weak, inadequate, overwhelmed, and discouraged.

The inference of the above is that everyone recognizes that Joshua stands confronted by an awesome mission. Not only must he lead the people into the land, grant them victory over their foes, and establish the foundations for moral and ethical government, but he must do all of that while laboring in Moses' long shadow. How awesome is the task of actualizing a national destiny first spelled out to Moses at Sinai (Ex. 19:5–6): "You shall be My treasured people from among all of the nations, My kingdom of priests and holy nation." God, Moses, the people of Israel, all reassure Joshua and bid him to "be strong and courageous," not to be overawed by the daunting mandate, not to be fearful to exercise his newly-acquired authority, not to be overwhelmed by the task of forging disparate tribes with sectarian concerns into a unified nation, not to be intimidated by the unavoidable prospect of conflict, warfare, and bloodshed. As if that were not enough, Joshua stands in need of reassurance also because he has been called upon to complete the work of Moses – the most storied leader in the history of the people of Israel, the only man to have brought tyrants down low and to have gone up to receive God's word "face to face," the most humble of men and yet the most supremely confident in the justness of his cause. How will Joshua succeed?

Joshua 1:10–18

Joshua Assumes Leadership

Having briefly surveyed Joshua's biography, we must now examine how Joshua goes about solidifying his leadership and living up to its mandate, instilling the people with direction and confidence. Recall the transitional nature of the first verses of the book and their implication of the awesome challenges that faced Joshua as he finally took hold of the reigns of leadership (Josh. 1:2): "Moses My servant has died. Now, arise and traverse this Jordan River, you and this entire people, to the land that I am giving to them, to the people of Israel." Not only was Joshua called upon to lead the people into the new land, settle them, and begin the process of their unification into a nation state, but he was also expected to deftly fill the overwhelming vacuum created by Moses' passing.

Bear in mind that Joshua's internal struggle to overcome fear and doubt is mirrored by the larger challenge of the whole people of Israel. They too stand confronted by the prospect of an awesome transition, finally and irrevocably leaving behind the simple, nomadic, and contemplative life of wandering tribes in the wilderness for the complex, settled, and concrete life of an established nation in Canaan. Clearly, their relationship with God must evolve accordingly, and a careful reading of the text will reveal the first, tentative steps in that direction.

THE FIRST COMMAND

> Joshua commanded the officers of the people, saying: "Pass
> through the midst of the camp and command the people: 'Pre-
> pare your provisions, for in three days' time you will traverse the
> Jordan River in order to inherit the land that the Lord your God
> gives to you as an inheritance.'" (Josh. 1:10–11)

With this brief directive, Joshua sets into motion an intricate series of
preparations that will culminate in the crossing of the Jordan River. In this
first interaction with the people as their leader, Joshua leaves no doubt
that he is in control of the situation and that he has a plan. The people
are told what they must do and what is going to happen next – there is
no ambiguity.

Significantly, although explicit scriptural proof is lacking, Rashi
cites an early tradition maintaining that Joshua's directive to prepare
provisions was pronounced to the people on the very same day that
the traditional thirty-day mourning period over Moses' death was
concluded (Deut. 34:8–9). In other words, Joshua wasted no time at
all in solidifying his command and impelling the people towards their
destiny. The period of mourning over Moses' death could have broken the momentum of the journey towards the land, and so Joshua
was careful to avoid that pitfall by seizing the first possible opportunity for going forward. As we shall see, the initiative and alacrity that
are evident in this, his first exploit as leader, are characteristic of his
overall approach.

"IN THREE DAYS' TIME"

While we consider the texts as an account of Joshua and his challenges,
we must remain cognizant of the larger picture, for the book is also the
story of the people of Israel. Let us consider, for example, the three-day
period during which the people were to prepare for their traversal of the
Jordan River. This particular time frame occurs in the Tanakh in other
contexts that together may shed light on the use of the motif here. The
following list of parallels should not be regarded as exhaustive:

On the third day, Abraham looked up and saw the place from afar. (Gen. 22:4)

On the third day, it was Pharaoh's birthday, and he made a feast for all of his servants. (Gen. 40:20)

Be prepared for the third day, for on the third day God will descend upon Mount Sinai for all of the people to see. (Ex. 19:11)

On the third day, Esther donned her royal garments and she stood in the inner court of the King. (Est. 5:1)

The first reference to three days' time is taken from the account of the *Akeda* or binding of Isaac. God had commanded Abraham, in the supreme test of the latter's trust, to take his only son to the land of Moriah in order to offer him as a sacrifice on one of its peaks. Abraham, his heart heavy with anxiety but steeled by steadfast faith, journeyed for three days until he reached the designated location. There, he prepared to carry out God's will, but at the last moment God stayed his hand.

The second example is from the story of Joseph's unjust incarceration at the hands of his master Potiphar, one of Pharaoh's chief ministers. While in prison, Joseph correctly interpreted the dreams of the butler and baker, foreseeing that in three days Pharaoh would release both of them from prison on the occasion of his birthday. The butler would be restored to his former position, while the baker would be unceremoniously hanged. Joseph implored the butler to bring his case before the king so that he too could be freed.

The third citation is from the account of the theophany at Sinai. Moses told the people to prepare themselves for the third day, for at that time God would manifest His awesome presence to them and proclaim His guiding words, the Ten Utterances.

The fourth reference, the only one of the above that is post-exilic, describes Queen Esther's bold and courageous plan to unmask the evil Haman and undermine his plan to annihilate the Jewish people. After three days of penitential fasting, she approached the king without being officially summoned, in an act that could have incurred the death penalty.

It is quite clear from the above examples (and others besides)[1] that "three days" in Tanakh implies a period of intense introspection, spiritual reflection, and concentrated preparation for an anticipated event that is potentially transformative. Thus, Abraham had much to ponder during his three-day journey, for he knew that at the designated time his relationship with his singular and beloved God as well as his adored and only son would undergo a quantum shift. Joseph, the butler, and the baker all anticipated the third day with anxious trepidation: Joseph yearned for freedom, the butler for restoration, and the baker dreaded his imminent death. The people encamped at Sinai and keenly prepared for the stated goal of their exodus, for God had told them that He would make them His own by transmitting His teachings to them; the third day therefore promised to transform their former status and to initiate their future destiny. Finally, Esther's three-day fast, filled with tension while charged with desperate hope, came to an end as she risked her life for her people by approaching the king unannounced.

Returning to our context, it is clear that Joshua's directive to the people to prepare for three days is not promulgated for simply practical reasons. Rather, during that three-day period of preparation, the people of Israel have an opportunity to reflect upon the events of the previous forty years: their abject slavery and sudden liberation, their despondency while wandering in the wilderness even while bearing the pledge of a new land, their shedding of complete dependency upon God, and the donning in its place of autonomous choice. For three days they will not only prepare their provisions but also ponder the past that they will soon leave behind and the future that they must embrace.

In our context, the climax of this three-day preparatory period will be the crossing of the Jordan River. Although we will later have opportunity to consider this momentous event in its own right, for now it is sufficient to note that to cross the Jordan River represents

---

1. See, for example, Genesis 42:18, II Samuel 1:2, I Kings 12:5, II Kings 20:5, Hosea 6:1-2, Ezra 8:31-32.

for Israel the potential for an inner transformation as profound as that experienced by their ancestor Abraham some five hundred years earlier. When Abraham was first summoned by God to abandon the land of Mesopotamia, his birthplace of Ur, and his family of incorrigible idolaters, he made that break by crossing the Euphrates and setting his sights on Canaan. The three-day period of preparation is therefore an opportunity for contemplation and introspection that concludes with a life-altering event.

To conclude this section, we raise a methodological point: By recognizing that "three days" is a motif that occurs in other biblical narratives, we introduce an important tool of interpretation. We are already aware that in our text tradition, commentaries interpret the text just as the ancient rabbis did before them. But now we note that the earliest interpretations of the biblical text are actually those of the Bible *interpreting itself*. The Tanakh does this by subtly utilizing common phrasing, imagery, or literary elements in different narratives, thus drawing our attention to the connections that may exist between far-flung contexts.

REUBEN, GAD, AND THE HALF TRIBE OF MENASHE

Having issued his directive to the people, Joshua now turns his attention to the so-called "Two and One-Half Tribes" and demands that they keep their word. In language that is almost identical to the Torah's account (see Num. 32), he reminds these tribes of their obligations towards the rest of the nation:

> To the tribe of Reuben, Gad, and half Menashe, Joshua said the following: "Remember the thing that Moses, God's servant, commanded you, saying – 'The Lord your God will grant you repose and give you this land.' Your wives, children, and flocks will remain in the land that Moses gave to you on the other side of the Jordan River, while all of your mighty men of war shall cross over before your brethren in order to help them. When God grants your brethren repose like you, so that they too inherit the land that the Lord your God gives them, only then shall you return to the land of your inheritance that Moses, God's servant, granted you on the eastern side of the Jordan River." (Josh. 1:12–15)

Recall that as the people of Israel approached the Jordan River from the east in their march towards the land, the two mighty Amorite kings, Siḥon and Og, the regional superpowers that controlled the extensive and fertile highlands east of the Jordan River, engaged them in battle. Moses and Israel defeated the two and conquered their territory. At that time, Reuben and Gad, tribes with extensive flocks, approached Moses and requested to remain east of the Jordan River in order to settle the lands. Initially, Moses, fearing a disastrous recurrence of the episode of the spies, expressed great consternation. Once he was convinced that these tribes would solemnly commit their warriors to cross over the Jordan River and assist in conquering the land of Canaan, he acceded to their request and even assigned part of Menashe to the eastern lands. These tribes swore a binding oath, and Moses entrusted Joshua, Elazar the Priest, and the remaining tribal chiefs with enforcing its provisions (Num. 32:28–30).

Joshua now invokes the terms of that oath and calls for its implementation. Significantly, in his brief remarks over the course of three verses, Joshua is careful to refer to Moses no less than three times, recalling the original oath with each mention. The overall effect is to suggest that the two and one-half tribes are called upon to comply because to do otherwise is to reject Moses' legacy, for it is Joshua who now stands in Moses' place. The potency of Joshua's leadership depends upon his ability to successfully take the place of Moses, and he therefore indicates that the objective of his rule will be to fulfill Moses' mandate. Reuben, Gad, and half Menashe indicate their readiness to comply by also recalling Moses:

> We will do everything that you command, and go wherever you send us. Just as we listened to Moses we shall listen to you, only may God be with you *as he was with Moses*! Any man who rebels against your command and fails to observe your words will be put to death. Be only strong and courageous! (Josh. 1:16–18)

In these eighteen opening verses of the book, Moses' name is mentioned no less than eleven times, an unusual concentration even for the lawgiver. Six of those references are in the context of God's charge to Joshua, three in the course of Joshua's own remarks to the people, and two in their response to him. Clearly, it is an indication of Moses' enduring memory, and the fervent hopes of God and the people that Joshua will succeed in his stead. The first chapter of the Book of Joshua concludes much as it began, by juxtaposing Moses' memory with the charge to be forceful and brave. The daunting challenges that await Joshua and the people on the other side of the Jordan River will soon have to be confronted, but they can be overcome if the example of Moses' life – his devotion to God, the Torah, and his people – can be followed.

THE TENSION OF TRANSITION

An expression of the tensions inherent in the transition of leadership is captured in a talmudic source, quoted by Rashi with some minor variations:

> During the period of mourning over Moses' death, over three thousand *halakhot* (laws) that had been communicated by him were forgotten by the people. Joshua enquired of God how to resolve them. God responded: "Moses My servant has died, and the Torah is called by his name. To tell you is impossible. Rather, go and preoccupy the people with warfare." (Rashi on Josh. 1:1)

In the more charged version preserved in the Talmud (Temura 16a), when Joshua is unable to restore the lost traditions after Moses' death and must therefore enquire of God, the people of Israel threaten to kill him!

This source captures the people's sentiments surrounding Joshua's succession. Moses was the "man of God," the ideal leader who was so profoundly connected to the deity that during his tenure, there was never a question regarding how to proceed. His death left a void so vast that it seemed incapable of ever being filled. Three thousand *halakhot*, a great number, were already forgotten during the brief thirty-day period of mourning over his demise! Significantly, in spite of Joshua's entreaties, God does not divulge the solution for the forgotten *halakhot*. In effect, the rabbis are intimating that Joshua attempted to take Moses' place and become a lawgiver in the image of his mentor, but was rebuffed by God. It is as if God says: "Moses My servant is dead, and you cannot be another Moses. You must be Joshua, and the guidance that you provide cannot and must not be the same. In Moses' stead, you have been chosen to lead them into the land and to inspire them in battle. The necessities of the hour are different, the needs of the people are no longer the same, and the nature of your leadership must correspondingly adapt. Preoccupy them with the warfare that is the challenge of the hour and do not attempt to restore the Mosaic past."

Joshua 2:1–24

Sending the Spies
to Jericho

The people of Israel are encamped on the eastern side of
the Jordan River. Joshua has already told them to prepare to cross
its meandering course. On the other side of the river, opposite their
encampment, is the gateway to Canaan from the east, the ancient city
of Jericho. Located in the arid Jordan Plain, Jericho is like a verdant
island in a wasteland sea, an oasis fed by a series of underground
springs. Modern study of its ruins has yielded impressive finds and
has determined that the original settlement of Jericho was one of the
first urban concentrations in the ancient world.[1] Its earliest levels have
been dated to the dawn of agriculture, more than ten thousand years
ago. By the time of Joshua, it had already been settled and resettled
many times.

---

1. The first studies of the site in the modern period were made by Charles Warren in
   1868; John Garstang excavated in the early 1930s. The most important excavations
   were carried out by Kathleen Kenyon between 1952 and 1958 on behalf of the British
   School of Archaeology in Jerusalem.

In preparation for Israel's first encounter with the Canaanites, Joshua deems it prudent to first send an expedition of scouts to ascertain the city's defenses as well as the morale of its inhabitants. Of course, his plan calls to mind a similar one initiated by his mentor Moses some forty years earlier. That pivotal mission ended in failure when the majority of the twelve spies returned with a negative report, the people of Israel panicked and demanded to return to Egypt, and God delayed their entry into the land until the generation of the Exodus died out. Joshua himself, as a former chief of the tribe of Ephraim, had been a member of that earlier expedition. He and Caleb son of Yefuneh of the tribe of Judah had been the only two spies who had spoken out in praise of the land and in support of trusting in God to attempt its conquest, but their encouraging words fell on frightened ears. The people, dejected and disheartened by the other spies' disparaging words, threatened to stone the two, and were only deterred by the sudden appearance of God's cloud of glory (Num. 14:10).

No doubt, that debacle was still vivid in Joshua's mind as he prepared to lead the people into Canaan for their second attempt. Let us examine Joshua's plan for sending his spies. By carefully comparing and contrasting it to that of Moses, we shall see how Joshua learned his lessons well, and was in fact very vigilant to avoid the pitfalls that doomed the earlier mission to failure.

AVOIDING DETECTION BY THE PEOPLE OF JERICHO

Joshua quietly [*ḥeresh*] sent two spies from the Sheetim and said: "Go see the land and Jericho." They went and arrived at the home of a harlot [*zona*] whose name was Rahab, and they lodged there. (Josh. 2:1)

It is perfectly understandable that Joshua sends the spies quietly, so that they can secretly infiltrate Jericho and uncover its weaknesses. In fact, some of the early sources quoted by Rashi fancifully read the Hebrew word for "secretly" – *ḥeresh* – as *ḥeress*, meaning "earthenware vessels," and remark that the spies were disguised as ordinary purveyors of pots and utensils, in order to avoid arousing the suspicions of the people of Jericho! While the image of pot sellers may be a fanciful midrashic flourish, Rashi's intent is clear: the spies are to do their utmost to avoid detection by the denizens of Jericho.

According to this reading, the primary purpose of the secrecy surrounding the mission was to ensure that the spies could slip into Jericho undetected, gather the necessary intelligence, and steal away again. This constitutes a marked departure from the spy mission initiated by Moses, where the text provides no indication that the spies were to attempt to conceal their movements or motives from the Canaanites. After all, a group of twelve men traveling together is going to be conspicuous under the best of circumstances. Even if we are to assume that the group split up in order to spy out different regions (as implied by Caleb's visit to Hebron – see Num. 13:22), we do find them all together collecting samples of the land's fruits, that they then convey back in plain sight.

Upon their return, Moses' spies exclaim that they felt as diminutive as grasshoppers in comparison to the towering Canaanite inhabitants, and conclude by remarking that the natives also regarded them as such (Num. 13:33). This indicates that the Canaanites were well aware of the spies' movements but that they apparently did not feel at all threatened by their presence. The implication of all this is that the mission of Moses' spies was not so much a military assignment as a morale booster. After all, hadn't God already reassured the people of Israel that they would inherit the land, and that He would assist them? What Moses' people lacked was not a strategic plan but rather strength of will, and his sending of spies was therefore meant to provide the people of Israel with encouraging reports about the land's fruitfulness, expansiveness, and allure. For Moses' spies to attempt to infiltrate into Canaan secretly was therefore unnecessary.[2]

Joshua's mission, on the other hand, clearly has a different agenda, for God has yet to inform him that the city of Jericho will be easily conquered when its defensive wall miraculously crumbles. Joshua is thus

---

2. A comprehensive treatment of Moses' spies also requires a careful comparison with his reminiscence of the episode on the eve of his death, in Deuteronomy 1:22–2:1. While many details differ from the Numbers version, the public nature of the mission is the same in both.

planning an assault on its barricades, and his sending of the spies therefore has clear tactical goals. If the spies are to succeed, they must enter the city quietly, quickly search out its weak points, and escape into the darkness undetected. This would explain both their infiltration under cover of night as well as their choice of lodgings. Nowhere would their presence be less conspicuous than at the home of a harlot, where people of all descriptions and backgrounds are wont to frequent, most of them with a great desire to maintain their anonymity. By staying at Rahab's house they might also be able to gather important intelligence about the city's notables, for no doubt Rahab hears much gossip during the course of her work. If nothing else, at least the spies can get a fairly accurate general impression of the city's mood on the eve of Israel's entry into the land. Whatever news is on the minds of the locals will find its way to Rahab.

UNANSWERED QUESTIONS

But if they aimed for secrecy, it is puzzling that the spies are discovered so quickly. The second verse of the chapter already indicates that the king of Jericho is informed of the spies' movements and quickly dispatches a party to Rahab's lodgings in order to arrest them. It seems that they had scarcely arrived and dropped their bags when the ominous knock of the gendarme could already be heard at her gates. Clearly, the city must have been on high alert, anticipating an attempt by Israel to infiltrate and search it out. Nevertheless, one would have expected the spies to have exercised more prudence in their behavior, and to implement Joshua's directive to maintain secrecy with greater success.

If we understand their premature discovery by the inhabitants of Jericho to have been due to a combination of the latter's high state of vigilance, excellent counter-intelligence, and the spies' lack of caution, we must submit that their decision to lodge at Rahab's house, built as it was into the city's defensive wall and offering a vista to the outside, was a remarkable stroke of luck. Further, her unexpected identification with the spies (to the degree that she was willing to aid them in their hurried escape into the night) was nothing short of miraculous. Had the spies unwittingly lodged within the city proper or else chosen a less sympathetic host, the mission could just as easily have ended disastrously with their humiliating capture. Surprisingly, however, when the spies return to Joshua with the report of their mission, they offer no indication that failure was a distinct possibility.

AVOIDING DETECTION BY THE PEOPLE OF ISRAEL

The above reading assumes that the primary thrust of the secrecy order was directed towards the people of Jericho. "Joshua quietly sent two spies from the Sheetim and said: 'Go see the land and Jericho,'" so that they would not be found out by the enemy. There is, however, another possibility that obviates some of the above difficulties introduced by this reading: the quiet sending of the spies was a calculated move by Joshua to keep the mission secret not only from the people of Jericho, but primarily from his own compatriots! Rabbi David Kimhi (Radak), quoting the much earlier *Targum Yonatan*, the authoritative Aramaic translation of the Prophets and Writings (second century, Israel), explains that:

> Joshua sent the men secretly so that the *people of Israel* would be unaware of the mission and therefore not discomfited by the thought of sending spies. But Joshua only sent them because he knew that they would be successful in their mission and would raise the spirits of the people of Israel with a positive report. (Radak on Josh. 2:1)

The brilliance of R. Kimhi's remark is cast into sharper relief when we again contrast Joshua's spies with those of Moses. Recall that Moses selected twelve men, one per tribe, all of them "leaders of the people of Israel," and each one designated by name (Num. 13:3). Recall also that although the text provided no description of their send-off, it emphasized their return:

> They came to Moses, Aaron, and the entire congregation of Israel to Kadesh in the wilderness of Paran, and they reported back to them and to the entire assembly and showed them all the produce of the land. They spoke to him and they said: "We came to the land to which you sent us and indeed it is a land flowing with milk and honey, and these are its fruits. However, the inhabitants of the land are very strong." (Num. 13:26–28)

Moses' spies offered their assessment that the conquest of the land was impossible, and the people of Israel responded with dreadful panic, crying out to return to Egypt. But Moses had made no attempt to conceal the mission of the spies at all. In fact, quite the opposite. They were dispatched to Canaan and received upon their return with a great deal of fanfare and flourish. We can see them in our mind's eye, leaders all, bedecked in their official regalia and proudly marching off towards the mysterious distant hills buoyed by the people's blessings for success. All of Israel watched them as they disappeared over the horizon, the portentous moment surging with destiny. If only they could have come back bearing a different message, with tidings of encouragement, with words of fortitude and hope!

LEARNING THE LESSON OF COVER-UP

Joshua remembers the moment all too well, and realizes in disquieting retrospect how tragic was the publicity of it all, how reckless and ill-advised. Almost forty years had elapsed since the fateful day of those spies' return, and Joshua now stands in Moses' stead, about to embark on his mentor's uncompleted journey. Sending his small party of two anonymous spies to Jericho in the gathering gloom of nightfall, Joshua wisely chooses a different course of action, tightly shrouding the mission in secrecy lest the news of it frighten the people of Israel. Significantly, when the spies return, the text indicates that:

> They descended from the hills, crossed [the Jordan River] and came *to Joshua* son of Nun, and described to *him* all that had befallen them. They said *to Joshua*: "God has given the entire land into our hands, for all of its inhabitants dissolve in fear before us!" (Josh. 2:23–24)

In this version, the spies make no contact with the rest of the nation, neither when they depart nor when they return. It is Joshua alone who is privy to their account, and if the spies indicate to him that their mission was unsuccessful, he can decide on the next course of action while the people of Israel remain blissfully unaware of the failure.

Armed with our alternative reading suggesting that it is primarily Israel that must be shielded from news of the mission, we can now retrace and reevaluate the spies' movements. The spies actually made a calculated choice to lodge at the house of Rahab, for they can already anticipate that detection by the unnerved people of Jericho is not out of the question. As they scan the city's outer wall from afar, they notice a series of beckoning windows belonging to peripheral dwellings that have been built into its fortifications. Such realities are not unheard of in the chronicles of ancient walled cities, where both congestion as well as thrift often led town planners to expediently incorporate perimeter houses into the ramparts. The nobility tended to dwell at the town's acropolis, located near its center and as far away as possible from attacking hordes that might surround the city wall. The poorest people, in contrast, would have to live next to or within the fortifications, and make do with less space, less air, less light, and more danger. For Joshua's spies, in search of the possibility of a quick and daring escape (did they come with their own coil of rope?), a house in the wall represents the best option.

In addition, is it not possible that Rahab's "hospitality" is known beyond Jericho's borders, so that the spies' seemingly random arrival at her well-trodden doorstep has actually been planned in advance? As we suggested above, her inn has a reputation for offering clients the discretion that they demand. And finally, her line of work has the added advantage of providing her with useful information concerning a whole array of perhaps pivotal personalities and their plans. As the sages colorfully describe it: "There wasn't a prince or noble who had not come to consort with Rahab the harlot" (Rashi on Josh. 2:11). Thus, rather than suggesting a heavy-handed lack of caution that leads to almost immediate detection, we may suggest in contrast that Joshua and the spies have done a remarkable job of gathering their intelligence in advance. They have succeeded in singling out a base of operations that has three distinct advantages, for it offers the spies the possibility of maintaining a low profile while vital information can be gathered, as well as providing them with the critical option of a quick escape. It is therefore not fortuitous circumstance that guides the spies to Rahab's door but rather deliberation and forethought. Their quick detection by alert informants and their betrayal to Jericho's king should therefore not be understood as the unexpected curtailment of their mission, but rather as a predictable development for which the two were already well-prepared.

COMPLEMENTARY INTERPRETATIONS

Was the secrecy of the spies aimed at the Jewish nation, or the people of Canaan? We may summarize by saying that both readings offered above are complementary. The spies are dispatched in secrecy to avoid triggering anxiety and disquiet among the people of Israel, for this concern is Joshua's primary one. Of course, they are also sent with orders to evade detection by the inhabitants of Jericho. With this twin mandate, the spies begin to chart out their mission. They will need to find a "safe house" from which they can reconnoiter, a location that at the same time can provide them with the option of flight. A harlot's lodging with access to the outer wall meets the criteria exactly. Their mission can be recast as a lightning strike into enemy territory, not with the necessity of avoiding detection, but rather with the objective of quickly collecting vital data while evading capture.

Of course, Joshua realizes that such an operation has the added advantage of sowing the seeds of even more apprehension in the town of Jericho, already on edge with reports of Israel's imminent arrival. To gauge the level of dread of its anxious inhabitants, we need only consider the text's observation that as soon as the king's search party left the safety of Jericho's gates (Josh. 2:7), "the gates were immediately closed." Jericho had already adopted the defensive posture of a city under siege, even before the people of Israel had crossed the swollen waters of the Jordan River. The nerves of Jericho were certainly not calmed by the news of Israelite spies who had succeeded in breaching the city's formidable battlements and then escaping into the ominous darkness without a trace.

Joshua 2:1–24

Rahab the Harlot

L ast chapter, we examined the narrative concerning Joshua's sending of spies to Jericho. In this chapter, we will again consider the spies' mission, but we will redirect our focus to the account's unlikely heroine, Rahab the harlot. The spies arrive at her house, it is there that they find refuge, and it is because of Rahab's quick thinking and courage that they are able to escape into the night.

Let us briefly recount the circumstances of Rahab's heroism. When news of the gendarmes' imminent arrival comes, Rahab quickly hides the spies. Rather than arousing more suspicion by denying any knowledge of their whereabouts, Rahab readily acknowledges to the king's officers that she had unwittingly provided lodging for "the strangers," and immediately deflects further questioning by averring that they had already fled into the night. She cunningly concludes her alibi with a patriotic flourish: "Pursue them quickly, so that you will capture them!" (Josh. 2:5), further dispelling any suspicions of collusion. In short, Rahab's response is quick, clever, and courageous. It is, of course, also treacherous. What prompts Rahab to turn her back on her own town and people, in order to win the confidence and pledge of the enemy? Why does she harbor the men and then abet them in their immediate escape?

WAS RAHAB REALLY A HARLOT?

It may come as a surprise to learn that some commentaries question whether Rahab was a harlot. It is true that the text explicitly describes her as Rahab *hazona* (Josh. 6:17), where *zona* elsewhere in Tanakh without doubt means a prostitute, or literally, "one who strays."[1] As a verb, the word is often used to convey the act of being unfaithful or traitorous, whether towards one's spouse or even towards God.[2] The meaning behind the usage is quite obvious: The prostitute is the exemplar of one who has no loyalty to any man, for she readily has relations with anyone who pays her hire.

Nevertheless, Rashi quotes the much earlier *Targum Yonatan*, who renders the phrase as "Rahab *pundekita*," where *pundak* means an inn and *pundekita* means an innkeeper. In other words, Joshua's spies did not arrive at the house of a harlot, for such a disreputable destination would be unthinkable for such reputable men. Rather, they lodged at an inn that served travelers, and Rahab was nothing more than the proprietress of the establishment. The linguistic justification for *Targum Yonatan*'s reading is the similarity between the grammatical root זנ"ה, related to prostitution or faithlessness, and the root זו"ן, meaning nourishment or sustenance. In a modest flight of interpretive fancy, Rahab *hazona* can therefore be construed as "Rahab the provider of food" or "Rahab who provides room and board." It should be stressed, however, that although these two roots share two common letters, they do not share a common stem, and in all probability are unrelated.

Of course, our story would probably not suffer terribly if indeed the spies had arrived at an innkeeper instead of at the house of a harlot, but such an interpretation would nevertheless put a serious strain on the straightforward reading of the text. More to the point, readers should be aware that *Targum Yonatan*'s interpretation is indicative of much broader trends in biblical exegesis, especially among those commentaries more prone to homiletical readings. The larger question concerns how to

---

1. See Genesis 38:13-18 and Hosea 1:1-9 for particularly egregious examples.
2. As in Numbers 15:39: "Do not stray after your hearts or your eyes that you stray (*zonim*) after."

approach phrases or situations that on the surface appear to cast pro-
tagonists in a less than virtuous light. When confronting such examples,
some commentaries (often basing themselves on much earlier traditions) adopt the approach of reinterpreting the noxious phrases more
benignly. Thus, for example, Rahab becomes an innkeeper; Ḥofni and
Pinḥas, the wayward sons of Eli, stand guilty only of delaying the sacrifices of childbearing women (1 Sam. 2:22); and Batsheva is already con-
ditionally divorced from Uriah when David takes her (11 Sam. 11:1–27).[3]

TREACHERY IN CONTEXT

It should be noted that here, in contrast to some of the above instances,
Rashi himself admits Rahab's true vocation! Recall Rahab's remarks:

> When we heard [of the splitting of the Sea of Reeds and of the
> victory over the Amorite kings Siḥon and Og] our hearts melted.
> No man has any spirit left to oppose you, for the Lord your God is
> God in the heavens above and on the earth below. (Josh. 2:11)

This complete loss of any will to fight was, apparently, especially obvious to Rahab, for as Rashi explains:

> She told them that no man even desired to sleep with a woman.
> Every nobleman and prince had visited Rahab the harlot. She
> was but ten years old at the time of the Exodus and had practiced
> prostitution for the entire forty years that had elapsed since then.
> (Rashi on Josh. 2:11)

As it turns out, understanding Rahab's real profession is not peripheral
to the story but rather essential for comprehending her motives. As a
zona, she is not only a paradigm of disloyalty but, more importantly, a
representative of all of those thankless members of society who tend to

---

3. Concerning this last glaring example, compare the talmudic tradition of Shabbat
   56a that exonerates David of wrongdoing with the more straightforward reading of
   Yoma 22b that finds him guilty. The exegetical debate is an ancient one.

be the most vulnerable and maltreated. Do we go too far in assuming that she, like most other practitioners of her profession, did not willingly choose her career but was coerced to adopt it through an unfortunate combination of misfortune and abuse? Stigmatized and marginalized, no prostitute can easily escape the vicious circumstances in which she finds herself. The disloyalty of the *zona*, who is faithful to no one and notoriously insincere, is the defense mechanism of a woman who has lived all of her productive years in the shadow of desperation and neglect. In other words, Rahab is able to cavalierly turn her back on her towns-people because they have long since turned their backs on her.

Perhaps this is the true meaning of the text's emphatic repetition that "she lowered them by the rope from the window, *for her home was in the side of the outer wall, and in the outer wall she dwelt*" (Josh. 2:15). To live in the outer wall implies not only a geographic location but a social reality as well. To dwell in the outer wall of the city is to be peripheral to the life of the city and most exposed to an enemy attack, thus marking Rahab as a marginalized inhabitant of Jericho. She owes nothing to them and they, in turn, can make no demands of her. How unproblematic it is for her to strike a deal with the spies for the preservation of herself and her immediate family, while fully cognizant that many of those around her will perish during the course of the Israelite conquest.

VALUE JUDGMENTS

What is most remarkable about our account is that it is completely devoid of any value judgment concerning Rahab's harlotry. This is in glaring contrast to numerous other examples in Tanakh, where to be a harlot is to stand accused of living a life that is immoral and corrupt. When the First Temple prophets decry Israel's waywardness and compare it to harlotry, their censure always includes references not only to idolatry, but also to theft, sexual immorality, and bloodshed (for examples, see Is. 1:21–23, Jer. 2:20–28, Ezek. 16:15–22). Here, however, other than indicating Rahab's line of work for purely narrative reasons, the text offers not a hint of criticism concerning its moral deficiency.

There must, therefore, be another dimension to Rahab that would explain the text's implied approval of her character. Recall how she successfully hid the spies on her rooftop and then deflected the suspicion of the king's officers, quickly redirecting the latter on a futile chase into the night after the suspects. Then, she ascended to the roof and haltingly presented her offer:

> She said to the men: "I know that the Lord has given you the land, for your dread has fallen upon us and all of the inhabitants melt before you. For we have heard how the Lord dried up the waters of the Sea of Reeds for you when you went forth from Egypt. Also, of your victory over Siḥon and Og, the two Amorite kings from across the Jordan River whom you utterly destroyed. We heard of these things and our hearts melted, and no man has any spirit left in him to oppose you, for the Lord your God is God in heavens above, and upon earth below. Now, therefore, pledge to me in the name of the Lord that having acted with kindness towards you, you in turn will deal kindly with my family. Provide me with a true sign. Preserve my father and mother, my brothers and sisters, and all that is theirs, and save our lives from death." (Josh. 2:9–13)

DAWNING AWARENESS

In her soliloquy, Rahab describes how fear and trepidation have seized the hearts of every denizen of Jericho. She recalls the astounding reports of two events in particular, the splitting of the Sea of Reeds and the defeat of the Amorite kings. Chronologically, the splitting of the sea and the drowning of Pharaoh's pursuing horsemen in its churning waters (Ex. 14) took place almost forty years earlier and was the culmination of the Exodus from Egypt. The defeat of Siḥon and Og, on the other hand, had happened but a few months previously, for Moses had battled them on the eve of his demise (Num. 21:21–22:1). Taken together, therefore, the two episodes constitute Rahab's bracketing of the entire Israelite experience; both were potent expressions of their God's prowess, a deity before whom the Canaanite city-states now trembled and quaked.

But Rahab does not conclude her opening remarks with these dry facts of history nor with her sober assessments of the town's flagging spirits. Instead, she closes with an exultant outburst that is quite unexpected: "For the Lord your God is God in heavens above and upon earth below!" This charged phrase, immediately followed by her request for preservation, raises the possibility that there is perhaps another way to understand Rahab's wonder and alarm as she brings to mind the events of the Sea of Reeds and the Amorite kings.

Recall that some four decades earlier, the people of Israel had left Egypt and confidently followed their leader Moses into the barren wilderness. Behind them, the Egyptian countryside lay in ruins, its people demoralized, and its god-king Pharaoh bent over in defeat. From an ethical perspective, the Israelite exodus was the liberation by God of hapless slaves from the cruel grip of state-sponsored slavery, and this event entered the annals of human history as the most forceful denunciation of man's heartlessness towards the weak and the downtrodden. Henceforth, every tyrant and totalitarian regime would stand condemned by its thundering message. The Exodus taught the world that there was an absolute moral law that no man, not even a god-king, could abrogate with impunity.

Similarly, the defeats of Sihon and Og were brought to Rahab's mind not simply as astonishing examples of how seasoned armies are sometimes overcome by inexperienced upstarts. Rather, Sihon and Og were referenced because they were the regional superpowers, merciless despots who bound many of the petty kings of Canaan in thralldom as their vassals (see Josh. 13:21). Their miraculous downfall at the hands of the Israelites was greeted on the Jordan River's western side not only with expressions of wonder but also with hushed sighs of relief.

Rahab ponders these two events, both of them indicative of a different "world order" than hers, both of them shining a ray of hope upon an otherwise dreary moral landscape. The overthrow of Pharaoh implied that even a serf was precious in the eyes of this unusual Israelite God; the defeat of Sihon and Og suggested that what was meaningful to Him had little to do with might and power, and much to do with decency and goodness. What revolutionary ideas these were in a polytheistic world drunk with dreams of bloodshed and plunder, and deaf to the cries of the vanquished and the oppressed.

THE WHISPER OF REPENTANCE

As the spies embark on their mission, the winds of spring go before them, bearing a message of vitality and promise. Facing them on her rooftop that looks out over the noisome city, under an ink-black canopy illuminated by a thousand points of silent light, Rahab surveys her small and nasty world, and her heart aches. The strangers speak of a God who cares, of a deity concerned with human destiny, of a being for whom injustice and oppression are anathema. Who understands better than her – the humbled prostitute – the pain of dwelling in the outer wall, the myriad acts of callousness and cruelty that compose the brutish streetscape of Jericho and its allies? Recounting the Sea of Reeds and Siḥon and Og, Rahab now realizes that there is another way. Jericho and the kings of Canaan may bravely try to oppose the military onslaught of Israel, but the message of their God will inevitably prevail. Pledging relief but demanding responsibility, their God's teachings will sweep away the rotting foundations of Jericho and send its ramparts tumbling down.

Her life a travesty, Rahab ponders her fate. To betray the spies will finally win her the empty accolades of the king of Jericho and the short-lived respect of those who uphold its "way of life." But to betray the spies is also to confirm the validity of their claims, that all of the idols of Canaan cannot comfort a broken heart nor restore a spirit made numb by the endless sight of selfish clients knocking at her dilapidated door. The spies are probably the first men to have arrived asking for her help instead of demanding her self-abasement. To betray them would mean to betray every remaining shred of decency and beauty left in the world.

Gathering her threadbare dignity about her, embracing the consoling words of her curious visitors, Rahab decides that all is not lost. Seizing the hope of a better future for herself, of a better life for her family, and ultimately, of a better world for all, she casts her lot with the Israelite spies and with their God:

> For the Lord your God is God in heavens above, and upon earth below. Now, therefore pledge to me in the name of the Lord that having acted with kindness towards you, you will deal kindly with my family. Provide me with a true sign. Preserve my father and mother, my brothers and sisters and all that is theirs, and save our lives from death. (Josh. 2:9–13)

How poignant are the comments of the *Mekhilta* (rabbinic *Midrash Halakha* on Exodus, third century CE) concerning this passage:

> When Yitro saw that God had taken the Israelites out of Egypt, he exclaimed: "Now I know that the Lord is greater than all other gods!" [Ex. 18:11]. Yitro himself had worshipped all manner of idolatry, for he states "all other gods." Naaman, however, acknowledged God even more, for he states "Now I know that there are no other gods on earth save for the God of Israel" [II Kings 5:15]. But Rahab the harlot surpassed both of them, for she said, "For the Lord your God is God in heavens above, *and* upon earth below!" (*Mekhilta* on Ex. 18:11)

LIFE-ALTERING TRANSFORMATION

The *Mekhilta* compares Rahab's exclamation to those of other seasoned idolaters who came to question their beliefs and values, to eventually reject them, and instead to sincerely embrace the God of Israel. Yitro, Moses' father-in-law, was the priest of Midian and loyally served the local desert fetishes of the southern Arabian Peninsula. When he heard of the Exodus and the Splitting of the Sea, of the oppressiveness of Pharaoh and of his overthrow by the concerned God of the Hebrews, he rejected his former faith and joined the people of Israel. Naaman was a ninth-century BCE Aramean warlord who had been stricken by a debilitating skin disease and was then cured by following the unassuming advice of the miracle-working prophet Elisha. As a result of that experience, he came to venerate the God of Israel, rejecting the worship of his own deities as so much empty ceremony.

Significantly for our purposes, the impetus for both Yitro and Naaman to begin their journeys of faith was their realization that God's intervention meant the existence of an aware and involved deity, who ruled the cosmos according to moral principles, and showed concern for those who suffered. In a similar vein, but to an even greater degree, Rahab's rooftop realization represents a transformative event that recasts her life and the lives of her loved ones. They will be extricated from the mire of Jericho in order to live.

Considering the matter from a literary standpoint, we note that the spies advise Rahab to make her household discernible to the Israelite invaders by suspending a crimson cord from its window (Josh. 2:18). In the original Hebrew, this is described as *tikvat ḥut hashani*, where the word for cord, *tikva*, comes from the same root that means hope.[4] The intimation is clear: Rahab's fateful decision represents not only the promise of survival but also the supernal hope afforded by the prospect of a new beginning.

The commentaries allude to our reading, perceiving repentance to be the catalyst that drives Rahab's decision. Commenting on the escape of the spies through her window, dangled by her saving cord, Rashi comments:

> Use of the definite article in the phrase "She lowered them by *the* rope through *the* window" [Josh. 2:15] is a reference to the very same rope and window that her paramours would use to ascend to her chambers. She thus proclaimed: "Master of the Universe! By these very things I transgressed, let me now achieve absolution by them!" (Rashi on Josh. 2:15)

Rashi understands that, by aiding the escape of the spies, Rahab decided to alter the fundamental trajectory of her life, abandoning Jericho and its turpitude and accepting Israel and its God. Rahab's transformed status is indicated by the text that describes her rescue after the fall of the city:

> They burned the city and all that was in it.... But Rahab the harlot and her family, everything that was hers, was preserved by Joshua. She henceforth dwelt among [*bekerev*] Israel until this very day, for she hid the spies whom Joshua had sent to search out Jericho. (Josh. 6:24–25)

---

4. That is, קִוְה. A similar double meaning is employed in Job 6:6, where Job describes the fleeting nature of his life: "My days fly by faster than the weaver's shuttle, only to end without hope." The word for "hope" is, as in our story, *tikva*, thus introducing a provocative second interpretation: The weaver's shuttle carries the thread horizontally through the stretched vertical cords of the fabric, and when it ends, the garment cannot be completed. Job therefore connects the truncated thread of the weaver with his own extinguished hopes.

It is noteworthy that the preposition "among" or *bekerev* used to describe her changed standing is the very same one consistently utilized by the Torah to emphasize the reception due to the new convert by his adoptive people Israel (see Deut. 16:11, 26:11, 29:10).

Some early sources actually go so far as to acclaim Rahab as the ancestress of prophets and priests:

> R. Naḥman said: Ḥulda the prophetess [see II Kings 22:11–20] was a descendent of Joshua ... R. Eina the Elder raised an objection from the following text: "Eight prophets who were also priests were descended from Rahab the harlot. These are Neria, Barukh, Seraya, Maḥseya, Yirmiya, Ḥilkiya, Ḥanamel, and Shalum [individuals all associated with the kin of Jeremiah, the First Temple prophet and priest, and almost all mentioned in Jeremiah 32]." R. Judah added: Ḥulda the prophetess was also one of her descendants. Said R. Naḥman: Rahab converted and became married to Joshua. (Megilla 14b)

According to the above source, not only did Rahab convert and become accepted by the people of Israel, but she became married to none other than Joshua their leader! Thus, although Rahab disappears from the biblical sources after the conquest of Jericho, her fateful decision to join Israel apparently lives on with surprising results.

Whether or not the above talmudic source represents an unassailable tradition, it is clear that for the rabbis the thought of Rahab the harlot becoming an earnest and legitimate convert and bringing forth illustrious descendants was not to be considered fantastical or obscene. This very fact offers the most striking evidence that our above analysis concerning Rahab's embrace of the spies and rejection of her townsfolk is correct. It was motivated by more than a calculated appraisal of Jericho's imminent capture and fall – it was motivated by repentance.

The lessons offered by this personal tale of Rahab the harlot are many, but the most important one of all is this: every person is capable of changing the direction of his or her life by willfully choosing a different moral path. The art of conscious living is to seize the more mundane occasions provided by our daily lives in order to come to our own self-realizations concerning who we really are and who we can yet become. Thus it is that the rejected and uncelebrated harlot becomes not only the instrument for her family's salvation but also the ancestress of Israel's most outspoken prophetic line.

Joshua 3:1–8

Crossing the Jordan River

fter three days in hiding, the spies return to Joshua and offer their forceful conclusion (Josh. 2:24): "They said to Joshua: 'God has given the whole land into our hands, and all of its inhabitants melt before us!'" Relieved and inspired by their words, Joshua wastes no time in preparing the people for their next challenge – the crossing of the Jordan River.

The Jordan River is a rather small, narrow watercourse, notwithstanding its gigantic proportions in the mind's eye of pilgrim and voyager. Its cold and fast-flowing headwaters originate in southern Lebanon and consist of three main springs that are fed by the melting snowpack of the Hermon mountain range. These tributaries converge and discharge into the northern end of the Sea of Galilee, or Kinneret. As the Jordan River flows out of the Kinneret's southern end, it begins its meandering and precipitous descent towards the Dead Sea, into which it empties after a drop in elevation of about 180 meters. The name Jordan River is derived from the Hebrew root יר"ד meaning "to go down," and is a fitting title in light of the river's downward course that ends at the lowest point on earth. The Jordan River's sluggish flow from the Kinneret to the Dead Sea, along the scrub-covered floodplain of a narrow rift valley, is three times longer than its air distance of about 120 kilometers. The entire length of the Jordan River, forming the natural eastern border of Canaan, is but a small part of the immense and earthquake-prone Great Rift Valley, a fault line that runs from Syria, through the Red Sea, and across East Africa to Mozambique. It must be noted that modern diversion and irrigation projects have reduced the flow of the Jordan River south of the Sea of Galilee by more than ninety percent.

> Joshua arose early in the morning and he and the people of Israel journeyed from the Sheetim and arrived at the Jordan River. They slept there prior to crossing. At the end of three days the officers passed through the camp. They commanded the people saying: "When you see the Ark of the Covenant of the Lord your God borne by the priests of the tribe of Levi, then you shall begin to journey after it. However, you shall maintain a distance from it of about two thousand cubits in measure. Do not draw close to it, so that you can be guided by it, for you have not journeyed by this route in the past." (Josh. 3:1–4)

Within the context of this three-day drama, one may be tempted to ask when the story of the spies could have actually taken place. Recall that in chapter one of the Book of Joshua, we saw Joshua take firm grasp of the reins of leadership, when he enjoined the officers to tell the people that they should prepare provisions (Josh. 1:11): "For in three days' time you shall traverse this Jordan River to enter and take possession of the land." In chapter two, Joshua sent the spies to Jericho and they initially lodged at the house of Rahab, then concealed themselves among the foreboding cliffs west of Jericho, returning to Joshua after three full days in hiding. Joshua received their report, and the next morning the people commenced their journey towards the Jordan River, and set up camp on its banks for the night. It is on the morrow "at the end of the three days" (Josh. 3:2) that the officers bid the people to follow the Ark.

All of these episodes cannot possibly be compressed into the initial three-day preparation period announced by the officers in chapter one, making it clear that the spies must have been sent by Joshua *before* that period began. In point of fact, the events of chapter two chronologically precede much or all of chapter one,[1] and the reticence of the text on that matter can only reinforce our earlier conclusions: The spies are sent secretly and the people of Israel are unaware of their mission. In this case, the narrative content of the story (the concealment of the sending of the spies) is cleverly mirrored by its stylistic features (the deliberate placement of chronologically later material at the beginning).

LED BY THE ARK

Now, confident in consequence of the spies' successful mission, the people of Israel stand ready to cross. They are to follow the Ark of the Covenant borne by the priests while maintaining a respectful distance. Because the Ark plays the central role in the crossing, it is critical for us to have some appreciation of its meaning. Recall that the Ark constitutes the principle vessel in the Tabernacle or *Mishkan*, that portable shrine constructed by the people of Israel during their wilderness sojourn and transported by them from place to place during the entire period of their wanderings. When the people encamp and the tent-like Tabernacle is erected, the Ark is placed in its innermost chamber, the Holy of Holies. The Ark and other vessels of the Tabernacle, including the elements of the building itself and the special garments worn by the ministering priests during the course of their service, are spelled out at length in *Parashot Teruma* and *Tetzaveh* (Ex. 25–28):

> They shall make an Ark of acacia wood, two-and-a-half cubits in length, one-and-a-half cubits in width, and one-and-a-half cubits in height. You shall cover it with pure gold inside and out, and place a golden crenellation upon its top. You shall prepare four molten rings and place them upon its ends, two rings on one side and two on the other. You shall prepare staves of acacia wood and cover them with gold, and you shall insert the staves into the rings in order to carry the Ark. The staves shall always

---

1. The thirteenth-century Rabbi Isaiah di Trani, in his comments to Joshua 2:22, explores this at length.

> remain in the rings and shall not be removed. In the Ark you
> shall place the testimony that I will give you. You shall make a
> lid of pure gold…. And place two *keruvim* of gold at each of its
> ends…. The outstretched wings of the *keruvim* shall cover the
> lid and they shall face each other…. I shall meet with you there
> and speak to you from upon the lid, from between the two *keru-*
> *vim* that are upon the Ark of the Testimony. From there I shall
> convey all of My commandments that you must tell the people
> of Israel. (Ex. 25:10–22)

The detailed directions for the Ark's construction describe three discrete elements: a chest-like wooden receptacle covered inside and out
with pure gold, a lid for the chest consisting of a rectangular block of
pure gold upon which sit two obscure figures called *keruvim*, and two
long poles of gilt wood for carrying the object. Concerning the function
of the Ark, the text speaks of two intertwined aspects. Firstly, the Ark
serves as the physical depository for the "testimony," the tablets upon
which were graven the Ten Utterances (see Ex. 31:18, 40:20). Secondly,
the Ark acts as the locus for the reception of God's commandments.
God communicates to Moses from the infinitesimal point in space that
lies between the outstretched wings of the *keruvim*.

THE SIGNIFICANCE OF THE KERUVIM

The most mysterious elements of the Ark, and the key to unraveling its
significance, are the *keruvim*. These two winged figures sit upon the lid
of the Ark at either end, but the Torah nowhere spells out their exact
form. Anglicized as cherubs, they are often portrayed as possessing
child-like features, a depiction that finds support in traditional Jewish
sources as well (see Sukka 5b). The *keruvim* are represented elsewhere
in the scheme, embroidered on the fabrics that constitute the building's tent-like cover (Ex. 26:1), as well as upon the special curtain that
divides the Holy of Holies from the rest of the building (v. 31). The only
other mention in the Torah of these curious creatures is in the description of the garden of Eden (Gen. 3:24), where the path to the tree of
life is closely guarded from the east by the "*keruvim* and the flaming,
whirling sword."

It is Nahmanides who provides the most convincing explanation for the meaning and purpose of the Ark in general and of the *keruvim* in particular:

> The text commands that the wings of the *keruvim* must be outstretched but does not indicate their purpose in the Tabernacle or why they are to be constructed in this way. The text continues by saying that the lid with its *keruvim* is to be regarded as an integral part of the Ark. The lid is to be placed upon the chest, within which are to be stored the [tablets of the] testimony. It shall function as My throne of glory, for there I will meet with you, and speak with you from upon the lid, from between the two *keruvim* when they sit upon the Ark of the Testimony. The Ark therefore resembles the "chariot" (*merkava*) that Ezekiel saw in his vision, when he states [Ezek. 10:20], "It was the same creatures that I saw beneath the God of Israel at the river Kevar, and I knew that they were *keruvim*." For this reason, God is called "He who is enthroned upon the *keruvim*" [1 Sam. 4:4] and their outstretched wings indicate that they are the chariot that bears the glory of God. (Nahmanides on Ex. 25:21)

For Nahmanides, the Ark of the Covenant is a chariot or vehicle that bears God's "throne of glory." Like an earthly monarch who sits upon a throne, God's presence is manifest upon His throne of glory, the Ark. Of course, God is incorporeal and therefore has no physical proportions. One cannot see Him enthroned atop the *keruvim*, but one can nevertheless experience His presence and perceive His commands. Eschewing the terminology of the mystics, we might say that the Ark expresses the possibility of introducing God's presence into the world. The *keruvim* are certainly not figurative, for the Torah explicitly outlaws idolatry as a most heinous offense. That they cannot be representational of the deity is also borne out by the simple fact that there are two of them, while the God of Israel proclaims absolute oneness as His creed (Deut. 4:15, 6:12). Rather, suggests Nahmanides, the *keruvim* are an attempt to portray the spiritual beings associated with God's intangible presence. The Ark therefore represents the "chariot" – the vehicle or means by which the experience of God in the material world can be achieved.

In other words, the Ark symbolizes our desire to bring God into our lives. In the Torah's frame of reference, this can only be done through the medium of God's teaching and the performance of His commandments. Therefore, the Ark contains only one thing: the stone tablets that spell out the unique obligations of the people of Israel, for these commandments are the central axis around which the relationship between God and humanity must pivot. God communicates to Moses from "between the *keruvim*," for the Ark is the symbol of His throne, denoting His ongoing presence and involvement in the world. That throne, in turn, rests upon the bedrock of the stone tablets, for the instruction etched upon them is the only means of bridging the chasm between God and man. Unique among all of the peoples of antiquity, Israel's most sacred object that resides in the most hallowed area of its national shrine is neither a molten image of a god nor a physical relic of a human saint, but rather a timeless text that is the antithesis of corporeality.

Nahmanides' approach sheds light on an otherwise inexplicable feature of the Ark that makes it special among the other vessels of the Tabernacle. "In the rings of the Ark shall the staves remain, they are not to be removed." All of the other vessels, such as the Table, the Menora, and the altars, had staves or poles that were inserted when the Tabernacle journeyed and were removed when it was set up at its new location. For all of the other vessels, therefore, the staves were nothing more than a practical and essential means of facilitating transport. In the case of the Ark, however, the staves must have an additional function, for they remain in the Ark even when it is at rest. It is probable that the injunction to maintain the position of the staves was an emphatic and concrete expression of the idea that the people of Israel, the human bearers of the Ark, have the special purpose of "bringing God's presence into the world." The Ark may indeed symbolize that God desires to be involved in our lives, the representation of His glorious throne constituting a promise of an immediate and intimate relationship. But unless human beings bear that Ark, unless the staves are carried by the people of Israel, God remains an inert and detached reality.

The staves must remain in the Ark always, to indicate that although the *keruvim* extend their wings in flight, they are by themselves incapable of animating our material world with God's presence. Their outstretched wings represent the possibility of vital interaction between man and God, but their lifeless gilded forms emphasize that the opportunity remains inherently latent. The potential to translate stasis into movement, to unleash a spiritual dynamic that alone can transform our concrete world, is the exclusive preserve of human beings who desire God and choose the good. We alone can initiate the Ark's motion by grasping the staves. The constant presence of the staves, their perpetual attachment to the Ark, highlights the role of humanity in general and the people of Israel in particular in the forging of the link between earth and heaven.

Returning to the account of the Book of Joshua, the procession of the people towards the land is led by the Ark not because it is a cultic or talismanic object, but because it signifies God's ongoing presence and involvement. He will lead them into the land and secure it for them, but they in turn must uphold the provisions of the tablets of testimony that serve as the foundation of His earthly throne.

AN UNUSUAL ORDER OF PROCESSION

According to the detailed directives governing the movement of the Israelite camp, spelled out at the beginning of the Book of Numbers (ch. 2), the Ark did not generally travel at the head of the procession. The tribes of Israel, bivouacked according to four ensigns that surrounded the Tabernacle from all sides, would break up camp at the first sign of the cloud of glory lifting off of the Tabernacle.

The first tribal grouping, comprising three tribes led by Judah, would begin to move in advance of the deconstructed Tabernacle, whose building elements then followed, borne by the Levitical families of Gershon and Merari. Another tribal grouping led by Reuben then set out, followed this time by the enwrapped holy vessels including the Ark, borne upon the shoulders of the Levitical family of Kehat. Finally the last six tribes, in two groups of three, led respectively by Ephraim and Dan, would journey. This protocol would allow the Tabernacle to be refabricated in advance of the Ark's arrival, so that it and the other holy vessels could be honorably positioned immediately upon their arrival (see Num. 2:1–31, 4:1–20, 10:11–28).

It therefore emerges that the directive to follow the lead of the Ark, as described in our passage from the Book of Joshua, is an unusual departure from the typical practice. The only other recorded instance is highly telling:

> On the twentieth day of the second month of the second year, the cloud lifted from upon the tent of testimony. The people of Israel traveled from the wilderness of Sinai, and the cloud came to rest in the wilderness of Paran. They traveled for the first time, according to God's word at Moses' command.... Moses said to Ḥovav son of Reu'el the Midianite his father-in-law: "We are going to the place that God has said He will give us; accompany us and we will deal kindly with you, for God has spoken good things concerning Israel."
> ...They traveled from God's mountain a distance of three days, and the Ark of God's covenant *went before them* at a distance of three days to seek out a place for them to rest. The cloud of God was upon them during the day when they traveled from the encampment. (Num. 10:11–34)

RELIVING THE PAST

The above passage, so wistful in retrospect, is the description of Israel's first attempt to achieve entry into Canaan. A short couple of months after the people had left Egypt, they arrived at Sinai. There they stood awestruck as God thunderously proclaimed His Ten Utterances, and there they remained encamped for over a year as they adapted to their new destiny. Finally, as the above passage from Numbers describes, the people traveled from Sinai towards the Promised Land. Moses, blissfully unaware that he himself would later be denied entry into the land, excitedly invited Ḥovav his loyal kin to join the triumphant march of the people to their destination. Falling into formation behind the Ark of the Covenant, Israel took its first tentative steps. But fate quickly overtook them as their subsequent complaints against God's providence spiraled out of control, soon thereafter spawning the devastating mission of the spies. The land that had beckoned to them from so near would remain beyond their reach for almost forty years.

Our narrative in the Book of Joshua consciously evokes those ruinous events and the dissipated years, but now in a new context of accomplishment and realization. Again, the Ark travels before the people of Israel as they confidently march towards the land, but this time success will be theirs. As Israel dutifully follows the gilded object at a respectful distance, they recall the failure of the first attempt to enter the land even as they realize the preciousness of being granted another chance to do things right. The episode of the Ark therefore highlights a broader theme that is evident in these early chapters of the Book of Joshua: the generation that stands poised to enter the land must first relive the failures of their fathers in order to recast them into triumph. We will take note of these many flashbacks as they unfold.

Joshua 3:9–17

The Theme of Passage

I n studying the crossing of the Jordan River, we have thus far considered the chronology of the events, examined the special significance of the Ark, and pointed out the parallel of the initial journey from Sinai. In this chapter, we will analyze the event in light of its most striking analog: the splitting of the Sea of Reeds and the passage of Israel through its midst "on dry land."

Let us begin by noting the procession of events as they unfold in the Book of Joshua, chapter three:

1. The people journey to the banks of the Jordan River and encamp overnight at its edge.
2. The officers enjoin them to maintain a respectful distance from the Ark.
3. Joshua tells the people to sanctify themselves in preparation for wondrous events on the morrow, but does not announce what those events will be.
4. God tells Joshua that He will exalt him in the eyes of all Israel and they will know that He will be with Joshua always, just as He assisted Moses.

5. Joshua announces to the people that when the feet of the priests bearing the Ark enter the waters of the river, the waters will immediately divide and form a dam-like wall.
6. The people journey, the priests enter the waters now swollen by the spring runoff, and the Jordan River divides at a location far off, "at the city of Adam."
7. The priests bearing the Ark stand steadfast on the river's eastern bank as the people of Israel cross before them.
8. The people of Israel emerge into the Promised Land at the outskirts of Jericho.

PARALLELS TO THE SEA OF REEDS

Superficially, this chain of events bears much resemblance to the account of the splitting of the Sea of Reeds, described in the fourteenth chapter of Exodus. Let us note the similarities by cataloging the events that led up to the splitting of the Sea of Reeds and then matching them to their Joshua analogs, indicated here by a bracketed number corresponding to the list above.

Recall that in Exodus, the people had scarcely fled the iron grip of Egyptian servitude when God redirected their natural route of escape to instead journey by "the way of the wilderness of the Reed Sea." Reaching its shore, the people were enjoined to encamp (1).

Suddenly, the sound of approaching chariots and horses broke the surreal nighttime silence, and the freed slaves cried out to God in alarm. Moses, himself unsure of God's plan of intervention, encouraged the people to stand steadfast and witness God's salvation, but left its specifics undefined (3).

God then told the people to begin to trek towards the ominous waters and informed Moses that He would soon be "honored" by the overthrow of Pharaoh and his host. The people of Egypt would thus know that He is the true and only God (4).

The mysterious pillars of fire and cloud, which had guided the people through the wilderness, now moved behind the camp in order to serve as a barrier between the Israelites and their Egyptian pursuers (7).

God caused the great eastern wind to blow all night long, and as dawn rose, the waters divided (6).

The people of Israel entered the sea on dry land (5), as its waters formed a "wall to their right and to their left." Pharaoh's horsemen and charioteers pursued them into its midst but as day broke, the Egyptian host was thrown into confusion and then drowned as the waters rushed back upon them. The people of Israel, led by Moses and Miriam, erupted in a spontaneous outpouring of joyous thanksgiving. Moses guided the people to safety as they left the sea and entered the wilderness of Shur (8).

As the above scheme clearly indicates, the crossing of the Jordan River is not simply an echo of the events at the Sea of Reeds, but is almost a perfect duplication, albeit in slightly different order. Before analyzing the specific details that are common to both events, let us first consider the broader themes. In simplest terms, the motif that links the two episodes most powerfully is the theme of passage. In the first story, the people of Israel, formerly enslaved and oppressed by the harsh taskmasters of the maniacal Pharaoh, journey forth to unexpected freedom. They mark their change of status at the banks of the Sea of Reeds. There, the bitter experience of brutal servitude is forever transformed, as their nemeses are swiftly and decisively vanquished. There will be no return to the physical bondage of the brick pits, though the mental effects of that trauma continued to live on in the people's shattered psyches for some time.

Some forty years later, the people of Israel again stand at a crossroads, for they are about to abandon their unsettled and insecure wilderness lives for the promise of "a good and expansive land, a land flowing with milk and honey, a land peopled by the Canaanite, the Hittite, the Amorite, the Perizite, the Hivite, and the Jebusite" (Ex. 3:8). The experience of ceaseless wandering from place to place, of expectantly setting up camp only to anxiously abandon it shortly thereafter, of aimlessly following an ephemeral pillar of cloud that never reveals the destination ahead of time, is to be finally terminated with the securing of a plot of rich, red earth. The allure of a rootless life – devoid of responsibilities greater than to the self and unburdened by the necessity to formulate concrete goals – may maintain its hold on the tribal confederacy for many years, but there can be no going back to the aimlessness of the nomad.

In both episodes, the symbolic act that serves to sever the past and secure the future is an act of passage through a body of water. The Sea of Reeds splits wide open to reveal the people's ineluctable destiny and the Jordan River stops midcourse to welcome Israel to its patrimony on the other side. In the process of passage, the former identity is shed and a new one takes its place. Not unlike an act of birth, the people of Israel emerge from the depths to embrace the glaring brightness of a new beginning. In both cases, the past with its crushing failures is jettisoned in favor of a promising but inscrutable future. It is God who initiates each process and guides it to its successful conclusion. Israel the enslaved becomes Israel the liberated, while Israel who wanders in the end secures rest.

ABRAHAM AND JACOB

Actually, there are other examples in the Tanakh of traversing bodies of water to initiate transformation. Recall that Abraham and Sara, denizens of the southern Mesopotamian city of Ur, were called upon by God to break with their familial and cultural moorings, and to instead follow His voice to the land of Canaan. This the two duly did, ultimately crossing the Euphrates River in their northwest journey. In the process, the two were eventually transformed into advocates of ethical monotheism, champions of the belief in a single God and His absolute moral code that devolves upon all of humanity. Abraham, who was henceforth known as "Abraham the Hebrew" or *Avraham HaIvri* (Gen. 14:13) is so called according to some rabbinic traditions because he hailed from the "other side of the River" or *Ever HaNahar* (see Genesis Rabba 42:8). His descendants, known as the Hebrews, or *Ivrim*, preserve in their ethnic designation this ancient tradition of passage associated with their forebear.

Jacob, the grandson of Abraham and Sara, is forced to flee the Promised Land to escape the rage of his brother Esau. In a striking reversal of Abraham's forward-looking and confident journey of faith, Jacob was alone and afraid, penniless and vulnerable, as he crossed the Jordan River and headed eastwards towards the land of Aram (Gen. 32:10). There, he sought refuge in the house of his uncle Laban and there he remained for a period of twenty difficult years. Eventually, he was again forced to flee and this time journeyed back towards Canaan with his family and flocks. Unsettled by the prospect of encountering his long-lost brother, Jacob prepared for a confrontation. Under the cover of darkness, he spirited his family to safety by crossing the "pass of Yabok," a tributary of the Jordan River located midway between the Dead Sea and Kinneret (32:23). Alone in the night, Jacob was suddenly confronted by an angelic figure who struggled mightily with him but could not defeat him. Jacob, injured but victorious, extracted a blessing from the mysterious phantom, who informed him that henceforth he would be known as Yisrael, for "You have struggled with angels and with men and have prevailed" (32:29). Once again, we have a passage of water, this time in both directions. Each time is associated with a transformation of destiny. Initially, Jacob's crossing of the Jordan River symbolized his exile; the crossing of Yabok was his restoration.

CONTRASTS VERSUS COMPARISONS

While it is useful to compare episodes in Tanakh in order to delineate and thus understand a common motif, it is even more important to take note of the contrasts, for these often hold the key to understanding the true nature of the events. Having considered the similarities between the events of the Book of Joshua and those of the Book of Exodus, let us now analyze the differences as well. First of all, we note that at the Sea of Reeds, God diverted the liberated Hebrews from their original route along the shoreline of the Mediterranean Sea. Those who travel from Egypt to Canaan would naturally follow this arterial coastal road, the so-called Via Maris or "Way of the Sea," which is called in the Torah "the way of the land of the Philistines" (Ex. 13:17). God, however, directed the people to go by way of the wilderness instead, thus orchestrating their unexpected arrival at the banks of the Sea of Reeds.[1] There, they

---

1. Maimonides, in his *Guide of the Perplexed* 3:32, masterfully explores the psychological dimension of this detour. The text in Exodus reports that God did not want the people of Israel to enter Philistine territory lest they "have a change of heart when they see warfare and return to Egypt" (Ex. 13:17). Maimonides explains that freshly freed slaves cannot possibly shed their oppressed identity in an instant and "washing the clay from their hands, at once engage the giants in battle!" The detour was

were told to encamp but were given no divine indications as to the significance of the detour. Joshua, in contrast, makes it clear to the people from the outset that their objective is to cross the Jordan River in order to enter the land. Their arrival at its banks opposite the gateway of Jericho is therefore eagerly anticipated and involves no unexpected surprises.

Next, we note that Moses' charge to stand steadfast (Ex. 14:13–14) was a spontaneous reaction to the people's alarmed outcries, while Joshua's directive to prepare for God's "wonder" is delivered from the outset with deliberation and foresight. At the Sea of Reeds, God ordered Moses to tell the people to go forward and indicated that Egypt would come to recognize His divinity. In the case of the Book of Joshua, it is Israel who will recognize that God is with them as He was with Moses.

At the Jordan River, Joshua announces to the people ahead of time that the river will cease its flow as soon as the feet of the priests bearing the Ark make contact with its waters. At the Sea of Reeds, the eastern wind divides the waters as Moses stretches his staff over them. Then, the waters part to form a tunnel-like passage. The pillars of cloud and fire hold off the pursuing Egyptian cavalry while the people of Israel hurriedly enter the water's midst. At the Jordan River, the river is dammed upstream from a far distance, "at the city of Adam" (Josh. 3:16). Adam is identified by many scholars with Tel ed-Damiyeh, an ancient town located near the important route that led from the Transjordanian highlands of the Gilead to the Canaanite city-state of Shekhem (modern day Nablus). It is situated approximately twenty-five kilometers north of the Plains of Jericho where the people actually crossed. Finally, we note that at the Sea of Reeds, Israel emerged into the wilderness of Shur, while at the Jordan River the people entered the Promised Land.

All of these contrasts can in fact be reduced to a single, fundamental and defining distinction that actually recasts the Sea of Reeds and the Jordan River as two widely divergent incidents: The events at the Sea of Reeds are concrete expressions of the people's *panicked and*

---

therefore a recognition of their limitations and the first step in the arduous process of transforming them into autonomous self-confident beings capable of conquering the land.

irresolute object status, while the crossing of the Jordan River is an act of Israel as a *disciplined and confident subject.* As we shall see, examining the matter from this perspective leads us to conclude that the events of the Jordan River and the Sea of Reeds have almost nothing in common, besides a superficial resemblance!

When the Hebrew slaves left Egypt, they displayed all of the trappings of liberation. Surging forward, they took their flocks and possessions with them, even bearing parting gifts of silver and gold from their former overseers. Joyously, they followed Moses, Aaron, and Miriam, and fell in motley line behind the guiding pillar of cloud. With wide and unbelieving eyes, they bid farewell to the dismal brick pits, to the sprawling building sites still stained with their sweat and toil, and to the toppled pharaonic figures of lifeless stone testifying to the downfall of a being they had only recently regarded as an invincible god. Not only did Pharaoh acquiesce to the terms of their departure, but he urged them to make haste!

THE MENTALITY OF SLAVERY

Israel's emancipation, however, had come about exclusively through divine intervention, for centuries of state-sponsored oppression had robbed them of any self-worth, resourcefulness, or hope. Stricken with a textbook case of slave mentality, the people of Israel played no role whatsoever in their liberation, and their first, tentative steps as free men were therefore fraught with great misgivings. Rather than marching defiantly forward from servitude with confidence and direction, as might have been expected from victorious revolutionaries, they were instead forcibly driven out of Egypt by a king and his people anxious to preserve the tattered remains of their empire: "The people of Egypt pressed the people [of Israel] to leave quickly, for they said, 'Else, we shall all perish!'" (Ex. 12:33). Even the matza, the quintessential bread of liberation, was not allowed to rise only because "They were thrust out of Egypt and could not tarry, nor had they prepared any provisions" (v. 39). If not for God's determination to bring forth the nation of Israel from the crucible of bondage in order to recast them as the bearers of His precious teaching, the Hebrews would have remained in Egypt forever – helpless, subjugated, and held in check by their own self-loathing.

Leaving Egypt, their new-found but fragile faith would not be enough to sustain them through the struggles that lay ahead on the road to true freedom. In order to nurture confidence, self-reliance, and the precious ability to exercise the moral will, the people needed to first be imbued with the knowledge that their fate was in the hands of a concerned and caring deity and not a callous and cruel despot. The highest goal of a slave is to mindlessly make bricks; the noble objective of a free man is to do what is right in the eyes of God. To truly transform a slave into a free man is a long and arduous process. It can only commence once the fear of and dependence upon the ruthless authority figure has been smashed.

Thus, God stealthily redirected the people towards the Sea of Reeds, there to irreversibly bring about the overthrow of their former oppressors, and to make it clear to Israel that there could be no return to Egypt or to its senseless and numbing servitude. Encamped on its shores, they suddenly heard the sound of whirling chariot wheels and pounding hooves, and they were thrown into a panic:

> They said to Moses: "Are there not enough graves in Egypt that you took us out to perish in the wilderness? What have you done to us to take us out of Egypt? Is this not the very thing that we said to you in Egypt, that you should leave us alone so that we might labor for Egypt? It is better for us to labor for Egypt than to perish in the wilderness!" (Ex. 14:11–12)

After much uncertainty, as the people cried out desperately, their backs to the sea and their faces turned in terror towards the pursuing hordes, God uttered the impossible directive: "Speak to the people of Israel and tell them to go forward … into the midst of the sea on dry land." They were bidden to place their fate (and faith) in God and to enter the parting waters, confident that they would emerge alive. In essence, however, their "decision" to follow God was a foregone conclusion. There was no other choice! Turning back to Egypt was impossible, the path in any case barred by the ominous pillars of fire and cloud. The inevitability of the situation is highlighted by the twice-repeated but otherwise superfluous remark of the Torah that "the waters formed a wall to their right and to their left" (Ex. 14:22, 29). Like the submissive objects that they still were, God thus forced Israel to enter the channel of the Sea of Reeds in such a way that offered them no alternative, no distraction, no escape, and only one direction of trajectory: forward.

At the shores of the Sea of Reeds, the Hebrews demonstrated precious little initiative, showing themselves utterly incapable of fighting back against their former oppressors whom they outnumbered by a margin of a thousand to one, even though their wretched lives hung in the balance.[2] Broken and paralyzed, they could only cry out to Moses and bemoan their bitter fate, chanting the familiar mantras learned during their centuries of servitude. God, in His compassion, offered them an alternative, a means of survival if they would but believe. In a charged and transcendent moment, their fortunes were forever altered as the Egyptian horsemen perished beneath the waves. Transformed the people were, but by a process imposed upon their stiff necks rather than embraced by their receptive ears. Emerging from the maw of the Sea of Reeds into the wilderness of Shur, a barren but introspective landscape, they stood ready to finally embark upon the long and painful journey to secure their real freedom, an exalted state of being infinitely more meaningful than the release from physical bondage that we mistakenly call "liberty."

---

2. For more on this, see the commentary of Rabbi Abraham Ibn Ezra to Exodus 14:13.

Joshua 4:1–24

The Jordan River
Crossing Revisited

L ast chapter, we considered the pivotal episode of the crossing of the Sea of Reeds, an event that forever transformed the Hebrew slaves and propelled them forward on the path towards real freedom. We carefully analyzed the textual cues provided in the Torah's description and arrived at the conclusion that at the Sea of Reeds the people of Israel, notwithstanding their exodus from physical servitude, were still plagued by a slave mentality that rendered them incapable of making destiny-charged decisions. God's orchestration of the events at the sea was a direct function of Israel's existential paralysis. It constituted a subtle form of divine coercion calculated to shatter the people's feelings of powerlessness and vulnerability in the face of Pharaoh's imperial might.

Tensely descending into the sundered sea, constrained by towering walls of water to their right and to their left, the people of Israel had no choice but to go forward, guided only by their tenuous trust in the God of history who had only just liberated them and taken them as His own. As evidenced by their own frightened outcries, they gladly would have returned to the numbing life of servitude and toil had the opportunity been offered. Instead, at the Sea of Reeds, God made it devastatingly clear that no such possibility would be brooked: "Moses said to the people: 'Do not fear. Be steadfast and witness God's salvation on your behalf this day, for as you witness Egypt this day, you shall never see them again!'" (Ex. 14:13).

Moses' response to the people as they stood transfixed by the crashing waves of the sea before them, and by the whirling wheels and pounding hooves of Egypt's menacing charioteers to their rear, was not only a decisive statement of his faith. It was also a resounding declaration that on no account must they return to the helplessness and hopelessness of subjugation to tyranny.

DEMONSTRATING CONFIDENCE AND WILL

Although the people would never again deny the intellectual certainty of that truth, it would take a generation for them to grasp its profundity. Raised in the hardship and deprivation of the wilderness, sustained only by their ongoing trust in God's providence and attention to His word, the people of Israel slowly internalized the fundamentals of freedom. For the first time, they needed to exercise their autonomous will in response to God's invitation that extended to them a higher calling and mission. Occasionally, they embraced His words, more often they refused, but all the while the inescapable lesson of what constitutes true nationhood under God was patiently borne home. For the slave, nothing is more real than the immediate, and nothing more exalted than a pause from toil. For the free man, there is an awareness of the past and an anticipation of the future, as well as an instinctive but undefined drive to find meaning. For the liberated nation, however, that too is insufficient. A nation needs a clear sense of destiny and a sustaining purpose, an understanding of its unique place in the world and the spiritual stamina to secure it.

A generation later, the people of Israel again stood at a crossroads. To enter the land was not only to settle it and enjoy its bounty, but more significantly to take on the sacred task of fashioning a nation-state committed to the fulfillment of God's teaching. To traverse the Jordan River was, therefore, more than a geographical relocation; it was a spiritual transformation as well. This time, in contrast to the Sea of Reeds episode, the people of Israel were expectant, self-assured, and fervent. Joshua's announcement of the impending crossing was received not with alarm and consternation, but rather with eager anticipation. There were no pursuing hordes pressing the people forward into the swirling waters, no menacing phantoms blocking their retreat and boxing them in. Ardently and enthusiastically, the people entered the riverbed, their sights firmly fixed on the Promised Land.

The constriction of the Sea of Reeds crossing, the narrow passage through the depths while hemmed in on either side by impenetrable cascades, is here replaced by an expansiveness that is experientially antithetical: "The down-flowing waters stood as a single wall, from very far away at the city of Adam that is located next to Zaratan. The waters descending towards the Sea of the Plain, that is the Salt Sea [Dead Sea], ended and were cut off, and the people crossed opposite Jericho" (Josh. 3:16). The seemingly superfluous reference to Adam and Zaratan indicates that the Jordan River ceased its downward flow quite far away from the actual point of crossing – since the city of Adam is located approximately twenty-five kilometers to the north. Thus, rather than crossing in a narrow line as at the Sea of Reeds (itself a sure recipe for panic when speed is of the essence), the people of Israel crossed the river as a front and entered Canaan along the length of the Jordan. The land beckoned to them and they responded, advancing across the dry riverbed without any of the alarm and terror that is necessarily associated with navigating through a constrained corridor.

The dynamic of initiative with which our account is charged is also indicated by the role of the Ark, as well as by the marked absence of the pillar of cloud. Recall that the Ark of the Covenant, borne on the shoulders of the priests, proceeded before the people until it reached the banks of the swollen Jordan. As soon as the feet of the priests came in contact with the river's waters, they miraculously ceased flowing and thus "parted" to expose its traversable bed. Incredibly, however, the priests bearing the Ark remained rooted to the spot as the people of Israel crossed *before* them (Josh. 3:17, 4:10–11). The priests and Ark were therefore located on the eastern shore (Transjordan), while the people now found themselves on the western side (Canaan). Again, this order of journey stands in direct contrast to the conventional "wilderness protocol," in which the pillar of cloud and Ark always preceded the people to their destination (see Num. 10:11–28). Completing the contrast, the pillar of cloud in fact disappears completely from the account, vanishing as a mirage into the void of the barren wilderness.

FROM HELPLESS OBJECT TO EMPOWERED SUBJECT

The implication of the omission is clear. If traversing the Jordan means to begin exercising true national autonomy, if crossing its waters implies a new status as liberated subjects, if entering the land entails shedding the protective prop of God's constant miraculous intervention in favor of His more subtle but no less real involvement in the prosaic activities of founding a state, then the pillar of cloud can no longer be ever-present nor the Ark constantly in front. God will continue to guide the people of Israel in all their endeavors, and the Ark that manifests His presence will not abandon them. At the same time, however, during the actual crossing into the land, the Ark must remain temporarily behind, to indicate to the people that settling Canaan will require a higher level of involvement on their part. They have not been guided to the banks of the Jordan only to maintain the helpless object status that characterized them at the Sea of Reeds. Here, they must complete the process of their liberation by demonstrating direction, resolve, and enterprise. Therefore, they *must* pass before the Ark. Though they enter the land while still under God's watchful gaze, it is by the exercise of their own autonomous will.

It should be obvious that the evolution from object to subject and from slavery to liberation is a lengthy process over time involving many incremental steps, and often plagued by setbacks. Any student of the Book of Numbers will recognize immediately that its narratives painfully trace this progression. No wonder, then, that as the people draw closer and closer to the land, the manifest involvement of God correspondingly decreases in order to inspire the people with the need for greater initiative by them. The rabbinic tradition preserved in the Talmud (Taanit 9a) highlights this: With Miriam's death, the wondrous well, said to accompany the people during the course of their wanderings, disappears forever.[1] With Aaron's death, the protective clouds of glory,

---

1. See Rashi to Numbers 20:2.

including the remarkable pillar of cloud that was always at the forefront
of the wanderings, dissipate with the rising dew.[2] With Moses' demise
and Joshua's ascent to leadership, the process is now accelerated. Poised
to enter Canaan, the people must recognize that God has charged them
with the responsibility for building a just society in their new land. The
Ark will still be with them, but as an expression of overt divine guidance, it will slowly recede into the background.

THE MOTIF OF HASTE

In essence, then, the true linkage between the Sea of Reeds and the
Jordan River is not about the superficial resemblance between the two,
but rather about how they together trace the process of Israel's maturation. These two bracketing events mark the long and laborious path
from abject slavery to real freedom, from Egypt to the land of Israel.
No wonder, then, that the text draws two other important parallels
between the accounts: "The priests who carried the Ark stood fast in
the midst of the Jordan River until Joshua finished telling the people
all that God had commanded him to speak to them, as Moses had
commanded Joshua. Then the people quickly traversed" (Josh. 4:10).
Here, incredibly, the confidence of the moment is captured by the fact
that the people *stand still* in the Jordan River until Joshua completes
his address! Marauding attackers do not threaten them, nor are they
fearful of being swept away by the raging spring runoff. This of course
stands in glaring contrast to the Sea of Reeds, where terrified Israel
expected to be overwhelmed at any instant either by Egypt's chariots and horsemen or else by the collapsing walls of water, with both
scenarios spelling their sudden doom.

Only after Joshua has completed his words, however, do the
people pass, but then they move quickly to go across the river. This
immediately calls to mind another episode of haste and hurriedness:

> The people of Egypt pressed the people [of Israel] to leave *quickly*,
> for they said, "Else, we shall all perish." The people baked their

---

2. See Rashi to Numbers 21:1.

> dough that they took forth from Egypt as cakes of matza and
> not leavened bread, for they were driven out of Egypt and could
> not tarry, nor had they prepared any provisions. (Ex. 12:33–39)

Or, as Moses recounts the event to the people in the Book of Deuteronomy: "Do not eat leavened bread but rather matzot, the bread of afflic-
tion, for seven days. This is because you left the land of Egypt in great
haste" (Deut. 16:3). The same theme thus connects the Exodus to the
Jordan River, but what a different kind of haste it is! At the Exodus from
Egypt, the haste of Israel suggested fear and alarm, an anxious escape
lest the god-king change his mercurial mind to enslave the Hebrews
again. How quickly therefore do they press forth from Egypt, driven
out by Pharaoh's momentary panic, God's unconditional decree, and
their own racing heartbeats.

At the Jordan River, the people also quickly proceed once Joshua
completes his words, but theirs is a rush of anticipation, of excitement,
of finally reaching the culmination of their long and arduous journey.
This time, their speed is occasioned by Joshua's impassioned address,
not preserved in the biblical text but recorded in the rabbinic tradition:

> While the people were yet in the Jordan River, Joshua said to
> them: "Realize that you are traversing the Jordan River in order
> to drive out the land's inhabitants … if you are prepared to do so,
> then good. If not, then the waters of the Jordan River will sweep
> you away!" (Sota 34a)

Here, then, there is a sense of mission that suffuses the event, a realization that entering and settling the land will require great effort and
no small amount of fortitude. This time, however, the people seize the
moment and cross over the Jordan River with alacrity, signifying their
willingness and desire to undertake the demanding task ahead of them.

THE "TENTH DAY" AND THE CLOSING OF THE CIRCLE

Finally, there is a temporal connection between the two rites of passage,
a seasonal link that draws them unmistakably together. The Passover of
liberation occurred in the springtime, for the Exodus took place in the

month of Nisan (March/April). The crossing of the Jordan River also takes place as the river overflows with the spring runoff:

> When the priests who carried the Ark of God's covenant ascended from the Jordan River and their feet touched the dry ground, the waters of the Jordan River returned to overflow their banks as before. The people ascended from the Jordan River on the tenth day of the first month and encamped at Gilgal to the east of Jericho. (Josh. 4:18–19)

The "first month" is the month of Nisan, the same month that the people had left Egypt forty years before. The tenth day is also significant, for on that very day forty years earlier the people of Israel had been bidden to take their paschal lambs, to expectantly await the dawn of deliverance as Pharaoh's formerly iron resolve crumbled with the onset of the final and most devastating plague:

> God said to Moses and Aaron in the land of Egypt: "This month shall be your first month, the first of all months of the year. Speak to the people of Israel and tell them to take a lamb for each household on the tenth day of this month." (Ex. 12:1–3)

Thus, we neatly close the circle as the process of the Exodus is finally completed with the entry into the Promised Land. Many challenges still face the people, not least among them to conquer and to settle its slopes. But at least one of the struggles, perhaps the most significant one, is behind them: They have become a people with divinely-inspired direction, with meaningful and worthwhile objectives, and with the patient resolve and national confidence to achieve them.

Standing now at the Jordan River, many among the people of Israel are old enough to remember all too well the events of the Exodus and the Sea of Reeds that they had witnessed as children. The elation of the Exodus was soon followed by foreboding, as they entered the wilderness and camped at the sea. Panic and dread seized them as the swirling dust of Pharaoh's whirling chariot wheels was spotted on the horizon, and then incredulity and alarm as the sea opened up and beckoned them to enter. Finally, they felt triumph and jubilation, as they emerged unscathed while their tormentors perished under the waves. What a series of sudden and extreme emotional and spiritual turns to be weathered by a people scarcely freed from bondage! How different the situation now, as the people of Israel cross at the termination of *three days of preparation* (see Josh. 1:11), cognizant of the challenges ahead and fully committed to engage them. We now appreciate Joshua's forceful directive to the people at that time to prepare their provisions for the traversal; it is nothing but the utter overturning of the panicked exodus, when the people baked matza because they had not prepared *any* provisions (see Ex. 12:39).[3]

THE ACCOUNT OF THE BOOK OF PSALMS

As we leave the banks of the Jordan River behind, it is worthwhile to consider briefly another biblical reference to this event, composed many centuries later but still infused with its intensity and grandeur. The song of thanksgiving from the "Hallel," or "Praises," is recited by the Jewish people to this day at moments of great national awakening:

> When Israel went forth from Egypt,
> and the House of Jacob left a foreign people.
> Judah was His sanctified one,
> Israel His dominion.
> The sea saw and fled,
> the Jordan River turned backwards.
> The mountains skipped as rams
> and the hills as young sheep.
> Why do you flee, O sea,
> why, O Jordan River, do you turn back?
> Why, O mountains, do you skip,
> you hills as young sheep?

---

3. The unusual Hebrew word *tzeda* or "provisions" is artfully employed in both accounts to highlight the contrast: leaving Egypt, they prepared no provisions and left in a panic. Three days before crossing the Jordan River to enter the land, they calmly arrange their provisions in anticipation.

Before the Master, tremble O earth,
from before the God of Jacob.
He transforms unyielding rock into a pool of water,
the adamant flint into a living spring. (Ps. 114)

In this moving chapter, the sea, river, mountains, hills, earth, and rock are personified and described as quaking before God's splendor and yielding to His irresistible commands. It is noteworthy that although the section clearly describes both the Sea of Reeds and the Jordan River, they are nevertheless presented under the single rubric of "going forth from Egypt." There is no explicit reference in this psalm to the entry into the land. This fact only reinforces our earlier analysis that these two pivotal events, though separated by a span of four decades, are part and parcel of the very same dynamic process. On the most profound level, the Exodus is not complete until the people of Israel are sincerely prepared to enter the land of Canaan, not as freed slaves, but as a cohesive nation inspired with a clear and meaningful set of national aspirations.

In our mind's eye, we can see the Jordan River part before them as the priests enter its frigid waters. Presumably the waters open up at their feet as the text suggests (Josh. 3:15), but how can we reconcile that with the equally unwavering claim of the next verse that:

The down-flowing waters stood as a single wall, from very far away at the city of Adam that is located next to Zaratan. The waters descending towards the Sea of the Plain, that is the Salt Sea [Dead Sea], ended and were cut off, and the people crossed opposite Jericho. (Josh. 3:16)

Where then did the waters cease and divide? Was it at the feet of the priests or at the city of Adam? Perhaps the answer is both, as suggested by a careful reading of the above thanksgiving hymn from Psalms, for it records that "the sea saw and fled, the Jordan River *turned backwards*." In other words, the waters may have parted at the point of the priest's entry into the river but they then continued to retreat upstream all the way to the town of Adam many kilometers away, and only then stood up as a towering and static wall. Like an imposing gate being majestically pulled open to admit an honored guest, the Jordan River is thus dramatically drawn back to reveal to the people of Israel their inescapable destiny. Traverse it they do, not as a frightened throng pressing single file through a narrow corridor, but rather as a confident multitude proudly marching across its exposed expanse to take their rightful place in the world.

Joshua 4:1–24

Memorial of the Twelve Stones

In contrast to the episode of the Sea of Reeds, at the Jordan River the people of Israel demonstrated confidence and resolve, initiative and trust. The priests bearing the Ark remained behind on the eastern shore of the river until all the people had passed, and only then did they too join their compatriots on the hallowed earth of Canaan to the west. Before Israel left behind the climactic moment and the waters of the river rushed back to fill the void, God bid Joshua to commemorate the event in a most unusual way:

> God said to Joshua: "Take twelve men, one from each tribe. Command them to remove twelve stones from the Jordan River, from the very place where the priests stand. Bring them over with you and place them at the location where you will sleep this night." (Josh. 4:1–2)

Joshua duly issues the directive, adding the following explanation:

> Let this be a sign among you for the time that your children will ask, "What then is the meaning of these stones?" You shall explain

to them that the waters of the Jordan River divided before the Ark of God's Covenant; when it passed into the Jordan River the waters divided. These stones shall therefore serve as a memorial for the people of Israel forever. (Josh. 4:6–7)

Significantly, Joshua does not only remove twelve stones from the waters of the Jordan River to be carried by the people to their destination, but places twelve *other* stones in their place:

The people of Israel did as Joshua commanded and carried twelve stones, according to the number of the tribes of Israel, from the midst of the Jordan River, just as God had spoken to Joshua. They carried them over to the place of their lodging. Joshua placed twelve other stones in the midst of the Jordan River, at the place where the priests stood, those who bore the Ark of the Covenant, and there they remained, until this very day. (Josh. 4:8–9)

JOSHUA'S INITIATIVE

This seeming departure from God's directives is easily resolved by Radak (in his commentary on Josh. 4:9): "Although the text does not state that God enjoined the placement of twelve additional stones in the river, we must assume that Joshua was so commanded." The effect of Joshua's additional act is to create a sense of repetition and reiteration that is echoed throughout the chapter: God's command to Joshua is followed by Joshua's directive to the twelve selected men. This is in turn followed by their removal of the stones, then by Joshua's supplementary placement of other stones, and finally by a report of the twelve taken stones being erected in Gilgal where the people camp. The entire account is concluded by another explanatory passage:

Joshua said to the people of Israel: When your children will later ask their parents the meaning of these stones, then you shall say to your children, "Israel traversed this Jordan River on dry land. The Lord your God dried the waters of the Jordan River from before you until you crossed, just as the Lord your God did to the Sea of Reeds, drying it before us until we traversed. This is in order that all the peoples of the world might know that God's hand is strong, so that you might revere the Lord your God forever." (Josh. 4:21–24)

THE TWELVE STONE MOTIF

The significance of twelve stones is obvious and is indicated by the text itself: they represent the twelve tribes of Israel (Josh. 4:4). In fact, this motif is found in at least two other places in Tanakh that shed much light on the usage here. The first occurred in the immediate aftermath of the revelation at Sinai some forty years before. As the people stood at the foot of the mountain and Moses prepared to ascend to its peak, God concluded a special covenant with the people of Israel and they agreed to observe His teachings. The passage in the Book of Exodus relates that:

> Moses came and told the people all of God's words and the laws, and the people answered with a single voice saying, "We will perform all of the things that God has said." Moses transcribed all of God's words, arose early the next morning and erected an altar at the foot of the mountain, and placed *twelve standing stones to represent the twelve tribes of Israel.* (Ex. 24:3–4)

In this passage, the twelve stones standing sentinel-like and steadfast next to the altar memorialize the acceptance of God's covenant by the people of Israel.

In a very different passage, from the period of the Aramean Empire's ascendancy some five centuries after the entry into the land, the twelve stones were again utilized to represent the twelve tribes of Israel. By this time, the people of Israel had shed their tribal divisions to become a nation, but a nation nonetheless divided into two disparate kingdoms. The southern kingdom, populated in the main by the tribe of Judah, was ruled by the descendants of David from Jerusalem the capital. The northern kingdom of Israel, comprised of the so-called Ten Tribes, had already begun its precipitous descent into idolatry and immorality, a downward spiral that would conclude with its destruction and exile. A lone voice still dared to proclaim the truth of God's teachings in the face of a hostile king and an estranged people: Elijah the prophet.

The sybaritic message of the false prophets of Baal, who made no appeals for social justice or moral development and in their place offered the numbing balm of empty and licentious ceremony, was forcefully opposed by the fiery Elijah, who single-handedly confronted 850 of them at Mount Carmel. With the people of Israel massed around the combatants, Elijah chided the false prophets who, try as they might, could not persuade Baal to send fire from the heavens to consume their sacrifice. After their noisy but unsuccessful attempts, it was Elijah's turn to stand before the people and petition God to respond:

> Elijah said to all of the people, "Draw close to me," and all of the people drew close to him. He then repaired the ruined altar of God. Elijah took *twelve stones according to the number of the tribes of Jacob, whom God had addressed by saying: "Israel shall be your name."* He built the stones into an altar in the name of God. (1 Kings 18:30–32)

In this context, the twelve stones of Israel constitute the very foundations of the sacrificial altar, the concrete expression of the noble attempt to bridge the daunting distance between humanity and the Creator.

Both passages thus link twelve stones with the twelve tribes, as if this ancient evocation of the people of Israel, Jacob's own sons, could somehow be petrified into permanence. In glaring contrast to Moses' twelve stone pillars, however, that embodied all of the promise of Israel's future, Elijah's altar stones are a sad and pathetic reminder of a different time, an earlier epoch before Israel had succumbed to the wiles of idolatry and renounced the Torah that was their heritage. And while Moses' stones stand apart and separate, as if anticipating the challenge of forging tribes into a nation, Elijah's are lovingly brought together by the prophet to suggest Israel's reconciliation after their division into separate kingdoms.

COMMEMORATION VERSUS CONTINUITY

Returning now to our passage in the Book of Joshua, we can better appreciate the symbolism of the twelve stones. Heaped up under the feet of the priests, the twelve stones speak of preserving the transcendent moment when the people of Israel stood united in purpose and unified in trust. The miracle of the Jordan River's traversal was made possible by Israel's faith. At the banks of the Jordan River, the often uncomfortable dialectic between human enterprise and divine intervention was harmoniously resolved: Guided by His Ark, the people of Israel followed with conviction and resolve, and God did not disappoint. The waters ceased to flow; the people took the lead and entered the riverbed, and emerged into Canaan as a nation.

But the crossing of the Jordan River was not intended to become a moment frozen in time and an ancient memory. Instead, traversing the river unleashed the dynamic of founding a state. Therefore, the stones could not remain rooted to the riverbed but had to also be borne into Canaan to accompany the people on their journey. Where the people lodged, the stones lodged with them, to indicate that life's most precious lessons of faith must not be reduced to static commemorations.

THE ALTAR AT MOUNT EIVAL

How illuminating that, according to a well-founded but otherwise astonishing rabbinic tradition, these twelve stones taken from the Jordan River are on that same day transported to Mount Eival (some sixty kilometers distant)! According to this tradition, they are used at Mount Eival to fashion the very altar enjoined by Moses' directive in the Book of Deuteronomy:

> Moses and the elders of Israel commanded the people saying: Observe all of the commands that I give you this day. On the day that you pass over the Jordan River into the land that the Lord your God gives you, you shall raise up great stones and cover them with plaster. You shall then write upon them all of the words of this Torah, so that you may come into the land that the Lord your God gives you, a land flowing with milk and honey.... When you traverse the Jordan River, you shall erect these stones that I command you this day at Mount Eival, and cover them with plaster. There you shall build an altar to the Lord your God, an altar of stones that have not been cut by tools of iron. The stones shall be whole for building the altar to God. (Deut. 27:1–7)

As Rashi indicates:

> God's command to transport the stones into Canaan was in
> accordance with Moses' directive to erect an altar at Mount Eival
> and inscribe thereon the words of the Torah. On that very day,
> the people came to Mount Eival, built the required altar, offered
> sacrifices and feasted, and then disassembled the stones and
> brought them to Gilgal where they lodged. (Rashi on Josh. 4:3;
> based on Sota 35b)

In other words, the stones taken from the Jordan River are used on that
very day to construct the ceremonial altar at Mount Eival. After the
assembly, that altar is dismantled and the stones are transported back
to Gilgal, where the people have set up camp.

It is of course difficult to reconcile the traveling distances
involved. Also, it must be noted that Rashi's tradition assumes that
the altar stones of Mount Eival are the very same stones upon which
the Torah is to be graven and are in fact equivalent to the Jordan River
stones, two assumptions that are by no means certain from the biblical
texts. For our purposes, however, what is significant is to recognize the
linkage between the twelve Jordan River stones and the hallowed altar
stones, the very same motif that we saw concerning Moses at Sinai and
Elijah at Mount Carmel. In the reading of the rabbis, the stones of the
crossing become the stones of the altar and upon them are inscribed the
words of the Torah. What a profound association between the people of
Israel, the teaching that they must exemplify, and their exalted mission
to apprehend God and serve Him.

THE TWO ACCOUNTS

Summing up, we note that this chapter provides two different account-
ings of the twelve stones, as well as two separate explanations. One set
of stones is *removed* from the waters of the Jordan River to be carried
by the people to their destination; another set is *placed* in the waters of
the river to remain there forever. According to Joshua's *first* explanation
of the twelve stones, they are a memorial of *God's intervention* through
the vehicle of the Ark of the Covenant:

> Let this be a sign among you for the time that your children will ask, "What then is the meaning of these stones?" You shall explain to them that *the waters of the Jordan River divided before the Ark of God's covenant*, when it passed into the Jordan River the waters divided. (Josh. 4:6–7)

According to his *second* explanation, however, the stones do not empha-size the miraculous nature of God's involvement in the splitting of the river, but rather focus upon *Israel's fortitude* in traversing its waters:

> When your children will later ask their parents the meaning of these stones, then you shall say to your children, "*Israel traversed this Jordan River on dry land*. The Lord your God dried the waters of the Jordan River from before you until you crossed, just as the Lord your God did to the Sea of Reeds, drying it before us until we traversed." (Josh. 4:21–23)

Taken together, there is a dual message to be communicated by the memorial of the twelve stones, and it addresses the unique spiritual task of the people of Israel. On the one hand, they must have steadfast and unshakable trust in God, rooted to the earth and immovable in anticipa-tion of His salvation. At the very same time, though, they must become the agents of their own deliverance by confidently traversing the waters at their own initiative, demonstrating not only absolute faith in God but enterprise and effort as well. Twelve stones, the crystallization of Israel's purpose in the world, are placed in the river's raging waters to remember the Ark's miraculous work and their firm faith, but twelve other stones are simultaneously transported to the new land to highlight Israel's own resourcefulness in securing and settling it.

THE SOARING ARK

The entwined strands of divine involvement and human initiative, the stones that remain and the stones that are removed, are beautifully captured in a striking rabbinic tradition preserved in the Midrash and Talmud concerning the Ark's passage through the Jordan River. By utiliz-ing a fanciful and grammatically unsubstantiated reading of the relevant verses (Josh. 4:15–18), the Midrash understands that when the priests heed God's command to ascend from the Jordan River after the entire people of Israel have already passed, they do not do so by advancing across the dry riverbed and exiting at its western shore as the people did before them. Rather, the priests and the Ark retrace their initial steps and leave the river from its eastern bank. As soon as they do so, of course, the river begins its raging flow anew, leaving them seemingly stranded on the opposite side: "Thus, the Ark was on this side and the people of Israel were on the other. The Ark carried its bearers and passed over the waters!" (Sota 34a). The contention of this talmudic source, in clear contravention of the straightforward reading of the verses, so unnerved Radak that he remarked:

> I am astonished by this midrash, for I see no exegetical reason to adopt its forced reading of the text.... Why indeed must the Ark carry its bearers and fly over? If such a miracle had in fact occurred, wouldn't the text have stated so explicitly?... Our sages who recorded this tradition understood their intent, and their wisdom is more profound than mine. (Radak on Josh. 4:11)

Radak can provide no convincing textual arguments in favor of the midrashic reading. While not discounting Radak's wonder, it seems obvious that this source did not intend for us to accept it literally, and certainly not as the plain reading of the text. In fact, there is a much more profound idea that this midrash communicates, choosing to do so through whimsical language and colorful imagery. As we saw earlier, the passage of the Jordan River is very much about the confluence of human initiative and divine response. The people of Israel sally forth with confidence and the Ark steps aside to let them go forward. In fact, the Ark itself, as we pointed out some chapters ago, is a static object unless it too is carried into the world by human beings. God desires us to take an active part in the process of deliverance that alone can transform our world. Having exerted the effort that God demands, attempted the task and become crowned with success, the human psyche begins to ponder whether in fact God was at all involved, whether perhaps His perceived role was illusory and our role alone was determinant. Perchance there is no more or no less than the human initiative that alone can redeem? Is it possible that all of life's triumphs are solely the product of our personal and national efforts?

The Midrash responds to this irksome thought with a resounding no. God is aware, God is involved, and God saves. It is true that the priests must bear the Ark in order for it to be a dynamic force. Without human initiative, there is no fulfillment of the Torah and no possibility of redemption. At the same time, however, the more perceptive minds realize that our abilities and successes are gifts of God, which He bestows in accordance with His will. To phrase the matter differently, the priests may be the bearers of the Ark, but on a more profound level the Ark *carries them.*

As the people of Israel stand on the Jordan River's western shore, they eagerly anticipate the arrival of the Ark to again take the lead. Suddenly, however, the waters resume their flow and the priests are left stranded on the opposite side. In a memorable moment, the Ark takes to the air, bearing aloft the priests and gracefully gliding over the waters. They alight on the western shore and take their place at the head of the procession. The import of the midrashic episode is clear to the people of Israel: The God whom they have pledged to introduce to a hostile world will help them overcome. Their arduous exercise of trust and initiative will not be in vain, because God will support their efforts and give them the strength to go on. When Israel carries His presence into the world, He bears them in turn and raises them aloft. The great expenditure of trust in God that is required in order to navigate a cruel and callous historical experience is not spent in vain; it is reflected back to us in the form of God's strength-giving support.

One final note: The above midrash provides us with an excellent opportunity to consider a methodological point. Often, when we come across an astonishing midrash, our immediate reaction is to dismiss it out of hand. This is not only a methodological error but a lost opportunity as well. The correct question to ask when confronted with a source of this type is not, "How is this possible?" but rather, "What more profound idea may the midrash be conveying?" Radak, although he declines to offer an alternative reading for the midrash, nevertheless alerts us to this necessary reorientation by invoking the ancient rabbis' wisdom. This is another way of saying that a non-literal reading of the midrash is in order. The message for us is clear: It is *not* the case that Midrash operates without any rules; it *is* the case that the rules of midrashic analysis differ from those of *peshat*.[1] In reading a midrash we search for the deeper insight that is couched in the fanciful language, in order to extract a more thoughtful message than might otherwise emerge from a straightforward reading of the biblical text.

---

1. The differences between a midrashic approach versus a peshatist approach to the biblical text are myriad and a fuller treatment of the subject is beyond the scope of this study. Nevertheless we can reduce the matter to a few salient points: (1) a midrashic reading is often impelled by non-contextual references, while a peshatist interpretation is grounded in the immediate context; (2) a midrashic approach makes prior assumptions about the characters, plot, or setting that a peshatist approach does not make; (3) a midrashic approach employs fantastic imagery or language in a way that departs from the *peshat*. In short, a midrashic approach employs the biblical verse as a medium for extracting additional meaning that it may not otherwise contain.

Joshua 5:1–9

Circumcision at Gilgal

Having successfully crossed the Jordan River, the people of Israel are now encamped on its western side, not far from Jericho. Last chapter, we considered the memorial of the double set of twelve stones, one set placed into the Jordan River and the other removed from the river to accompany the people to their new camp. At the time, Joshua indicated the dual purpose of the commemoration: on the one hand to indicate God's miraculous intervention through the agency of the Ark, and on the other hand to emphasize Israel's steadfast trust in fearlessly crossing into the Promised Land. The similarities to the Sea of Reeds were numerous, but, as we discovered, the two pivotal events were more properly appreciated in contrast. The theme of contrast will continue to preoccupy us as we begin the study of the next episode, for the text deliberately invites us once again to recall events associated with the Exodus:

> When all of the Amorite kings on the western side of the Jordan River, and all of the Canaanite kings on the seashore heard that God had dried up the waters of the Jordan River before the people of Israel until they had passed, their hearts melted and they had no more spirit in them to fight the people of Israel. (Josh. 5:1)

For the people of Israel, the traversal of the Jordan River's waters was an important transformative act that highlighted the shedding of their wilderness existence, a life characterized by minimal initiative on their part and maximal overt intervention by God. Henceforth, they would be expected to demonstrate greater resolve and enterprise, while still remaining cognizant of God's central role in securing a successful outcome. For the peoples of Canaan, on the other hand, the miracle at the Jordan River had a very different purpose: to instill fear, dread, and surrender.[1]

UNDERSTANDING THE TOPOGRAPHY OF CANAAN

Before we embark on the chapters of conquest and settlement, it is important to be aware of some salient geographical and political features of the Canaanite landscape. The land of Canaan west of the Jordan River has a variety of climatic and topographic zones. Although constituting a relatively small land mass, Canaan forms the natural bridge between Africa and Asia and contains a great diversity of landscapes. The snow-covered peaks of the Hermon range to the north give way to the verdant and rolling countryside of the Galilee, which then abruptly descends to the fertile and hot valleys of the Kinneret basin. From here, the landscape rises again to form the limestone hills of the central region and the arid and barren cliffs of the Negev to the south. From west to east, the flat and mostly traversable Mediterranean seashore yields to the foothills that rise to form the central hills, but then the landscape suddenly cascades into the Jordan rift and finally trails off into the desolate and stark deserts to the east. The crest of the central hill country constitutes the watershed, dividing the fertile coastal valleys and western

---

1. Significantly, Israel anticipated this Canaanite dread when they triumphantly sang at the Sea of Reeds: "May dread and fear fall upon them, may Your mighty power silence them as stone, until Your people will traverse O God, until the people whom You have acquired will traverse!" (Ex. 15:16). Little did Israel realize at the time that forty years would elapse before their hopeful vision would come to pass. In any case, our context provides striking confirmation of the earlier analysis: the Sea of Reeds and the Jordan River are two critical nodes along the continuum of Israel's spiritual development. The ancient rabbis continued the theme in their startling reading of Ex. 15:16 preserved in the Talmud, Berachot 4a.

hill terraces that are watered by the rain clouds spawned by the Mediterranean, from the inhospitable and desiccated wilderness to the east. The contrasts of this land are highlighted by the fact that while the Sea of Kinneret is the only substantial body of fresh water in the area, the Dead Sea (only 120 kilometers to its south) contains the highest salinity of any sea in the world.

The variegated terrain of Canaan had the pronounced effect of making political unity difficult to achieve at all periods of Canaanite (and later, Israelite) history. The tribes that inhabited Canaan tended to form independent city-states that controlled their immediate regions and little else. Frequently, these cities were in conflict with each other and rarely cooperated on matters of regional importance. During no period of Canaanite history do we find the development of political models based upon allegiance to an absolute and central authority, such as were to be found to Canaan's southwest in Egypt or to its northeast in Mesopotamia. Those other two realms were both characterized by great and undifferentiated river valleys: fertile grounds for nurturing absolutist models that could control and manage the resources successfully.

In Canaan, the Amorite tribes that originally hailed from Asia Minor and the lands northeast of the Jordan inhabited the hill country, while the fertile coastal plains were settled and extensively farmed by the more materially advanced peoples whose towns dotted the seaboard all the way up to Phoenicia. The above-cited verse is quite precise in speaking of numerous Amorite kings and Canaanite kings, for the land was effectively carved up among assorted petty fiefdoms. The importance of this fact for the people of Israel should now be obvious: The task of conquest will be made easier by the absence of any united front that can oppose them. The confederacies of Canaanite city-states hurriedly hatched in the aftermath of the fall of Jericho and the Ai (Josh. 10:1–5) present much less of a threat than a cohesively united polity. As we shall see, the conquest of Canaan will unfold as the successive falls of individual towns and cities.

CIRCUMCISION OF THE PEOPLE – TWICE

This brief introductory verse is quickly passed over as the text suddenly refocuses our attention on another matter entirely:

> At that time, God said to Joshua: "Make blades of flint and cir-
> cumcise the people of Israel on a second occasion." Joshua made
> blades of flint and circumcised the people of Israel at the Hill of
> Foreskins. This is the matter concerning the circumcision per-
> formed by Joshua. All of the people who had left Egypt, the males
> of military age, had perished in the wilderness on the journey after
> having left Egypt. All those who had left [Egypt] were circum-
> cised, but all those who had been born in the wilderness while
> traveling, after the Exodus from Egypt, were not. (Josh. 5:2–5)

The mass rite of circumcision performed by Joshua at this time was
meant to rectify a striking omission: the males who had left the land
of Egypt some forty years before had been circumcised, as the day of
liberation drew near, but all those subsequently born and raised in the
wilderness were uncircumcised. Although the relevant texts in the Book
of Exodus fail to say so explicitly, they imply that during the enslavement,
the commandment of circumcision had fallen into neglect. The paschal
sacrifice, presented on the very eve of the Exodus, could not be brought
by males who were uncircumcised (Ex. 12:43–50), and therefore a mass
rite of circumcision must have taken place a short time before the flight
from Egypt. During the course of the wilderness wanderings, all the
circumcised adults who had left the land of Egypt eventually perished
in consequence of the episode of the spies. Those who had been born
in the wilderness, on the other hand, remained uncircumcised, as the
command of circumcision was again apparently disregarded. Therefore,
the males who entered the land were in need of performing it anew.

Our text thus sets up a double parallel in which the uncircumcised generation of the enslavement corresponds to the uncircumcised
generation of the wilderness, while the circumcision of the Exodus is
like the circumcision of the entry into Canaan. To understand the ramifications of the above, it is necessary to briefly revisit the command of
circumcision as it is presented for the first time in the Book of Genesis:

> When Abram was ninety-nine years old, God appeared to him
> and said: "I am Almighty God, walk before Me and be pure of
> heart. I will fulfill My covenant with you and shall increase you

greatly.... Your name shall no longer be Abram, but rather Abraham, for I have made you the father of a multitude of nations.... I will give you and your descendants after you the land of your sojournings, the entire land of Canaan as an inheritance forever, and I shall be their God."

God said to Abraham: "You shall observe My covenant, you and your descendants forever. This is My covenant that you shall observe between Me and you and your descendants after you: all of your males shall be circumcised. You shall remove the flesh of your foreskins, and it shall constitute the sign of the covenant between Me and you. At the age of eight days shall all of your males be circumcised forever.... He who remains uncircumcised and does not remove the flesh of his foreskin shall be cut off from among his people, for he has abrogated My commandment." (Gen. 17:1–14)

THE ESSENCE OF THE IDEA

The passage above, describing the special relationship between God and the aged Abraham, suggests that the covenant sealed between them both shall be indicated on the bodies of Abraham and his descendants by the physical mark of circumcision. Without digressing to discuss the substantial literature devoted to explaining this unusual commandment,[2] it should be obvious that at its most essential core, circumcision speaks of identification with a larger group of people. As individuals, people may lead unconnected lives, but when a group of them is provided with a similar indelible physical mark on their bodies, that cannot but imply their coming together in some sort of communal or national association.

---

2. For more on the rationale of circumcision, see Maimonides in his *Guide of the Perplexed* 3:49, where he offers two powerful insights. The first sees circumcision as an attempt to positively shape male character by tempering sexual drive; the second speaks of the collective identity that is created when people share the same ineradicable mark. For the purposes of our discussion, we have adopted the second interpretation. Other *Rishonim* who dealt with the issue include the *Sefer HaḤinukh* in Mitzva #2, Radak in his comments to Genesis 17:11, and Seforno in his comments to Genesis 17:13.

The descendants of Abraham, the people of Israel, were henceforth identifiable as a separate faith community. No wonder that God's command is accompanied by Abraham's change of name, because from now on his household will be similarly charged with a new destiny and mission. The covenant between God and Abraham is one in which Abraham's descendants will be responsible for upholding God's commands, and He, in return, will relate to them as His special people. Since that covenant is eternal, and can never be abrogated by either party, it is marked with an indelible sign on the body that is bound up with the male's reproductive capacity. Individuals may die, but the nation that is forged through their common ideals lives on in perpetuity.

What is especially meaningful for our purposes is the progression in God's unfolding revelation to Abraham: The promise of the covenant is followed by the change of name. This is succeeded by God's oath to maintain an eternal bond between Abraham's descendants and the land of Canaan, and the passage then concludes with the command of circumcision and the consequences of non-compliance. In other words, the nation-in-the-making that will champion God's covenant will be charged with a unique role that will be most effectively realized in its own land, the land of Canaan. The land isn't simply a convenient backdrop for the covenant, but rather the key to its comprehensive fulfillment. The individual descendants of Abraham will henceforth be identified as a people with a crucial role to play in the larger scheme of human history. Their ultimate success in the world will depend upon the structures and institutions that only national autonomy can provide.

It is therefore eminently reasonable that the two mass rites of circumcision occur at these moments of intense national identification. As the people prepare to leave Egypt, they are for the first time regarded as a nation and not only a collection of tribal units. As they enter the land some forty years later, they are about to embark on a new stage of nationhood, for their collective yearnings will now become capable of attainment. Our text, however, does not indicate why the rite of circumcision, though regarded as a vital and venerable command, had been neglected by the people of Israel during the course of their wanderings.

An ancient talmudic tradition quoted by Rashi begins to shed some light on the omission:

On the eve of the Exodus from Egypt, a great multitude was circumcised together, and the rite described in the Book of Joshua
therefore constituted the second time that the ceremony was
performed. During the entire forty years of the wanderings, the
northern wind did not blow, and thus there was no day that was
deemed fit for executing the procedure. (Rashi on Josh. 5:2 based
on Yevamot 72a)

According to this source, the northern wind is a particular climatic
condition associated with dispersing cloud cover and thus creating the
ideal conditions for accelerating the healing process. Under normal circumstances, its curative effects are felt on most days. Its unprecedented
absence for such a lengthy period was deemed sufficient grounds for a
protracted delay in fulfilling the command of circumcision.

RASHI AND RADAK

It is not the aim of our textual investigation to ascertain the scientific
basis of this tradition. For our purposes, what is significant is to recognize that by ascribing the negation of the rite of circumcision to
the absence of the northern wind, the onus for the omission is clearly
removed from the people of Israel and seemingly placed on God. The
Creator who marshals the forces of nature and bends them to His will
decided, in accordance with His inscrutable wisdom, to hold back the
therapeutic powers of the northern wind. The people of Israel were
consequently denied the opportunity to perform an ancient command
that they would have otherwise, apparently, fulfilled with fervor. Rashi
offers no convincing explanation for the divine decision to alter the
prevailing weather patterns in a manner that prevented the people of
Israel from maintaining this singular sign of the covenant vouchsafed
to Abraham.

Radak is also reticent concerning the underlying assumptions of
the above talmudic tradition, and is content to instead provide a more
rational explanation:

It is also possible to explain that the people did not fulfill the
rite of circumcision for all of those years because the verse states

that "they encamped by God's command, and they broke up
camp at God's command" [Num. 9:20]. Thus, they never knew
in advance the day that they would travel. If the newborns would
have been circumcised and would have then had to travel on the
day of their circumcision, they would have become endangered
en-route. (Radak on Josh. 5:2)

Since the fundamental objective of the wilderness experience was to
nurture the people's recognition of the necessity to rely upon God, their
travels were conditioned by inexplicable divine fiat and by no other dis-
cernable criterion. When the cloud of glory unexpectedly lifted off of the
Tabernacle, the people of Israel followed, and where it just as abruptly
came to rest, there they set up camp until the next round of the journey (Num. 9:15–23). The inherent instability that characterized their
nomadic lives made the fulfillment of the commandment of circumcision impossible, lest performing it lead to endangering the well-being
of the newborn children.

    Like Rashi before him, the explanation of Radak also has the
convenient effect of shifting responsibility for the annulment of circumcision to God, but offers us no additional insight into the possible divine
motivation. A closer reading of the relevant talmudic passage may assist
us in better understanding the matter. The Talmud offers no less than
three possibilities as to why Israel did not fulfill the commandment of
circumcision during the forty years of wandering:

> Why weren't the people circumcised? It may be because they suf-
> fered weakness due to journeying, or it may be because the north-
> ern wind did not blow. Thus have we learned: "For all of the years
> that the people of Israel were in the wilderness, the northern wind
> did not blow on their account." Why not? It may be because the
> people were in a state of reproach, or it may be because it would
> have scattered the clouds of glory. (Yevamot 71b–72a)

A careful reading of this passage indicates not only the source of
Rashi's explanation, but that of Radak as well. "Weakness due to jour-
neying" is very similar to Radak's contention that the unpredictability

of camp life made it hazardous for the command of circumcision to be observed by the people. Significantly, though, the Talmud devotes most of its attention to the alternate view concerning the northern wind, but here provides a reading that varies considerably from the understanding furnished by Rashi. The pivotal phrase that Rashi omitted is "because the people were in a state of reproach," where the exact nature of the reproach and its underlying causes are cryptically absent from the text. Why were the people of Israel in a state of reproach for the duration of the wilderness experience? Why should this impact on the command of circumcision? Is there any textual basis in the Book of Joshua or elsewhere for this elusive talmudic explanation?

THE TORAH'S STARTLING TIME FRAME

All of us are well aware that from the moment of the Exodus until the entry into the land of Canaan, some forty years elapse. The pivotal episodes of the entire period, the trials and triumphs, successes and failures, are described at great length in the narrative sections that constitute much of the Book of Exodus and the Book of Numbers. The Torah devotes a great deal of attention to the events leading up to the Exodus, to the subsequent journey from Egypt to Sinai, to the revelation of God's ten guiding principles at that mount, to the debacle of the Golden Calf and God's forgiveness, and to the people's energetic endeavors to craft and erect the Tabernacle. The people remained at Sinai for almost a year and there they received the bulk of the Torah's commands, as contained in the Book of Leviticus. Finally, as the Book of Numbers opened, they were bidden to break up camp as the cloud of glory lifted off of the Tabernacle and the Ark of the Covenant began its trek towards the land. As they approached its borders and reached the oasis of Kadesh Barnea, the spies were sent to search out the land but they returned with frightening reports of Canaanite invincibility. The people fell prey to their inflated claims, surrendered their trust in God, and that entire generation was consequently condemned to wander aimlessly in the wilderness and to expire.

Almost forty years later, the Torah again picks up the thread of the narrative with the description of the people's arrival at the wilderness of Tzin, "in the first month" (Num. 20:1) of the fortieth year. There, Miriam dies, Moses and Aaron strike the rock and are condemned to perish, but the inexorable march of the people of Israel towards Canaan continues. Skirting the territory of Edom, Moav, and Ammon, they find themselves east of the Jordan River and in direct confrontation with Siḥon, the mighty king of the Amorites whom they defeat in battle. Og, king of the northern region of Bashan, is vanquished next, leaving the people encamped on the Jordan River's eastern stretches with no opposition barring their entry into Canaan.

What is most astonishing about the above schematic survey of these forty years is that it indicates that *the Torah passes over thirty-eight of those years in almost complete silence!* Thus, we know a lot about the period associated with the Exodus and the arrival and encampment at Sinai, we know a fair amount about the successful second march towards Canaan, but we know next to nothing about the intervening period – from the debacle of the spies until the people's arrival at the wilderness of Tzin – a span of almost four decades. As Rabbi Abraham Ibn Ezra succinctly puts it: "The Torah mentions not a single episode or prophecy [to Moses] except those that occurred during the first year or the fortieth!" (Ibn Ezra on Num. 20:1). The great majority of the Torah's narratives and commands, the numerous chapters that comprise four of the five books of Moses, are thus properly compressed into the startling time frame of two years: the year of the Exodus from Egypt and the year of the entry into the land. The intervening period, during which a generation came of age, lived out its useful years and perished, is shrouded in utter darkness.

In the Book of Deuteronomy, aged Moses, his life ebbing away, recounts the history of Israel. He remembers well the sending of the spies, the promise and the disappointment, and God's stern sentence against the people:

> None of these men, this evil generation, will live to see the good land that I swore to their ancestors to give them…. Your young children, whom you said would be taken as spoil, the children who know not yet how to tell good from evil, they will enter it. I will give it to them and they will inherit it. (Deut. 1:35, 39)

Moses recalls the journey from Kadesh Barnea whence the spies had been initially sent, to the brook of Zered at the gateway to Canaan from the east. A distance that could have easily been traversed in a period of days stretched out interminably to become almost forty years. Wistfully, Moses recalls them:

> The years that passed from the time that we left Kadesh Barnea until we came to Naḥal Zered were thirty-eight years, until all of the adult men of military age had perished from among the people, as God swore to them.... When all of them had completely died out, then God spoke to me saying: "Today you pass by the border of Moav at the city of Ar." (Deut. 2:14–18)

A careful reading of the above verse indicates that Moses implies a subtle linkage between the death of the generation of the wilderness and the renewed communication of God to him. Or, as Rashi puts it, echoing sentiments preserved in the much earlier rabbinic midrash of the *Sifra* (Parshata 1, 2:13):

> From the episode of the sending of the spies until this point, the text of the Torah does not record that "God spoke to me [Moses]" but rather that "God said to Moses." This indicates that during those thirty-eight years, the people of Israel were in a state of reproach, and God's communications to Moses were not characterized by affection. This teaches that the spirit of God inspires the prophets only for the sake of the people of Israel. (Rashi on Deut. 2:16–17)

Rashi's penetrating comments reveal the true nature of the "prophetic gift," namely that God inspires people with His word as a function of the needs of His people Israel. At the same time, Rashi's interpretation provides us with the key for advancing our investigation. As long as the people of Israel were in a state of reproach, a period that lasted thirty-eight years, God's communications to Moses were correspondingly austere and abrupt. This is the very same state of reproach that our above talmudic source associated with the cessation of the rite of circumcision.

WEAVING TOGETHER THE STRANDS

Earlier, we noted that as long as the people of Israel were in the wilderness, they did not observe the command of circumcision. Now we have learned that during this very same period, God addressed Moses in a tone that lacked tenderness and warmth. These are the very same thirty-eight years that the Torah passes over in deafening silence. Recall that the vast majority of the Torah's narrative events and commands are associated with either the first year after the Exodus or the final year before the entry. The intervening vacuum of thirty-eight years constitutes the futile lifespan of a generation condemned to die; they perish in a barren wilderness that swallows them up without leaving even a textual trace. And what was the event that triggered this fatal chain? It was the sending of the spies.

Earlier, we devoted much time to contrasting Moses' spies to those of Joshua. What concerns us here, however, is that earlier episode's axiological implications: When the people of Israel frightfully embraced the spies' tainted report, they rejected God's precious gift of the land of Canaan. To recall their words at that sorry juncture:

> The people raised their voices and cried that night. The whole people of Israel railed against Moses and Aaron, and said: "If only we would have died in the land of Egypt, or in this wilderness, if only we would have died! Why does God bring us to this land to die by the sword, leaving our wives and children as plunder. Surely it is better for us to return to Egypt!" Each one said to his fellow: "Let us appoint a leader and return to Egypt!" (Num. 14:1–4)

Or, as poetically described in the psalms, written some four hundred years later:

> They rejected a desirable land
> and did not believe His word.
> They slandered in their tents,
> they did not listen to the voice of God.
> He swore to them
> to cause them to perish in the wilderness. (Ps. 106:24–26)

When the people of Israel turned their backs on the land of Canaan, notwithstanding God's longstanding oath to secure it for them, they suffered His harsh reprimand. With the explicit statement of His displeasure and disappointment there is the stark realization by the people that there will be no clemency for their indiscretion, no moderation of their sentence, and no hope for pardon. God's oath will instead be fulfilled to their children, who will be nurtured on the steadfast trust that only the experience of the wilderness can provide.

In the meantime, the northern wind ceases to blow; its healing breezes desist and die away, to be replaced by the stifling feeling of God's distance and utter remoteness. To their dismay, the people of Israel realize that what yesterday was palpably within reach is today unachievable. Turning to the sole remaining comfort, God's guiding laws, they become aware that one of the most solemn and meaningful of their national rituals could no longer be performed without great and intolerable danger: the command of circumcision. The mark that had set them apart on the eve of their national awakening as they prepared to leave Egypt, the ancient expression of their national identity and of God's perpetual covenant, the sign that had been bestowed upon their forefather Abraham as God lovingly extended to him the eternal gift of the land of Canaan, was now, like the fertile earth that sadly beckoned beyond the hot sands of the Sinai, beyond their grasp forever.

From a purely technical perspective, the formal commandment of circumcision devolves upon individuals and is completely independent of any actual geographic link to Canaan. The Talmud and codes make it crystal clear that circumcision is *never* dependent upon residing in the land (see Mishna Kiddushin 1:9). Nevertheless, as a conceptual ideal, circumcision implies a national identity and its corollary of an autonomous existence in a homeland. Therefore, when Israel readies to leave Egypt, transcends individuality, and forges their national identity, it necessarily follows that they must perform circumcision, although they have neglected the command for some time. Their bodies marked with the seal of God's covenant and minds seared with its eternal promise, they venture forth to secure the land and the mission that He swore to their ancestor Abraham.

When the spies return and Israel rejects that future by vociferously declining God's gift of Canaan, it necessarily follows that His barring of their entry into the land will be accompanied by the onset of circumstances that will render circumcision incapable of fulfillment. Could it be that the people can angrily rebuff the land "flowing with milk and honey," promised to their forebears and sealed by solemn oath, but can yet stand ready to observe the ancient rite of circumcision that is so fundamentally bound up with the awareness of their national mission and its ancient and organic connection to the soil of Canaan?

God, in His mercy, spares them the unbearable pain of explicitly renouncing their offers of fulfillment. Instead, He precipitates conditions that will make circumcision impossible. The north wind ceases to blow, Moses' prophecies are bestowed with brusqueness, and the people of Israel enter the gaping jaws of a wilderness that will swallow up any memory of their lives. The linkage of the events is not at all arbitrary, for all of them together delineate the contours of the people's anguished "state of reproach" of which the ancient rabbis spoke. All hope is not lost, however, for the children of that generation will grow to maturity and merit to graciously accept the gift of the land.

Now crossing over the Jordan River, finally overcoming the collective curse cast on those thirty-eight depleted years, standing on the very land that God had promised to their parents and had now given to them, the people of Israel listen attentively as God finally seals that sorry chapter forever:

> For forty years the people of Israel trekked through the wilderness, until those adults of military age who had left Egypt and had not hearkened to God's voice perished. God had sworn to them that He would not show them the land that He had sworn to their ancestors to give us, a land flowing with milk and honey. Their children who were established in their place were therefore circumcised by Joshua.... God said: *"On this day I have rolled off the reproach of Egypt!"* Therefore they called that place Gilgal until this very day. (Josh. 5:6–9)

Joshua 5:10–12

Passover and Manna

In our last study, we investigated the wider ramifications of the mass circumcision performed by the people of Israel immediately after they had crossed the Jordan River. We carefully considered the startling biblical admission that the rite had not been performed in the forty years since the people had left Egypt, and were able to link the people's negation of the practice to their divinely-imposed estrangement from Canaan. Having embraced the report of the spies soon after the Exodus and been consequently condemned to perish in the wilderness, the people's performance of the ceremony of circumcision, with its age-old underlying ties to national identity and national homeland, would have constituted a glaring contradiction in terms. As evidence for this reading, other related sources were adduced: the ancient rabbis' otherwise obscure claim that the drawn-out absence of the curative northern wind precluded the observance of circumcision, the well-founded rabbinic tradition concerning God's grudging manner of communication with Moses during that same thirty-eight year wilderness sojourn, and the undeniable textual confirmation provided by the fact that the Torah's narratives record nothing (or next to nothing) of those intervening years.

Taken together, the implication of the above seemingly disparate elements is clear: for Israel to be distant from Canaan's soil and the attendant possibility of national autonomy, for Israel to stray from its God-given comprehensive mission that is inextricably bound up with a homeland, is for Israel to become but a shadow of itself. Banished from the Jordan River's western bank by a reckless lack of trust, the people reaped the bitter harvest of their indiscretion and were no more. The most fundamental manifestation of their identity as a people, the precious command of circumcision, was subtly placed by God beyond their grasp, in order to indicate in no uncertain terms that the ethereal exile of the wilderness could never substitute for the tangible challenge of settling the land. Therefore, as soon as the people of Israel resume the thread of their story as a nation by traversing the river's rushing waters under Joshua's able leadership, finally closing the ignominious chapter of the spies' infamy, they enthusiastically fulfill the commandment of circumcision en masse.

THE PASCHAL SACRIFICE – A SYMBOL OF NATIONAL RENEWAL

What immediately follows in our narrative should now be readily com-- prehensible: "The people of Israel encamped at Gilgal, and they performed the Pesaḥ [Passover] on the fourteenth day of the month at evening, at the plains of Jericho" (Josh. 5:10). On the eve of the Exodus from Egypt, the rite of the paschal sacrifice was preceded by the mass circumcision of the males, who were otherwise disqualified from participating (see Ex. 12:42–50). Here, as well, Joshua circumcises the people and they then prepare the paschal lamb without delay.

Like circumcision, many of the detailed prescriptions of Passover plainly attest to its overriding national dimension. Chronologically, it ranks among the first of the commands that were given to Israel as a people. The Exodus from Egypt signaled not only the emancipation of oppressed slaves, but also their adoption of a shared destiny that was to culminate in their becoming a nation. Accordingly, the Torah mandates that the paschal sacrifice is ideally to be consumed in a group setting, and that individuals are to be discouraged from offering and consuming it in isolation.[1]

---

1. See Maimonides, *Mishneh Torah*, Laws of the Paschal Sacrifice, 2:1-2.

While the wistful descriptions of the Mishna in Pesaḥim 5:5–7 relate, in strict historical context, to the offering of the paschal lamb during the late Second Temple era (first century, CE), the observance was a national event of epic proportions throughout the lengthy period that the Temple stood in Jerusalem. As the Temple's sacred enclosure filled to overflowing with Jewish pilgrims drawn from the four corners of the globe, the experience of the Exodus was relived. Understood in this light, Joshua's Passover offering is the most definitive statement yet of Israel's ongoing transformation from tribal wilderness nomads to a united nation settled in a homeland. But what of its link to the observance of circumcision, a connection made explicit not only by ritual laws enshrined in the text, but by the historical precedent of Egypt as well?

Circumcision is a painful experience, and its adherents must be ready to suffer that pain in order to testify to their association with each other as well as with a common destiny. On the most fundamental level, circumcision acts as an identifying mark that links together unrelated individuals to form a community or a nation. That first paschal lamb prepared in Egypt was also about identifying marks, for its blood marked the homes of God's followers. Eaten in units of family and clan, this sacrifice – more than any other – eloquently spoke of larger, national affiliations. Therefore, it was precisely these two commandments that ushered in the Exodus, for they both spoke of assuming a national identity predicated upon the recognition of God and adherence to His teaching. It is most fitting, therefore, that these two observances constituted the merits by which the people of Israel secured their redemption from Egyptian bondage.

As we saw earlier, the text in the Book of Exodus makes the celebration of the paschal sacrifice *contingent* upon being circumcised, for both observances are expressions of the same religious and national themes (see Ex. 12:43–44). Significantly, the offering of the paschal sacrifice and the observance of circumcision are also the *only* two positive commandments in the Torah that carry the penalty of spiritual excision (or in Hebrew, *karet*) from the community of Israel for their non-fulfillment. One who willfully abrogates either of these rites has rejected any connection to the destiny of the people of Israel, and is therefore spiritually expelled from their midst.

THE ABROGATION OF PASSOVER IN THE WILDERNESS

How telling that the traditions indicating that circumcision was abrogated by the people for the thirty-eight year period of the wilderness sojourn also record that a similar fate befell the observance of Passover! While the Torah itself records that the people of Israel did perform the paschal sacrifice during the second year of their exodus, as they prepared to break up their encampment at the foot of Mount Sinai, the ancient rabbis' careful reading of that relevant text revealed more ominous undertones:

> God spoke to Moses in the wilderness of Sinai, in the first month of the second year of their exodus from the land of Egypt, and said: "The people of Israel shall observe the paschal sacrifice at its appointed time. On the fourteenth day of this month at evening you shall perform it in its correct time, in accordance with all of its decrees and ordinances." Moses told the people of Israel to observe Passover. They observed Passover on the fourteenth day of the first month in the evening while in the wilderness of Sinai, according to all of the matters that God had commanded Moses so did the people of Israel perform. (Num. 9:1–5)

Echoing the rabbinic surprise at the fact that this Passover section chronologically precedes the census recorded at the beginning of the Book of Numbers (that took place "on the first day of the second month of the second year") and must therefore be regarded as out of order, Rashi comments:

> Why didn't the book begin with this section? It is because it contains allusions to Israel's reproach, namely that during the entire forty year period of the people's sojourn in the wilderness, they performed only this one paschal rite! (Rashi on Num. 9:1)

We must therefore amend our earlier list of "wilderness negations" to include one more item. Not only did the Torah pass over the four decade span of the generation of the wilderness in utter silence, not only did the northern wind die down for that time and thus prevent the observance of circumcision, not only did God fail to address Moses during that era in tender tones of prophecy. Tradition asserts that the inviolable observance of the paschal sacrifice, the very service that, more than any other, recalled Israel's election as God's chosen, was abrogated and forsaken as well. Passover remained for almost four decades disregarded, with the notable exception of the rites celebrated during the second year of the Exodus *as the people prepared to take their leave of Sinai and journey towards the land of Canaan* – a stirring march tragically cut short by the dispatch of the spies.

In a stunning flashback to those singular events of the Exodus, and in a shattering reversal of their aborted trajectory, the people of Israel now perform these two thematically related observances in quick succession. This time, though, they fulfill circumcision and offer the paschal lamb not as reluctantly liberated slaves who were forcefully thrust out, but as a mature people who willingly embraced God's unceasing guidance in the wilderness and now stand ready to mark the dawn of true nationhood with their entry into the land.

Significantly, the celebration of the paschal sacrifice is one of the few holiday celebrations that is referenced throughout the entire biblical period. In our context, of course, we find it prepared by Joshua (3:2–12) when the people of Israel cross the Jordan River to enter the land, in the thirteenth century BCE. Later, the rites are celebrated by King Hezekiah (II Chron. 30:5–15), the resolute and righteous eighth-century BCE king of Judea who attempted to gather in the remnants of the northern kingdom of Israel on the eve of the Assyrian exile. Later still, the inspiring seventh-century BCE religious reformer King Josiah (35:16–19) called for the observance of the paschal sacrifice, as the storm clouds of Babylonian invasion began to gather on the horizon of Jerusalem. Finally, towards the end of the biblical period, Passover is observed by the nascent community of fifth-century BCE Jews who return to Zion under the aegis of Cyrus king of Persia (Ezra 6:19–22).

Although there is no evidence to suggest that the paschal sacrifice was completely unobserved during the intervening periods, as it was during the course of the wilderness wanderings, it stands to reason that its impact must have been less pronounced. We do know from the biblical text itself that the long intervening periods in between those brief bouts of inspired leadership were more often than not characterized by national stagnation, as well as moral and spiritual decline. In contrast, all of the above paschal celebrations occurred at pivotal moments of national and religious renewal, and were initiated by an inspired leader animated by his relationship with God.

CESSATION OF THE MANNA

Standing outside of Jericho's gates, the people are now ready to embark on the conquest of Canaan. One final episode separates Israel from its first encounter with the Canaanites:

> On the morrow of the Passover,[2] the people ate matzot and roasted grain prepared from the produce of the land, on this very day. The manna ceased on the morrow when they ate from the land's produce, and the people of Israel had no more manna. Therefore, that year they ate from the new produce of the land of Canaan. (Josh. 5:11–12)

This fleeting reference to the cessation of the manna serves as a fitting conclusion to the entire first five chapters of the book. Up until this point we have in large measure focused upon the glaring contrasts between the Exodus from Egypt and the entry into Canaan, between fearful slaves and proud free men, between uncertainty that leads to failure and resolve that leads to triumph. We have considered the many parallels that span this chasm of forty years: Joshua's leadership and Moses' guidance, the spies of Jericho and the spies of Canaan, the traversal of the Jordan River and the crossing of the Sea of Reeds, and the rites of circumcision and paschal sacrifice. We are ready to take our leave of what might be called the "Introduction to the Book of Joshua – Overcoming

---

2. The matter of *mimaḥarat hapesaḥ* (on the morrow of the Passover) in verse 11 may be related to a much larger discussion concerning the controversial phrase of *mimaḥarat hashabbat* in Leviticus 23:15. See the context in Leviticus and Mishna Menaḥot 10:3. Rashi and Gersonides both derive support from our verse for the rabbinic tradition concerning the counting of the seven weeks until Shavuot, while Radak does not.

the Demons of the Past" in order to consider the book's next section: the conquest of Canaan, a prolonged account that begins with the battle of Jericho. But before doing so, the text first indicates that the miraculous manna, the remarkable food that sustained Israel for a generation, abruptly terminates.

We must once again turn back to the Exodus in order to appreciate the significance of the manna's cessation. Recall that after the people left Egypt, bearing no more provisions than the unleavened cakes on their backs, they were guided to the Sea of Reeds. There, God caused the sea to miraculously open up, and the people of Israel traversed it on dry land while the pursuing Egyptian hordes drowned in its chilly depths. Leaving its banks, the people entered the inhospitable wilderness of Shur. After a fruitless three-day journey in search of water, they came to the bitter waters of Mara but could not drink them. Crying out to God, they were miraculously provided with liquid refreshment, as Moses healed the bitterness. Continuing to march, they then came to Eilim, a well-watered oasis, but soon were enjoined to leave its pleasant landscape and journey through the barren wilderness of Sin. Exactly one month had passed since the people had left the brick pits of Egypt, until they cried out to God for food:

> God said to Moses: "Behold, I will cause sustenance to rain down from heaven for you. The people will go out to gather it each day, so that I might prove their resolve to see if they will follow My Torah or not."...The house of Israel called the substance "manna".... They consumed it for forty years until they came to a settled land, they ate the manna until they came to the boundary of the land of Canaan. (Ex. 16:4–35)

The entry into the wilderness of Sin, and into the wilderness experience of desolation, deprivation and despondency, was signaled by the onset of the manna, the sustaining symbol of God's guidance and care. For the entire period of the wilderness sojourn, the people of Israel were nurtured on this ethereal substance as they ingested the profound meaning of God's providence. No matter what else happened, the manna never failed to fall and the people were never disappointed. If there was a lone constant in the drawn-out saga of the journey through the wilderness, it was the delicate manna that daily covered the margins of the Israelite camp. If there was a single indication of God's miraculous intervention and ongoing support from on high, it was the manna that fell daily from the heavens like supernatural rainfall.

Taking their leave of the wilderness forever, now standing firmly on Canaan's substantial soil, the people of Israel have completed the journey and reached their destination. The miracles of the Exodus, the Sea of Reeds, and the wilderness have drawn to a close and Israel must now build its national life in its land like any other people. Of course, God's involvement in the process is just as real, His concern and kindness just as immediate. But the overt nature of His involvement must necessarily recede into the background so that the people of Israel can exercise their newfound maturity to choose, to err, and to learn from their errors in order to succeed in the future. It cannot be otherwise, and the miraculous manna must perforce cease, just as Israel enters the land and completes the dual rites of circumcision and Passover that signal the dawn of nationhood. The four decades of the wilderness, the expiration of one generation as another generation came of age and took its place, is thus bracketed by the experience of the manna. With the entry into the wilderness, the manna begins to fall and with the entry into the land, it ceases.

Joshua 5:13–6:1

The Angel of the Lord

Leaving behind the shores of the Jordan River, the great national observances of circumcision and Passover, the manna and all of the other wilderness associations, we now turn our attention to the book's second section, the story of Canaan's conquest. In length, this part of the book is roughly comparable to the first, extending from the beginning of chapter six until the end of the "kings list" of chapter twelve. As a study of military strategy, the account is riveting. But as an exploration of moral and ethical issues, this section of the Book of Joshua is perhaps the most challenging. We will explore both aspects and a good deal more, as we consider the most striking progression of these chapters: the remarkable transformation of Israel from a nomadic conglomeration of disparate tribes into a disciplined, cohesive, settled nation.

APPEARANCE OF THE ANGEL

Having crossed the Jordan River, Israel now stands at the outskirts of Jericho, and their successful campaign against the city is introduced with the appearance of a mysterious, phantom-like figure:

> When Joshua was encamped at Jericho, he suddenly saw a man with drawn sword standing opposite him. Joshua approached

him and said: "Are you on our side or on that of our enemies?"
He responded: "No, for I am the captain of God's legions and
have now arrived." Then Joshua fell upon his face to the ground
and said: "What does my master ask of his servant?" The captain
of God's legions said to Joshua: "Remove your shoes from upon
your feet, because the place upon which you stand is hallowed
ground," so Joshua did so. As for Jericho, it was completely closed
up because of the people of Israel; none came out and none
entered. (Josh. 5:13–6:1)

Although the figure appears in the guise of a man, Joshua quickly comes
to realize that he is confronted by something else entirely, for the captain
of God's legions is none other than an angel. In the Tanakh, an angel of
any sort generally indicates a direct communication from God to man.
In our context, the angel appears in the guise of a warrior and grasps an
outstretched weapon, as Radak explains:

> For this is to indicate might and triumph. In a similar vein, the
> angel appeared to Jacob our father and wrestled with him. Jacob
> prevailed and was thus strengthened as a result of the occurrence
> and realized that his victory over the angel presaged his triumph
> over Esau [see Gen. 32:25–30].... So too, this angel appeared
> to Joshua with his drawn sword in the manner of a victorious
> hero. Thus, God says to Joshua in the aftermath of the episode:
> "Behold, I will give Jericho, its king and mighty men, into your
> hand." (Radak on Josh. 5:12)

According to Radak, the appearance of the warrior angel is to indicate
to Joshua that his forces will prevail against Jericho, notwithstanding the
city's vaunted defenses. Having noted that this exchange takes place at
a transition point in the book, as the focus shifts from the narratives of
passage to the account of the land's conquest, we may extend Radak's
comments to address the entire campaign against the Canaanites. Israel
will prevail because God's assistance will be extended to them and to
their leader Joshua.

MOSES AND THE BURNING BUSH

The dialogue between Joshua and the angel is obscure. In response to his query concerning the content of God's communication, the angel cryptically commands him to remove his footwear "because the place upon which you stand is hallowed ground." This expression immediately calls to mind God's unexpected appearance to Moses at the episode of the burning bush (Ex. 3:1–10). After Moses had been drawn to God's mountain by the remarkable bush that burned but was not consumed, God called to him but bid Moses to remove his footwear and maintain his distance in deference to the holiness of the site. That vision constituted the beginning of Moses' calling. From that point onwards, in spite of his mighty protests to the contrary, Moses was appointed by God as His emissary to Pharaoh.

The deliberate association may therefore indicate that Joshua as well now stands at the brink of assuming a more comprehensive leadership role. Though he has led the people since Moses' demise, his unique task – as spelled out by God Himself in the Book of Numbers (27:15–23) – was "to lead the people out [to battle] and to lead them back in." In other words, Joshua does not fully assume the mantle of leadership of Israel until they are poised to engage the Canaanites in battle. And that is now, with Jericho's ramparts looming menacingly on the horizon.

REMOVING FOOTWEAR

In the case of Moses, the sanctity of the environs was manifest: the site of God's revelation to him was none other than the mountain in the wilderness of Ḥorev associated with His presence, namely Mount Sinai, where the people of Israel would later receive the Torah. It is unclear, however, how the holiness of a location in space translates into the necessity to shed one's shoes. Although rabbinic tradition as recorded in the Midrash (Exodus Rabba 2:13; see also Zevaḥim 24a) clearly links the episode of Moses with that of Joshua, it does not shed light on the underlying idea:

> Wherever the Divine Presence manifests itself, it is forbidden to don one's footwear. Similarly, we find with respect to Joshua, "Remove your shoes from upon your feet," and similarly the

> priests who ministered in the Temple at Jerusalem did so bare-
> foot. (Exodus Rabba 2:13)

Perhaps, as some commentaries maintain, the unusual rite suggests leaving behind the mundane and the soiled that adhere to the soles of the shoes (both in a literal and a figurative sense), before treading on holy ground.[1] Or, as others maintain, it may be an expression of modesty, as if the person must descend to ground level in preparation for the encounter with the absolute. Then again, it may suggest the attempt to forge some sort of organic connection with the holy ground itself, as if by standing barefoot on hallowed earth one could transcend the artifice and superficiality of human existence and experience the authenticity of the divine.

Whatever the case may be, the injunction to remove one's shoes seems perfectly reasonable in the episode of Moses. It also seems readily comprehensible in the setting of the ministering priests at the Temple. But it is quite unintelligible in our context of Joshua. What is the hallowed earth that Joshua stands upon presently, if not the land of Canaan where he and the people have been carelessly treading for a number of days? Why does the angel appear to him only now, on the eve of Israel's first battle against the city-states of Canaan? How do the heartening words of the angel relate to his threatening posture?

Perhaps the answer lies in the explanation of Radak quoted above. Joshua and the people are about to embark upon a new phase of their mission, namely, the conquest of Canaan. As we all realize, there may be such a thing as a justified war, but there is no such thing as a kind one. In warfare, combatants clash, blood is shed, and innocents cruelly perish. We euphemistically and with sterile detachment refer to "casualty figures" and "collateral damage," but we are actually describing precious lives nastily cut short, with stunned survivors left to gather the embers from among the ashes. The battlefield may crown a victor but it does not ennoble him.

It may be that Joshua, who had prevailed against Amalek in his younger years and was therefore no stranger to bloodshed, had been

---

1. See the commentary of Rabbi Ḥizkiya ben Manoaḥ (thirteenth century, France) on Exodus 3:4.

pondering these same tragic truths when the angel appeared to him bearing assurances of God's intervention and assistance. How would he lead Israel into the battle for their survival, while at the same time impressing upon them the dignity and inestimable worth of the human being? How would the army of the Hebrews be inoculated against the type of gratuitous and sadistic wartime brutality that was widespread in the ancient world and no less common today? Enter the emissary of God bearing a drawn sword and a profound message: The land of Canaan, from time immemorial a flashpoint of conflict, is yet hallowed ground. The empires and civilizations that were forever vying to rule this land bridge between Africa and Asia, a corridor that constitutes a critical conduit for commerce and for culture, played out their petty passions on its slopes, strewing them with death and destruction. But the sanctity of the land, its potential to radiate God's healing words to a devastated world, could not be expunged.

Joshua and Israel will prevail, the city of Jericho will fall, and the Canaanites will be defeated. But the people and their victorious armies must never lose sight of the land's sanctity, of a man's inherent worth, of the vision of a better world in which warfare is archaic and killing obsolete. Canaan's city-states, materially advanced and cultured though they were, never succeeded in advancing that vision even one tiny increment, because it was an idea that was antithetical to their polytheistic values. The angel of the Lord, however, addressing Joshua on Jericho's outskirts, makes it absolutely clear that his mission must be different. God may countenance justified bloodshed, but He will not tolerate wanton cruelty. The concept of Canaan's hallowed earth implies an intimation of the divine, and a corresponding necessity to tread upon that land with greater care and heightened sensitivity. What is tolerable and considered natural in other lands, namely viciousness, violence, and cold-hearted cruelty, all committed in the name of victory, is wrong when perpetrated by God's nation, and out of place when committed in the land that is the focal point of God's concern.

Support for this reading is found in the paragraph breaks of the original Hebrew text, which connects the angel's message of holiness to the conquest about to unfold. The verses read:

> The captain of God's legions said to Joshua: "Remove your shoes from upon your feet, because the place upon which you stand is hallowed ground," so Joshua did so. As for Jericho, it was completely closed up because of the people of Israel; none came out and none entered. (Josh. 5:15–6:1)

In contrast, the conventional notation of chapter and verse unexpectedly wrenches the above verse from the episode of the visiting angel, using it instead as the opening verse of chapter six. As we pointed out earlier, the traditional spacing of the Hebrew text is often at odds with the conventional divisions of chapter and verse, which are of much later non-Jewish origin. The discrepancy in this case is particularly telling. In light of our above analysis, we must conclude that the opening verse of chapter six must be read as the conclusion of the section of the visiting angel. The angel comes to communicate not only an assurance of divine assistance, but also God's demand for responsibility and decency. It is as if the angel says in the name of God: "Fight against Jericho and defeat it, but never forget that you must not surrender your humanity in the process. Overcome the foe; do not perpetrate acts of gratuitous violence in defeating him or gloat over his downfall." These are critical lessons for a people about to initiate wars of conquest.

Joshua 6:2–26

The Fall of Jericho

After the departure of the mysterious angel, God Himself addresses the Israelite leader, confirming the angel's words and indicating to Joshua how the city is to be attacked and conquered:

> Let all the fighting men circle the city once, repeating the procedure for six days. Seven priests will bear seven rams' horns before the Ark, and on the seventh day you shall encircle the city seven times, as the priests sound the horns. As the sound of the rams' horns persists, when you hear the sound of the horn, then all of the people shall shout very loudly. The wall of the city will fall in its place, and the people shall then attack it from all sides. (Josh. 6:3–5)

THE ENCIRCLEMENT OF THE CITY

As Joshua implements the plan, a number of other pertinent details emerge. The Ark is indeed preceded by the priests sounding the rams' horns, but the priests themselves are led in the procession by a vanguard of elite fighting men, identified by rabbinic tradition with the members of the tribes of Reuben, Gad, and Menashe (see Josh. 6:9 and Rashi's commentary), the very tribes who swore their allegiance to Joshua in chapter one of the book by undertaking to fulfill Moses' oath. The rear-guard of the procession is manned by another fighting force associated with the tribe of Dan (see 6:13 and Rashi's commentary), who during the course of the wilderness peregrinations traveled at the rear of the camp in order to round up any Israelites who fell behind (see Num. 10:25).

Thus, there are four elements in the march-past: the vanguard, the priests, the Ark, and the rearguard. The central two are linked by the Tabernacle: the priests minister there before God's presence, which is represented by the Ark. The bracketing two, in contrast, are represen-tatives of the tribes of Israel, those associated with the lands east of the Jordan (Reuben, Gad, Menashe), as well as those who are set to reside on its western side (Dan). In essence, this first pivotal battle is initiated by a force that constitutes a microcosm of the people and their God, united in purpose and bonded by a common destiny. As knowledgeable readers, we may surmise that as the campaign to secure the land progresses and other Canaanite cities fall, some tribes will suffer from the sore tempta-tion to abandon the more comprehensive national concerns in pursuit of their own sectarian interests. For this very reason, the attack on Jericho is carried out in a manner that emphasizes the overriding importance of maintaining national cohesiveness in the face of the common threat.

The method of encirclement is an effective tool of psychologi-cal warfare against the inhabitants of the city, who watch with alarm as the Israelites file by silently, led by their God and proceeded by the shrill sound of the rams' horns (see Radak on Josh. 6:3). The strategy is calculated to foster palpable anxiety among Jericho's defenders, as each passing day brings another circuit of the city by the voiceless enemy, but no overt hostilities. The denizens of Jericho will have plenty of time to ponder the ominous intentions of the Israelite God, whose disciplined troops maintain their unnerving composure as the cool morning still-ness is shattered by the piercing blasts of the seven horns.

THEME OF SEVENS

But from Joshua's and the people's point of view, the most remarkable feature of the encirclement of Jericho concerns the repeating motif of the number seven: seven priests, seven rams' horns, seven days of circling the city, and the culminating act of circling seven times on the seventh day as the walls come tumbling down. The "seven" theme is found elsewhere, typically in the case of hallowed times. Thus, the weekly Sabbath (mirrored perhaps in the seven-branched Menora of the Tabernacle and Temple – see Ex. 25:31) is celebrated on the seventh day, the national holidays of Passover in the spring and Sukkot in the fall (separated by exactly seven months) are of seven days' duration, and seven weeks link the observance of Passover – the anniversary of the Exodus from Egypt – to the celebration of Shavuot, the harvest festival known as the "Feast of Weeks" that traditionally commemorates the revelation at Sinai.

The motif of seven also recalls the agricultural calendar that is spelled out in the Book of Leviticus 25:1–24, in which six years of planting and harvesting are followed by a seventh year of release, during which no farming work takes place and the earth lies fallow and untended. Seven such cycles constituting forty-nine years are followed by the remarkable year of the Jubilee, which is inaugurated by the blast of the ram's horn on the solemn day of Yom Kippur. In the year of the Jubilee, all ancestral lands excepting those of walled cities, though they may have been sold to others during the course of the intervening period, revert to their original owners, and all bonded servants are set free to return to their homes.

Although Radak rejects the attempt to provide a rationale for the motif of seven in our passage and instead directs the reader to more mystical possibilities, the most plausible explanation for the theme is that it highlights recognition of God and consecration to His holy name. Thus, the six days of labor are designated for man to pursue his mastery of the natural world, but the seventh day is "a Sabbath unto the Lord your God" (Ex. 20:8), set aside for the pursuit of more lofty spiritual goals. The national commemorations of Passover, Shavuot, and Sukkot recall God's overt involvement in the Exodus and during the sojourn in the wilderness, as well as commemorating His proclamation of the ten guiding principles at Sinai. Additionally, the three festivals call to mind God's ongoing providence, in bestowing seasons of planting, harvesting, and ingathering so that humanity might prosper. The agricultural cycle of seven years is to convey that not only is time hallowed by God's command, but that also material space, the mundane soil and its produce, are to be dedicated to His service. There is nothing in the world, no man and no clod of earth, which remains disconnected from its source. This is proclaimed by the shofar blast on the Day of Atonement of the fiftieth year of the Jubilee, that calls upon all of the people of Israel and even their landed property to "Return!"

In all of the above cases, whether of time or space, the Sabbath, holidays, or the years, the number seven constitutes a complete cycle whose progress must be directed towards God. The seven days of the week, the seasons of the year, and even the septennial successions of the farmer's hoe turning over the moist earth, are not meaningless repetitions undifferentiated in their numbing sameness, but rather unique opportunities for communion with God. These constant temporal and spatial reminders gently but persistently declare that our short life spans, conditioned as they are by relentless cycles of time and space, can easily be crushed and consumed by incessant repetition unless some higher purpose informs them.

THEME OF SEVEN IN THE CONQUEST OF JERICHO

The motif of seven in our context affirms to the Israelites that victory is God's alone, for they will prevail not by force but rather by His decree. By encircling seven times, by sounding the seven horns for seven days, the battle is to be dedicated to God, to impress upon Joshua and his army that although they are enjoined to exercise autonomy, to employ military strategy, to carefully plan, and to cautiously execute their plans, the day, in the end, will be won by God's intervention. Significantly, according to a well-founded rabbinic tradition, the cycle of warfare that the encirclement of Jericho introduces continued unabated for a period of seven years until the land was conquered (see Josh. 14:10, and Rashi's commentary). The battle of Jericho underscores a theme that will inform the entire period of Israel's conquest of Canaan and subsequent biblical history:

> These [wage war] with chariots and those with horses, but we proclaim the name of the Lord our God. They are bowed and fallen, while we rise up and are strengthened. Lord, save us! The King will answer us on the day that we entreat Him. (Ps. 20:8–10)

But there is more. By indicating that the victory over Jericho is God's alone, the army of Israel comes to appreciate that their campaign must be waged for more noble causes than power and plunder, the twin pillars of "justified" warfare in the ancient world. No wonder that in this paradigmatic battle against the Canaanites, Joshua vigorously pronounces an otherwise inexplicable ban against their bodies and possessions:

> The seventh time as the priests sounded the horns, Joshua told the people, "Shout out, for God has given the city to you! The city and all that is in it shall be consecrated (*herem*) to God. Only Rahab the harlot and all that are with her in her house shall live, for she concealed the spies that we sent. As for you, observe the ban (*herem*), lest you succumb (*taharimu*) and take from the ban (*herem*), for in so doing you shall place the camp of Israel under a ban (*herem*) and discomfit it. All of the silver and the gold, the bronze and the iron shall be holy to God, and shall be placed in the treasury of God".... At that time, Joshua pronounced an oath saying: "Cursed be the man before God who arises and rebuilds this city of Jericho, for he shall lay its foundations with [the death of] his firstborn and set its gates with [the death of] his youngest child!" (Josh. 6:16–19, 26)

The people of Israel are to take no booty from the spoils of Jericho, no human slaves to do their bidding, no precious possessions to fill their coffers, no material souvenirs of their crushing victory. Instead, all proceeds of the enemy are to be consecrated to God and to His Tabernacle. The commentaries disagree as to whether this ban of Joshua was enjoined by God – though no such explicit reference in the text can be adduced – or whether in fact Joshua himself pronounced it of his own volition. It is clear, though, that the *inspiration* for such a ban is in our account, for it is none other than the blatant motif of seven that we have been discussing. It is a short and direct route from the seven-fold encirclement of the city, with its overtones of divine involvement and human dedication to His name, to Joshua's pronouncement that completely consecrates the city and its contents to God's honor.

THE CITY LED ASTRAY TO EMBRACE IDOLATRY

Elsewhere in the Tanakh, there is a striking parallel to the overthrow of Jericho, and it concerns not Canaanites but rather Israelites after they have settled the new land:

> If you hear reports concerning one of the cities that the Lord your God gives you to dwell in, that ignoble men from your midst have led astray the people of their city saying: "Let us go and serve other gods" that you have not known. You shall diligently investigate and enquire carefully. If it is true that this abomination has taken place in your midst, then you shall slay the inhabitants of that city by the sword, and destroy (*haḥarem*) it and all that is in it, including its animals, by the edge of the sword. You shall gather up all of its spoils into its central square and completely burn them with fire unto the Lord your God. The city shall be a desolate ruin forever, never to be rebuilt. Let nothing of the ban (*haḥerem*) adhere to you, in order that God may turn away from His burning anger and grant you compassion and increase, just as He swore to your ancestors. Therefore, hearken to the words of the Lord your God to observe all of His commandments that I command you this day, to do what is upright in the sight of the Lord your God. (Deut. 13:13–19)

The above passage constitutes one of Deuteronomy's many harsh invectives against idolatry, perhaps its most harsh. Although in the narrow sense the verses speak of Israelites who have embraced idolatry, the analogies that otherwise exist between the *Ir HaNidaḥat* – the city led astray – and Jericho cannot be mere coincidence. In both cases, the city under discussion is to be utterly destroyed, its inhabitants including animals completely slaughtered, their possessions and the city's plunder to be entirely shunned, and its ramparts and houses never to be rebuilt. In both cases, the recurring word in the passage is a cognate of *ḥerem*, translated according to various contexts as "banned" (Deut. 7:26), "utterly destroyed" (20:17), or "wholly consecrated" (Lev. 27:28). In both cases, the point of the severe reaction is to secure God's favor. What might be the significance of the correspondence?

The obvious and indeed only linkage between the city led astray and Jericho is idolatry. The *Ir HaNidaḥat* is a hypothetical Israelite city whose inhabitants have wholeheartedly embraced the worship of other gods, after the manner of the Canaanite city-states of which Jericho is the exemplar. The unforgiving punishment that is to be meted out to its Israelite population is the Torah's standard response for the deliberate abrogation of the prohibition of idolatry. The striking analogy to Jericho is meant to drive home the following fundamental truth: an Israelite city that endorses idolatrous worship is no different than its Canaanite counterparts and will suffer the same ignominious fate.

In a contrasting vein, Rahab and her family are preserved by Joshua when Jericho falls. Thus, while these particular people of Canaanite stock are saved, cities whose inhabitants are of Israelite stock can yet be doomed. This contrast in and of itself is enough to make absolutely clear that Joshua's war is not a racial and genocidal campaign of ethnic cleansing but something else entirely: a war against *idolatrous values*. We will continue to analyze and to substantiate this fundamental axiom as we go on to study the upcoming chapters of conquest.

Joshua 6:27–7:26

Israel's First Setback: Akhan's Trespass

Last chapter, we considered Israel's first encounter on the battlefield with the Canaanites. In truth, due to overt divine assistance, it was not much of a battle. After circling the stout ramparts of Jericho for seven consecutive days, the walls of the city came crashing down, and the Israelites easily captured it and laid it waste. In the years 1952–58, the site of Jericho was extensively excavated by the British archaeologist Kathleen Kenyon on behalf of the British School of Archaeology in Jerusalem. Her investigations established that the earliest settlement at the site dated from the tenth to eighth millennium BCE, making Jericho one of the earliest urban concentrations in the world. Her research also demonstrated that the massive fortifications of the town dated from the middle Bronze Age, centuries before Israel's incursion into Canaan towards the end of the Bronze Age. Additionally, the biblical claims of the entire wall falling away were unsubstantiated by the archaeological record, which found no evidence of the complete collapse of the outermost fortifications.

Careful readers of the Book of Joshua will have already noted that the text nowhere indicates that the *entire* wall of the city gave way. Quite the contrary: Recall that of all of the city's inhabitants, only Rahab the harlot and her extended family, crowded into her humble dwelling, were preserved. Rahab did as she had been instructed by the escaping spies, tying the scarlet cord in her window to alert the invading forces of Israel that the inhabitants of her home were to be preserved (Josh. 2:18–19). However, earlier the text clearly indicated that Rahab's domicile "was in the city wall, for she dwelt in the wall" (v. 15). In other words, the fact that immediately after the fall of the city wall, the spies hurried to Rahab's house to rescue her and her family indicates that parts of the wall must have remained intact. This conclusion is drawn by Radak:

> The text states that "the city wall will crumble in its place," but what about the house of Rahab that was located in the city wall? It is not likely that she and her family were preserved although their house was destroyed, for the text would have not passed over such a miracle in silence. Also, Joshua commanded the spies to "go to the *house* of the harlot and save them" [Josh. 6:22], imply-ing that her house was intact and did not fall. Rather, it would seem to me that the entire city wall did not collapse, but only that section that faced the Israelite forces. There they attacked, while Rahab's house was situated in another section of the wall that did not fall. (Radak on Josh. 6:5)

Often, perceived conflicts between the text and the excavation record are due to erroneous readings of the text, rather than faulty scientific scholarship. We may even go so far as to argue that as an unintended but important byproduct, archaeology can assist us in testing the accuracy of a textual reading. The popular perception of the proverbial walls of Jeri-cho completely and utterly tumbling down is now known to be incorrect. What Radak was able to glean from an extremely thorough, conscientious, and rigorous study of the relevant texts, without recourse to empirical evidence, was corroborated six centuries later by the excavator's spade.

Sometimes, though, the opposite is true – the fault of incongru-ity lies not with the interpretation of the text but rather with the erro-neous methodology or incorrect conclusions of the excavator. As some archaeologists have pointed out, there exist examples of Canaanite towns with fortifications from the middle Bronze Age that continued to be settled into the late Bronze Age without substantial updating of their fortifications. Alternatively, other scholars have interpreted the evidence in the hill country to suggest that the Israelite incursion into the land actually took place earlier than is commonly assumed, while Jericho was still fortified and settled.[1] As a rule, we welcome the contributions of archaeology to biblical study with anticipation but also circumspection. There is no doubt that archaeology and its related fields have much light to shed on the understanding of the biblical text. However, under no circumstances should the foundations of one's faith be predicated upon its conclusions, which are notoriously subject to adjustment, revision, and sometimes complete reinterpretation in light of new finds and theories.

TENUOUS SELF-CONFIDENCE

Leaving behind the ruins of Jericho, the book now shifts its attention to the trespass of Akhan. Bear in mind that until this juncture, the tone of all of the narratives has been entirely positive. Joshua has deftly navigated the transition of leadership without mishap and the people of Israel have admirably succeeded in overcoming the disastrous failures of their forebears. The incident of Akhan is therefore a watershed, for it marks the first time since Moses' death that the people experience disappointment and dejection. Curiously, though, God does not directly inform the people that they have failed; rather, it is a confluence of circumstances that bears the lesson home.

> Joshua sent men from Jericho to the Ai, east of Beit El. He said to them: "Go and spy out the land." The men went and spied out the Ai. They returned to Joshua and said: "It is not necessary for all of the people to go. Let two or three thousand men go to strike at the Ai. Do not tire out all of the men, for they [the people of

---

1. See Y. Meitlis in *Excavating the Bible* (Savage, MD: Eshel, 2012) and L. Levine and A. Mazar (ed.) in *The Controversy Over the Historicity of the Bible* (Jerusalem: Yad Ben-Zvi, 2001) for comprehensive overviews of some of the issues as well as various solutions.

the Ai] are few in number." About three thousand of the people went there, but they fled before the men of the Ai. The men of the Ai smote about thirty-six men and pursued them from before the gate until the Shevarim. They struck them down at the descent, and the heart of the people melted and turned to water. (Josh. 7:2–5)

We begin by noting that Joshua dispatches spies to reconnoiter the Ai, following the precedent of Jericho. His miraculous victory over Jericho has not at all infected him with overbearing self-assurance. Also, the spies return with a reasonable and levelheaded assessment that contains none of the swaggering language employed by the first set of spies sent to search out Jericho. The overall effect is to suggest that the attack on the Ai is planned and executed with care and forethought.

What follows is therefore doubly shocking. The outgunned men of the Ai, although shaken by the astonishing news of Jericho's miraculous capture, easily succeed in repelling the Israelite onslaught and even inflict a number of casualties. The fragile nature of Israel's confidence is indicated by the fact that although only thirty-six men of Joshua's strike force are killed, out of a contingent that numbers three thousand, nevertheless the people are thrown into a panic. Their melting hearts that faint away recall Rahab the harlot's description of the terrified people of Jericho, whose stout "hearts turned to water" when they heard of Israel's triumphs (Josh. 2:11). The defeat at the Ai should therefore be regarded as the complete reversal of the victory at Jericho.

JOSHUA'S REACTION

Most astonishing of all, however, is Joshua's impassioned reaction. Tearing his clothing, he falls before the Ark of the Lord along with the elders of Israel. They place dust upon their heads, which, when coupled with the rending of garments, is employed elsewhere in Tanakh as a sign of abject grief and mourning (for example, see I Sam. 4:12, II Sam. 1:2). Joshua cries out to God:

> Oh, Almighty Lord God, why have You caused this nation to pass over the Jordan River, only to give us up into the hands of the

Amorites who will destroy us? If only we had desired to remain on the Jordan River's other side! Please, Almighty God, what shall I say after Israel has fled before its foes? The Canaanites and all of the inhabitants of this land will hear of it and turn against us, obliterating our name from the land. What shall You then do for the sake of Your great name? (Josh. 7:6–9)

Joshua's words, defeatist in tone, recall long-forgotten events that had been all but expunged from Israel's collective memory. The last time we had seen him tear his clothing in mourning was at the debacle of the spies sent by Moses, a doomed expedition in which he had taken part. When ten of those spies returned with their hopeless message, only two members of the group opposed them: Joshua and Caleb. But realizing that their words of encouragement could not stem the people's panic (see Num. 14:5–6), the two "tore their garments" as Moses and Aaron "fell down upon their faces before the whole congregation of Israel."

As for Joshua's outcry, including the remarkable yearning to have not entered Canaan, similar words had been expressed by the people only in that most aggrieved moment of overwhelming defeat:

The whole congregation raised their voices and the people cried that night. All of the people of Israel complained to Moses and Aaron and said to them: "If only we would have died in the land of Egypt, or in this wilderness, if only we would have died! Why does God bring us into this land to perish by the sword, our women and children to be despoiled? It is better for us to return to Egypt!" (Num. 14:1–3)

Both Joshua's actions as well as his words recall the formative event of forty years before that had recast Israel's history. During the entire course of the introductory narratives that constitute the first five chapters of the book, there was not even one single explicit reference to the episode of Moses' spies. This is in spite of the fact that so many of those introductory episodes were unambiguous analogs to Israel's earlier failures. It is almost as if the grotesque phantom of the spies, sublimated, submerged, and never entirely overcome, had to be confronted one last time in order to finally purge it from the national consciousness forever. All of its painful hallmarks – the panic, disbelief, hesitation, and despondency – are reassembled here at the battle of the Ai, crying out for a more satisfying resolution. In considering Joshua's pleas, we may note in contrast that never had Moses, even in his most dejected moments, questioned God's motives in bringing the people forth from Egypt, causing them to enter the wilderness, or directing their emergence from it in preparation for crossing the Jordan River!

INVOKING GOD'S GREAT NAME

Unlike his condemned compatriots, however, who could not see beyond their own fear to somehow overcome, Joshua's concluding invocation of God's great name indicates that his deliberate references to the spies carry other connotations besides hopelessness. Like his mentor before him, who assuaged God's wrath by appealing to His special relationship with Israel (see Ex. 32:11–14, Num. 14:11–20), Joshua recalls the insoluble link that binds God to His people. God's presence in the world, His great name, is a function of Israel serving as the bearer of His message; their destruction as a people would spell the end of His involvement in human history. If Israel disappears, then there is no one else to champion the exalted cause of ethical monotheism, no other nation to proclaim God's oneness or the absolute morality that is its necessary and most important corollary. In effect, Joshua proclaims that notwithstanding Israel's failures, there must be divine forgiveness and the opportunity for rectification, if not for Israel's sake then for the sake of God's own "survival." In the final analysis, then, Joshua's declaration is not a mournful dirge of defeat but rather a cautious call to go forward.

God's response is swift and direct. Calling upon Joshua to rise up, God informs the leader that:

> The people of Israel have sinned *and have also* abrogated My covenant that I commanded them, *and have also* taken from the consecrated property, *and have also* stolen, *and have also* denied, *and have also* placed [it] in their vessels. The people of Israel will not be able to stand before their foes, for they will flee from

before them, for they have become banned. I will no longer be with you if you do not destroy the banned matter from your midst. (Josh. 7:11–12)

This stark formulation, employing five usages of the "and have also" (*vegam*) in a single verse, implies a list of indiscretions in ascending order: the perpetrator has sinned, constituting an abrogation of Joshua's directive, by taking from the spoils. This act of theft has required the perpetrator to subsequently deny the wrongdoing and finally to resort to the hiding of the looted items. Severe consequences for the crime, in the form of defeat at the hands of the Canaanites, will not be waived until the people of Israel apprehend and punish the guilty party.

This divine rejoinder actually constitutes a concise formula of one of the Tanakh's most abiding principles, a tenet that serves as a foundation for the remainder of biblical history and beyond. In effect, God declares, there is a cohesive bond between the destiny of Israel as a people and their moral and ritual conduct. When the nation of Israel as a whole sincerely observes God's laws and fulfills His commands, then they enjoy the success and triumph that are the products of His direct involvement in human history. But when they stray from His directives and replace His guiding teachings with false gods of their own making, then they experience all of the failures that natural circumstances would otherwise confer. The fortunes of the individual typically follow more convoluted pathways, so that evil people may enjoy victory while the righteous sometimes perish, but the national fate unfolds according to this more perceptible axiom. Taking from the spoils of Jericho therefore brings defeat upon the people in spite of the fact that there is absolutely no logical connection between the misdeed and the defeat at the Ai.

The divine communication goes on to specify how exactly the guilty parties are to be revealed:

Arise and sanctify the people and tell them to prepare for tomorrow, for thus says the Lord, God of Israel: There is contraband in your midst. You will not prevail against your foes until it is removed from your midst. In the morning, you shall draw close according to your tribes. The tribe that is singled out by God

> will then draw close according to clans. The clan that is singled
> out by God will draw close according to families, and the family
> singled out by God will draw close according to male members.
> The one who is singled out in the ban will be burned by fire, he
> and all that he possesses, for he has transgressed God's covenant
> and has committed a base act in Israel. (Josh. 7:13–15)

The passage above describes the remarkable process by which the perpetrator was to be exposed. Although the text is silent concerning the
precise mechanism, it is clear that the process involved some sort of consecutive sorting of elements from the larger to the smaller, and finally to
the single individual. The early traditional sources suggest that it was the
Ark of the Covenant or perhaps the breastplate of the High Priest containing the twelve tribal gems that served as the "polygraph" (see *Pirkei
DeRabbi Eliezer*, chapter 38). For instance, as the twelve tribal represen-
tatives filed past the Ark, the tribal prince of Judah was ensnared so that
he was paralyzed to escape its embrace, indicating that a member of his
tribe was responsible. The clan heads of that tribe then appeared before
the Ark, and one of them again became trapped in the Ark's "force field."
This winnowing process continued until the actual guilty individual was
singled out. Alternatively, the tribal leaders may have presented themselves
before the High Priest, and, according to this tradition, the gem of the
tribe of Judah darkened, indicating that it was a member of Judah who was
responsible. The clan heads of that tribe then appeared before the High
Priest and drew lots, and the lot of the guilty clan was chosen, and so on.

    While it is not possible to ascertain the exact nature of the selec-
tion method, whether it depended upon the Ark of the Covenant or
else the breastplate of the High Priest, the fundamental implication is
the same: It is as if God Himself actively singled out the perpetrator, for
both the Ark and the breastplate are regarded as the barometers of His
presence and involvement in the world, and in the life of the people of
Israel. As we explained in an earlier chapter, the Ark is an expression of
God's throne and the symbol of His sovereignty on the terrestrial plane,
while the breastplate that is always worn as part of the High Priest's regal
garb of service indicates the unique relationship that exists between God
and the people of Israel.

INEXPLICABLE LARGER BLAME

On the next day, Joshua arose early and initiated the grim process. Sure enough, the tribe of Judah was singled out, followed by the clan of Zeraḥ, the family of Zavdi, and finally by the heart-stopping selection of Akhan son of Karmi, son of Zavdi, son of Zeraḥ of the tribe of Judah. Under Joshua's gentle prompting, Akhan readily admitted his trespass and described his indiscretion:

> Akhan answered Joshua, saying: "It is true. I have sinned against the Lord God of Israel and have done such and such. I saw in the spoils a Sumerian robe, two hundred shekels of silver, and a gold ingot of fifty shekels weight. I coveted them and took them. Behold, they are hidden in the ground under my tent, while the silver is underneath." Joshua sent messengers and they ran to the tent. Behold, it was buried in his tent and the silver was underneath. They brought it forth from the tent and presented it before Joshua and before all of the people of Israel, pouring it out before God. (Josh. 7:20–23)

Akhan's sincere admission is admirable but not surprising under the circumstances. We are perhaps more startled by the description of the stolen goods. While the robe may have been a fine example of Babylonian craftsmanship, and the silver and gold a not insubstantial amount, it is difficult to understand the intense divine displeasure ignited by such a trifling act of pilferage. After all, there were probably many thousands of Israelite soldiers that overran Jericho, and much booty to be had. Of all of them, only Akhan dared to abrogate the ban imposed by Joshua. Viewed in the larger perspective, his act of indiscretion seems almost inconsequential. Most astounding of all, however, is the incongruity between Akhan's act of petty theft and the accusation that God leveled earlier against all of the people:

> The *people of Israel* committed treachery and took from the ban.... God said to Joshua..., "The *people of Israel* have sinned and have also abrogated My covenant that I commanded them, and have also taken from the consecrated property, and have also stolen, and have also denied and have also placed [it] in their vessels.

The *people of Israel* will not be able to stand before their foes, for they will flee from before them, for they have become banned. I will no longer be with you if you do not destroy the banned matter from your midst." (Josh. 7:1, 10–12)

What a lengthy litany of iniquity, what a detailed list of wrongdoing, what a damning indictment against all Israel! How are we to reconcile the text's sweeping censure, God's broad condemnation, and the people's bitter defeat by the inhabitants of the Ai, with the simple fact that in actuality only one person took some minor items from the spoils of Jericho?

THE PRINCIPLE OF CO-RESPONSIBILITY

In order to comprehend the matter, we must again return to the method that God indicates for the singling out of the criminal. Since ultimately it is only by miraculous intervention that Akhan is selected, would it not have been easier and more efficient for him to be named from the outset as the guilty party? The dramatic literary effect notwithstanding, why was it necessary to go through the lengthy process of exposing him, a process that, as we stated above, was predicated upon the sifting out of a single individual from the series of larger groups of which he is part?

Rabbinic tradition, basing itself upon the episode of Akhan and other relevant texts, formulated a principle that lies at the foundation of Jewish nationhood, a unique characteristic of Israel that sets it apart from most other peoples. That principle is this: all Jews are co-responsible for each other, and Jewish individuals are regarded as being organically connected to the larger group.[2] There is no such thing as living a Jewish life

---

2. See *Midrash Halakha Sifra* on Leviticus 26:37 (Beḥukotai, Parshata 2, chapter 7:5) for the earliest formulation of the principle that "All Israel are co-responsible one for the other." The principle, limited in Sanhedrin 27b to situations where one is able to prevent one's fellow from wrongdoing, has important halakhic applications. Rashi, for instance, in his comments to Rosh HaShana 29a, invokes the principle to explain the matter of reciting a mitzva blessing on behalf of another even if one has already fulfilled one's own obligation.

that is indifferent to the larger community or aloof from the trials and triumphs of the nation. In essence, our rabbis taught that while there are a number of discrete dimensions to human existence, all of them are nevertheless intertwined and complementary.

Thus, a Jew first of all lives his life as an individual before God. He is responsible to God for his personal conduct and his private moral decisions. Even the intensely individualistic exercise of his autonomous will must be in accordance with God's laws. At the same time, however, the Jew must live his life conscious of the larger community of which he is part. He must share in their moments of joy and not distance himself from their suffering. There is a communal aspect to his existence that is more than simply a function of living among others and learning to respect social norms and conventions. It is rather an expression of his intense connectedness to all members of the community, their shared purpose and objectives, and the collective destiny that binds all of them together as one.

But even beyond this, there is a still additional facet to Jewish living that transcends the narrow concerns of the individual and even overshadows the general affairs of the community, and that dimension is the national. Inspired by its power, we do not speak of the Jew or of the Jewish community, but rather of the people of Israel. The individual may perish and disappear, the community descends to oblivion, but the nation that is bound in a covenantal relationship with the Creator will live forever. The nation of Israel has a mandate that is comprehensive and all embracing, and every Jew has a part to play in its successful realization. No member of the nation can forever deny his affiliation with that mandate, for it is seared into his very flesh by the mark of circumcision and into his mind by the events of our collective history.

During the long centuries of exile, the Jewish people were dispersed to the four corners of the globe so that they came to adopt the culture and speech of the people among whom they lived, and of necessity their own national identity became subdued. Nevertheless, the deep-seated concern of the Jew for his far-flung brethren, in spite of being separated from them by great geographic distance, language, or customs, is a powerful indication that the ember of nationhood still burns brightly in the Jewish heart.

It is precisely this aspect of Jewish living that animates the ancient story of Akhan. While it may be the case that, strictly speaking, only he was guilty of the crime of trespass, in essence the whole nation shares in his blame. We are not speaking of his immediate accomplices who must have seen him commit the crime or else heard of it indirectly through other sources. Rather, we are speaking of the co-responsibility of all members of the nation for each other. As part of the nation even Joshua must be held accountable, for he too is part of organic Israel. The method of ascertaining Akhan's guilt can now be appreciated: In the end, he is singled out, but not before the process of his arrest emphasizes the concentric circles of concern that form the basis of every Jew's identity – the family, the community, the tribe, and the nation.

These spheres of identity, like the proverbial layers of an onion, are separated and ranked according to their distance from the core. Those that are closest to Akhan are held more accountable than those that are on the periphery of his crime. It is Akhan's immediate family and personal possessions that bear the brunt of his punishment. The commentaries disagree concerning the precise fate of his children – do they suffer immolation or only public humiliation?[3] Whatever the case, all agree that their anguish is most severe and their shame most intense. Can it be otherwise? No crime is committed in a vacuum, and in order for a criminal to successfully carry out and then conceal his nefariousness, active assistance or at least acquiescence of loved ones is often necessary.

This is the powerful lesson of Akhan's downfall: All human acts, whether of omission or commission, whether of good or evil, whether of selfish greed or altruistic love, impact upon the larger familial, communal, national, and even global reality. It is the glory of man and sometimes his infamy that God has assigned to him such a central role in the unfolding of the human saga, and woe to the person who lives his life oblivious to this overarching truth. All the more so when that

---

3. Rashi concludes from a careful comparison of Joshua 7:15 and 7:24-25 that Akhan and his animals were stoned, his possessions burned, but his sons and daughters were not harmed. Radak disagrees and explains that Akhan's children suffered his fate.

life is lived according to the Torah, when it is lived as an authentically Jewish life, for in that dimension of living every minor and mundane act, every insignificant and insipid deed, every breath, and even every passing thought carries with it the potential for astounding consequence. It is not enough to mourn over Akhan's tragic end, to bewail his cruel fate and the unfortunate circumstances of his "being caught." Rather, like Joshua and the people of Israel, we must take away from his cautionary tale the precious gift of living our lives with an awareness of others, with a consciousness of the community and nation that are affected by our deeds, and that, by the immutable laws by which God governs the world, affect us in turn.

Joshua 8:1–29

Victory over the Ai

I n the previous chapter we considered the trespass of Akhan and its terrible consequences for the entire people of Israel. At the core of the cautionary tale was the indispensable concept of Jewish nationhood, according to which the fortunes of the larger community or even the nation are sometimes affected by the acts of the individual or the few. Having crossed the Jordan River and begun the process of settling the land, the twelve disparate tribes will need to quickly assimilate the painful lesson of Akhan if they are to survive as a state.

Recall that Akhan's act of indiscretion was directly responsible for the subsequent defeat of the people at Ai, when the outnumbered inhabitants of that town routed the Israelite attack force and even inflicted casualties upon them. Now that Akhan's crime had been uncovered and the people had witnessed the awful spectacle of his punishment, they were enjoined by God to renew hostilities against the Ai, this time buoyed by His promise of victory.

God offered Joshua words of encouragement – "Do not fear, nor be afraid" (Josh. 8:1) – words first pronounced to him by his mentor Moses when Joshua was designated as the next leader of Israel (see Deut. 31:8). Joshua, however, does not take the divine assurance of triumph as an invitation for passiveness but instead prepares extensively in accordance with God's terse directive to "place an ambush behind the city" (Josh. 8:2).

This time, Joshua chooses thirty thousand fighting men and accompanies them as they march to strike the town from its northern perimeter. At the same time, five thousand men are selected from among that larger force and sent under cover of darkness to wait in ambush on the town's western outskirts.[1] Joshua's remaining twenty-five thousand troops, who make no attempt to conceal their movements, attack the city but then feign retreat. The inhabitants of the town as well as those of the adjoining town of Beit El, believing that another easy victory over the Israelites awaits them, give chase and leave their cities exposed. Quickly, the five thousand concealed fighters emerge from their lair and attack the open town of the Ai, setting it ablaze. Realizing that they have been trapped, the fighters of the Ai and Beit El find themselves caught between the two Israelite armies and are slaughtered to a man. Altogether, twelve thousand are slain, and only the king of the Ai is taken as prisoner.

Besides providing us with an excellent insight into Joshua's brilliance as a military strategist, the battle of the Ai also indicates that the Israelite leader takes no chances this second time around. Recall that at the first battle of the Ai, Joshua had unconditionally accepted the words of his spies who maintained that a small force of perhaps "two or three thousand" would be more than sufficient to subdue the Ai, and that there was therefore no need to "weary all of the people" (Josh. 7:3). Here, Joshua employs a force that numbers ten times the cautious estimate of the spies!

JOSHUA'S CRITICAL SIGNAL

There is one important detail that must not be overlooked, for it provides us with one of the book's key insights into the mysterious workings of divine providence. This victory, in marked contrast to that over Jericho, seems to be the exclusive result of Joshua's clever scheme and his men's fearless implementation. Here, there is no active participation of the

---

1. So explains Gersonides on Joshua 7:13. Rashi and Radak, interpreting the repetition of 7:12 as an additional step, speak of two ambush forces to the west of the city!

Ark of the Covenant, no silent encirclement of the town's ramparts, no miraculous crumbling of its impregnable defenses. Rather, the defenders of the Ai are overrun by an irresistible combination of overwhelming force and perfectly executed strategy. The Israelite fighters feign retreat and thus draw out the men of the Ai after them; the smaller ambush force rapidly deploys at the exact moment of the town's defenselessness and then seizes it without encountering resistance. They quickly set it on fire and the men of the Ai are suddenly confronted by the demoralizing spectacle of their town, as well as their visions of speedy victory, going up in smoke. Losing their will to fight, they are easily overcome by the pincer movement of Israel's forces and conquered.

But how does Joshua's smaller ambush force know the precise moment when to leave their concealed location in order to seize the town? After all, to deploy too early will result in the strategy being discovered and the ambush force neutralized. To deploy too late will endanger the larger Israelite army whose feigned retreat could become a real rout. Either way, the task of conquering the Ai and neighboring Beit El will be immeasurably harder. It is Joshua himself who provides the critical signal. Accompanying the larger force that feigns retreat in order to draw out the fighters of the Ai and Beit El, Joshua is able to maintain visual contact with the concealed ambush group of five thousand. Perhaps he cannot see them as they lie in wait on the town's western outskirts but they can see him:

> Joshua raised the spear that was in his hand towards the town. The ambush force quickly arose from their [hiding] place and ran towards the town as he lifted his spear. They entered the city and captured it, setting it ablaze. (Josh. 8:18–19)

Thus, the timely deployment of the ambush force is a function of the "flare" that Joshua sends up. When they see his outstretched spear, they know that the city gates have been left wide open by its over-confident defenders. Really, then, it is Joshua's symbolic gesture that wins the day; afterwards the victory unfolds in a perfectly naturalistic manner. But how does Joshua know when to raise his spear? Is it no more than the intuitive sense of timing with which great military men are blessed?

"God said to Joshua: '*Stretch out the spear that is in your hand towards the Ai*, for I give it into your hand.' And Joshua raised the spear that was in his hand towards the town" (Josh. 8:18). In an act reminiscent of Moses raising his staff over the waters of the sea (Ex. 14:26–27), God commands Joshua to raise the spear. Parenthetically, we should note that the staff of the lawgiver shepherd has been replaced in this scene by the spear of the inspired general, highlighting the changed circumstances of Joshua's leadership. In any case, when Joshua raises the spear, the force in ambush who patiently await just that signal swiftly leave their hiding place and attack, prevailing against the town and heralding a crushing triumph for Israel over its foes.

While it is clearly Joshua and the people of Israel who make the necessary preparations, fight the battle and achieve victory, their success in the end is due to God's covert intervention. Inspired at precisely the right moment, Joshua raises the spear and the rest of the plan unfolds with perfection. The military historian who hypothetically observes the battle from the outside sees only Joshua's stroke of brilliant timing and the people of Israel's determined attack, but the more perceptive onlookers who possess deeper insight into the true nature of the miraculous are able to discern the hand of God. In glaring contrast to God's obvious involvement at Jericho, therefore, the battle of the Ai introduces a new stage in His evolving relationship with Israel. Just as He indicated to Joshua, He will always be with them and will not abandon them to the cruel designs of their foes. But unlike the obvious and irrefutable proof of His salvation that was provided by the plagues, the Exodus, the splitting of the Sea of Reeds, the crossing of the Jordan River, and the victory over Jericho, here God begins to retreat behind the veil of natural events. This is in order to allow the people of Israel the opportunity to forge their own path, to make autonomous decisions, and to learn the difficult lessons of their own mistakes.

But let no man of Israel make the error of equating divine silence with divine absence, as if a dearth of miracles indicates His detachment, unawareness, impotence, or nonexistence. The freedom given to man to exercise his autonomous will without hindrance is a unique invitation that is afforded only to the human species. It is an opportunity to seek God and to find Him, as an act of human initiative and out of the yearning for a better world. God patiently awaits our overture and yearns to respond in kind. His response, however, is concealed under multiple layers of cause and effect. Sometimes, as in our case, it consists of nothing more than a confluence, a convergence of circumstances that is a function of precise timing. And often, God's quiet participation is overshadowed when human hubris shrilly takes credit for the victories, while assigning the defeats to the cruel but arbitrary fates. The sensitive souls, though, can sense His constant involvement and see its unmistakable impact throughout human history.

TAKING FROM THE SPOILS

Like Moses before him, who raised his hands aloft at the battle against Amalek and kept them held high to inspire his people to victory (Ex. 17:11–12), "Joshua did not let down his hand that grasped the spear until all of the people of the Ai had been subdued" (Josh. 8:26). Significantly, in that battle against the marauding Amalekites who had attacked the defenseless and tired Israelites soon after they had left the land of Egypt, it was Joshua himself who had been selected by Moses his mentor to lead the people to their improbable victory (see Ex. 17:8–13). Here too, Joshua's raising of the spear serves as more than the signal to the five thousand men who lie in ambush anxiously awaiting his order to attack. The raised spear symbolizes victory and reminds the people of God's critical involvement in that process. They are inspired to prevail against the foe because they know that God will not let them down.

In the aftermath of the victory, the people of Israel are permitted to take from the spoils of the town, thus providing another important contrast to the battle of Jericho. While some commentaries see in this license a prudent concession by Joshua in light of Akhan's earlier failure,[2] others detect another sign of the subtle shift towards more hidden divine involvement. At Jericho, the victory was God's alone. It was precipitated by His Ark, the symbol of His earthly throne, and resulted from the miraculous collapse of the city's fortifications. Assuming, as some commentaries do, that God nowhere enjoined the harsh ban against the

---

2. See Rashi on Joshua 7:10.

booty of Jericho that Joshua pronounced, we must instead posit that it was only natural for him to interpret the miraculous circumstances surrounding the Israelite triumph as an invitation to dedicate the victory's proceeds to God: "All of the silver and the gold, the vessels of brass and iron, shall be sanctified to God. It shall be brought to God's treasury" (Josh. 6:19).

Here at the Ai, the groundwork for the success was laid by Joshua's meticulous planning and the people's spirited fight. While God in the end provided the critical catalyst for the victory, it was a triumph that belonged to all of Israel. Therefore, the spoils are also given to them (as indeed they are in every other battle that is henceforth described in the book), to stress the significance of their initiative and to highlight their involvement.

The victory over Ai thus provides us with an important lesson into the trajectory of the Book of Joshua, as it traces the anxious arc of decreased supernatural involvement and increased human initiative. This dynamic tension, in marked contrast to the miraculous tone of the vast majority of the wilderness narratives of the Ḥumash, defines the rest of the Book of Joshua, the remainder of the biblical books, and the post-biblical history of the people of Israel until this very day. Like Israel of old, we must not lose sight of the fact that God is always aware, always involved, and always able to intervene at the decisive moment, albeit in a concealed manner. God's involvement is shielded from dim minds that equate trust with phony catechisms and predicate faith upon the supernatural house of cards known as miracles.

The message of the battle of the Ai is in fundamental opposition to that of the shallow practitioners who would magically fashion belief by applying the quick fix of divine wonders that in the final analysis cannot transform a recalcitrant heart of stone into one of flesh. Only the patient nurture of our trust that God is present in our lives can help us appreciate that God not only cares about us but that He guides us towards recognition of His concern.

The Duplicity of
the Givonites

After the town of Ai is captured and its defenders routed, its ramparts are burned to the ground. The king of Ai is taken prisoner, subsequently executed and hanged, but then his body is removed from the gallows as evening falls. This is in general accordance with the provisions spelled out in Deuteronomy. But while the deuteronomic legislation applies to Israelite criminals, Joshua applies it to the defeated Canaanite king:

> If there is a man who is guilty of a capital crime and he has been executed, then his body shall be hanged upon a tree. Do not allow his body to remain upon the tree all night but rather you shall surely bury him on that day. It is an affront to God to leave him hanging. Do not defile your land which the Lord your God gives you as a possession. (Deut. 21:22–23)

The account of the victory over Ai concludes with a description of the public assembly at Mount Eival. There, the people of Israel offer sacrifices upon the altar of whole stones that are inscribed with the words of the Torah, while Joshua reads out the deuteronomic laws, the "blessings and the curses."[1] All of this is a direct fulfillment of Deuteronomy 11:26–30 and 27:1–26. The elements of the assembly – the participation of all Israel, the proclamation of God's instruction, the recording of a text on the altar stones, and the offering of sacrifices – all recall the events at Mount Sinai. At that time, all Israel gathered at the base of the mountain (Ex. 19:3) to hear God's declaration of the Decalogue (v. 17), the text was recorded upon the tablets of stone (24:12), and sacrifices were presented (vv. 4–5). The implication is clear – the assembly at Mount Eival was a conscious re-enactment of the revelation at Sinai and a pointed reminder to all Israel that success in Canaan would depend upon Israel's willingness to transmit Sinai's values.

At the same time, by linking the capture of the Ai and the killing of its king to the convocation at Mount Eival, the book highlights the moral dimension of the conflict, emphasizing that Israel's wars of conquest must not be exercises in wanton bloodshed, unrestrained plunder, and cruel vengeance. While the inhabitants of the Ai are necessarily put to death in the course of the battle, their king, the symbol of their might and power, is dispatched without recourse to torture and his body is shortly thereafter removed from the gallows and buried without mutilation. These represent two telling departures from the conventions of ancient warfare.

The final verses of the section (Josh. 9:1–2) describe the response of the kings of Canaan to the above events. All of them, those of "the mountains, the plains, the coast of the Great Sea all the way to Lebanon," determine to battle Joshua and Israel with unified resolve. Could it be that the Canaanite kings were discomfited not only by Israel's crushing military victories but also by the moral absoluteness of their divinely ordained laws? Is it not plausible that the polytheistic foundations of

---

1. In the early 1980's, Prof. Adam Zertal of Haifa University announced that he had discovered Joshua's altar on Mount Eival. The find generated much controversy and continues to be debated. See his article, "Has Joshua's Altar been Found on Mount Ebal?" in *Biblical Archaeology Review* 11:01 January/February 1985 for a fascinating account.

Canaanite society, providing king and subject alike with complete license to shape ethics according to expediency, also began to quake and tremble with the fall of Jericho's buttresses and Ai's bolted gates?

THE STRATEGY OF THE PEOPLE OF GIVON

Shortly after the fall of the Ai, we read of a curious diplomatic mission:

> The inhabitants of Givon heard about all that Joshua had done to Jericho and to the Ai. They also employed clever strategy, and disguised themselves as emissaries. They took faded sacks for their donkeys, and worn-out wineskins that were cracked and mended. They donned old and patched footwear and worn-out clothing, and took bread and provisions that were dried out and decayed.
>
> They approached Joshua at the encampment at Gilgal and they said to him and to the people of Israel: "We have come from a far-off land to conclude a pact with you.... We are your servants...who hail from a very distant land and come to honor the Lord your God, for we have heard of His exploits and all that He did in Egypt, and to the two Amorite kings east of the Jordan River, Siḥon king of Ḥeshbon and Og king of the Bashan who dwelt in Ashtarot. Our elders and the people of our land told us to take provisions for the journey and approach you, saying that we are your servants and wish to now conclude a pact with you." (Josh. 9:3–11)

The town of Givon and its hamlets of HaKefira, Be'erot, and Kiryat Ye'arim (Josh. 9:17) are situated about ten kilometers north of Jerusalem. Jerusalem and Hebron are important centers in the Judean hill country, while Yarmut, Lakhish, and Eglon are situated in the foothills that guard the western approaches to that hill country from the coastal plain. Geographically, Givon is associated with these southern kings (10:3). Alarmed like the rest of their southern Canaanite brethren at the uncontested Israelite triumphs, the people of Givon adopt a different approach. While the other Canaanite city-states form a confederacy in order to militarily oppose the looming threat, the Givonites sue for peace. Disguising their messengers as ambassadors from a distant land, they secure an oath of non-aggression from Joshua and the tribal leaders, who anchor their pledge with "the name of the Lord, God of Israel" (9:19).

The Givonites implement their plan brilliantly. Concealing their true intentions with convincing disguises, they choose their words carefully. Like Rahab who expressed her sincerity by recalling the mighty deeds of the God of Israel, the Givonite ambassadors claim to come in homage to His great name. They mention the Exodus from Egypt and the victories over the Amorite kings but pointedly omit any reference to the more recent victories over Jericho and the Ai. These glaring omissions serve to bolster their questionable claim of having traveled from a far off land; no doubt, while the victories over Jericho and Ai were unfolding, the emissaries were in transit and therefore unaware of more recent events.

In the end, the ruse is discovered. To their dismay, Joshua and the people of Israel ascertain that in fact the people of the "far-off land" are none other than the Givonites who dwell scarcely thirty kilometers from the Israelite encampment at Gilgal. But bound by their oath, Joshua and the elders are prevented from attacking their involuntarily-acquired allies. To abrogate their treaty now would constitute a desecration of God's name by which they had vowed. Instead, Joshua designates them as "hewers of wood and drawers of water" for the congregation of Israel and the Tabernacle.

The motivation of the Givonites seems straightforward, as they themselves explain:

> Joshua summoned them and said: "Why did you deceive us by saying that you were from a place far away from us, when in fact you dwell in our midst?" They responded: "Your servants heard of all that the Lord your God had commanded His servant Moses, to give the land into your hands and to destroy all of its inhabitants from before you. We were afraid for our lives because of you, and therefore did this thing." (Josh. 9:22–24)

Fearing for their lives, aware of God's pledge to Moses that He would drive out Canaan's inhabitants and seeing the unfolding fulfillment of His pledge before their very eyes with the fall of Jericho and the Ai, the

Givonites realized that military resistance would be futile. They therefore attempted to preserve their cities through guile. What is more puzzling is Joshua's initial surprise at the Givonites' conduct. After all, if the threat of death was indeed suspended over them as ominously as they said, isn't their duplicity perfectly intelligible? Why, then, does Joshua wonder about their motivation for implementing their crafty plan?

THE TALMUDIC TRADITION

Joshua's bewilderment provides indirect support for the rabbinic tradition first mentioned in the Jerusalem Talmud and adopted by many of the later authorities:

> Joshua sent three proclamations to the inhabitants of the land of Canaan, before the people of Israel entered the land. The first stated: "Whosoever wants to leave, let him do so." The second stated: "Whosoever wants to conclude peace, let him do so." The third stated: "Whosoever wants to wage war, let him do so." The Girgashites decided to evacuate…to Africa, the Givonites concluded peace, and the other thirty-one kings of Canaan waged war and were defeated. (Y. Shevi'it 6:1)

Contrary to the straightforward reading of the text, which describes the uninvited entry of Israel into the land and their immediate and unannounced embarkation on a campaign of conquest, the above tradition insists that actually the people of Canaan were forewarned about the Israelite incursion and were provided with the opportunity to deflect its course. While the casual reader may dismiss this talmudic tradition as a fanciful attempt to morally justify the war of conquest, as if the Israelites really offered their enemies an opportunity to avoid defeat, it must be emphasized that support for the tradition can be found in the Book of Joshua itself. As we saw earlier, the narrative indicates that in the aftermath of the Israelite victories over Jericho and Ai, "All of the kings that were on the [western] side of the Jordan…gathered together to battle Joshua and Israel as one" (Josh. 9:1–2). While not explicitly suggesting that there were other possibilities open to the Canaanites, these verses do make it clear that the prevailing outlook was that engaging Israel in warfare was the preferred approach. Thoughts of evacuation or surrender were far from their militant minds.

A more unassailable reference can be found in chapter eleven, which summarizes the Israelite campaign and its overwhelming achievements:

> Joshua conquered all of this land – the hill country, the Negev, the land of Goshen, the plain and the rift valley, the mount of Israel and its plain…. *There was not a single city that concluded peace with the people of Israel, except for the Hivites who dwelt in Givon.* Rather, everything was taken in war. God had strengthened their resolve in preparation for the war with Israel so that they might be utterly defeated and shown no compassion, so that they might be destroyed as God had commanded Moses. (Josh. 11:16–20)

These verses make it absolutely clear that the other Canaanite cities could have followed the example of the Givonites and sued for peace. Instead, they chose to steel themselves for battle and were therefore responsible for its consequences. It is unclear whether the three proclamations mentioned above were sent simultaneously or one after the other. Perhaps the first, sent while the people of Israel were en route to the Jordan River, called upon non-combatants to withdraw. The second may have been sent when Israel was already encamped on its banks, and invited the remaining Canaanites to surrender peacefully. The third, conveyed as Israel crossed over, made clear that the war of conquest would soon be underway. This reading, implied by Maimonides in Laws of Kings 6:5, understands that as Israel drew closer and closer to the probability of conflict with the cities of Canaan, the tone of the proclamations became more and more urgent.

Alternatively, perhaps all three communications were sent at the same time and offered the Canaanite city-states any one of the three outlined options. This alternate reading of the source is supported by the parallel account preserved in the Midrash:

> R. Samuel b. Naḥman explained: "Joshua sent a proclamation to every city that he planned to attack in which it was written that, 'Whosoever wishes to go, may do so. Whosoever wants to

surrender peacefully, let him. Whosoever wants to wage war, so be it.'" (Deuteronomy Rabba 5:14)

Either way, the above talmudic source and its variants go a long way to explain Joshua's surprise at the duplicity of the Givonites. If in fact they had been offered the possibility of surrendering peacefully, why did they risk arousing the wrath of their vanquishers by securing their survival through deception?

THE WINDS OF WAR

While the commentators offer a number of intriguing explanations for the Givonites' conduct, a rather simple possibility emerges from our larger context. Recall that the narrative of the Givonites is introduced by the assertion that all of the Canaanite kings had decided to battle Israel as one (Josh. 9:1–2). Recall, also, that the verses in chapter eleven pointedly indicate that only the Givonites, of all of the land's inhabitants, sued for peace. Finally, note that in the aftermath of the Givonite treaty struck with Israel, the southern kings launched a punitive assault against the towns of Givon (10:1–5). It was an attack that was blunted and ultimately repelled only by an unexpected Israelite counter-attack.

The implication of these citations is clear: The greatest impediment to the adoption by the Givonites of more honest methods to secure a pact of non-aggression with Israel was not Joshua's intransigence (a possibility itself negated by the talmudic tradition), but rather the unified Canaanite front that opposed any compromise with the Israelites. The town of Givon was thus forced to adopt subterfuge in order to avoid arousing the ire of the other Canaanite kings who would have opposed such an overture of peace tooth and nail. Unable to publicly declare their willingness to surrender to Israel for fear of immediate and overwhelming retribution at the hands of their adamant brethren, the Givonites instead sent their emissaries secretly and in disguise. Once they were in possession of the precious Israelite pledge of support, they discarded the pretense. The Canaanite attack was indeed forthcoming, but so was the Israelite defense. Had the Givonites sued for peace openly, they would have been attacked and overwhelmed by their countrymen long before Joshua and the Israelites might have come to their aid.

Joshua 9:3–27

Introduction to the
Wars of Conquest

T o appreciate the episode of the Givonites, we must consider
a passage from the twentieth chapter of Deuteronomy that discusses
the topic of warfare. According to the Torah, warfare must be waged in
accordance with divinely-delineated principles. The Israelite combatants are expected to adhere to guidelines that govern their conduct in
conflict and that set limitations on their behavior.

The passage opens with an injunction to be fearless even in the
face of overwhelming odds and to trust in God's deliverance, for He
can prevail just as surely as He liberated the Israelite slaves from their
much more powerful Egyptian overlords. The text goes on to single out
a number of individuals who are exempt from waging non-defensive
wars, namely the builder of a new house, the planter of a new vineyard,
or one who betroths a new wife. The final exemption pertains to the
one who is "afraid and faint of heart" (Deut. 20:8), who is sent home in
order not to undermine the morale of the fighting troops.

The next section in the chapter addresses the treatment of the
enemy forces:

> When you draw near to a city to wage war against it, then you
> shall first proclaim peace. If they respond in kind and open the
> gates for you, then all of the people that are in the city will pay
> tribute and serve you. If they do not surrender peacefully but
> rather fight against you, then you shall besiege them. When
> God gives the city into your hands, then you shall smite all of
> its men by the sword. But the women, the children, the animals
> and all of the goods that are in the city you may take, for so shall
> you consume the spoils of your enemy that the Lord your God
> gives you. Thus shall you do to all of the cities that are very far
> from you, that are not the cities of these nations here. But from
> the cities of these people that the Lord your God gives you as
> an inheritance, you shall not spare any soul. Rather, you shall
> completely destroy them, the Hittite, the Amorite, the Canaanite,
> the Perizite, the Hivite, and the Jebusite, just as the Lord your
> God commands you. This is in order that they not teach you to
> perform all of the abominations that they do in the service of
> their gods, for then you shall transgress against the Lord your
> God. (Deut. 20:10–18)

The concluding verses of the chapter address the treatment of the enemy's land, and put forth the remarkable prohibition against cutting down
the fruit trees of the besieged city. In so doing, the Torah effectively outlaws a "scorched earth" policy of wanton and reckless destruction, even
as the enemy forces are besieged and conquered.

TREATMENT OF THE ENEMY

It is the middle section of the passage that concerns us here, for it
outlines how the Israelite army is to relate to their adversaries on the
battlefield and in the aftermath of victory. At the outset, the text asserts,
an enemy city must be offered the option of surrender. If the terms of
surrender – tribute and servitude – are accepted, then none of its inhabitants are to be harmed. If, on the other hand, the enemy city insists on
warfare, it may be attacked and all of the combatants may be killed. The
women and children civilians, though, may not be hurt but can be taken
captive, and the city's goods may be taken as spoils. But concerning the

cities of the Canaanites, the cities of "these nations" that are comprised of six specific tribal groups, the passage draws a sharp distinction. In the event of warfare, none of the inhabitants of such cities are to be spared, lest they lead the conquering Israelites astray by enticing them to worship their gods and to perform the licentious rites associated with that worship, thus distancing Israel from God.

There is an inherent ambiguity in the text of the passage, and the commentaries are in sharp disagreement concerning the most plausible reading. Recall that in discussing the treatment of the "far-off" enemy city, the text outlines two separate contingencies: Firstly, an overture of peace must be extended. Secondly, in the event of warfare, only the male combatants may be killed. In sharp contrast, the passage then goes on to insist that a distinction must be drawn between these "far-off cities" and the "close cities," between non-Canaanite combatants and Canaanites. In the event of warfare, non-Canaanite civilians are not to be harmed, whereas Canaanites are to be wholly destroyed: "You shall not spare any soul." *What is unclear, however, is whether the peace overture that must be extended to non-Canaanite cities must also be proclaimed to Canaanite cities,* or whether instead the Canaanites are not to be offered any possibility of surrender at the outset.

Textually, the resolution of the matter is a function of interpreting the phrase: "Thus shall you do to all of the cities that are very far from you, that are not the cities of these nations here." This directive follows immediately after the description of the peace overture, its rejection, the ensuing battle and conquest, the killing of the male fighters, and the preservation of the women and children. Does this phrase modify everything that precedes it, including the opening verse that insists on offering peace terms? If so, then the implication is that peace overtures are to be denied to the Canaanites – thus shall you do, extending offers of peace and protection of civilians, to all nations far from you, but not to the Canaanites who constitute "these nations here."

On the other hand, perhaps the phrase modifies *only* the action to be taken in the event of actual warfare, thus implying that the offering of peace terms is to be applied equally to the Canaanites as well, that they too are accorded the opportunity to surrender and to thereby spare their populations from the harsh consequences of defeat. In this case, the opening passage applies to *all* enemy cities including those of the Canaanites: "When you draw near to a city to wage war against it, then you shall first proclaim peace. If they respond in kind and open the gates for you, then all of the people that are in the city will pay tribute and serve you." According to this reading, a difference between non-Canaanite and Canaanite cities is only enjoined in the event of warfare that follows a spurned offer of peace: Non-Canaanite civilians may be spared, but all Canaanite civilians are to be killed.

RASHI AND NAHMANIDES

It is Rashi who adopts the more straightforward but also more severe first reading and understands that the overture of peace had to be extended only towards those cities that did not lie within Canaan's borders. According to Rashi, the nations that inhabited Canaan were not to be offered any possibility of surrender, but were instead to be wholly obliterated (see his comments to Num. 21:22, Deut. 20:10, as well as his explanation to the talmudic passage in Sota 35b). While raising troubling moral issues, Rashi's explanation has the distinct advantage of readily explaining the motives of the Givonites. As members of the Hivite tribe, one of the so-called "seven nations" that inhabited the land of Canaan, the Givonites were therefore slated for extinction. Their ruse was a desperate attempt to avoid that eventuality by instead securing an oath of preservation from their unsuspecting vanquishers. According to Rashi, we must recast Joshua's puzzlement as an expression of astonishment at the audacity of the Givonites, rather than perplexity concerning their rationale: "Joshua summoned them and said: 'Why did you deceive us by saying that you were from a place far away from us, when in fact you dwell in our midst?'"

As for the rabbinic sources that indicate that on the eve of the Israelite invasion Joshua sent a vanguard of messengers to the nations inhabiting Canaan bearing triple proclamations of retreat, surrender, or war, we must submit that according to Rashi the possibility of surrender was extended to the Canaanites only *before* Israel crossed the Jordan River and began to fight. Once they crossed over, however, the option of surrender was no longer offered. As we saw last chapter, not all of the variant sources of this rabbinic tradition would accord with Rashi's reading.[1]

In contrast to Rashi's explanation, Nahmanides avers that the overture of peace spoken of in Deuteronomy 20 was extended to all enemy cities, including those of the Canaanites:

> Indeed, the passage from Deuteronomy distinguishes between both types [of enemy, but only insofar as combat is concerned]. The injunction to extend an offer of peace, however, applies even to obligatory wars such as those waged against the seven nations of Canaan. After all, didn't Moses send a communiqué of peace to Siḥon the king of the Amorites [Num. 21:21 and Deut. 2:26–30]? Surely, Moses would not have abrogated the commandments enjoined by this passage of "Destroy them utterly" [Deut. 20:17] and "Spare not a soul!" [v. 16] Rather, there is a difference between the Canaanites and non-Canaanites only when the terms of surrender are refused and battle is joined. In that case, the women and children of "far-off" cities are to be spared, while those of Canaan are to be killed. (Nahmanides on Deut. 20:10)

Concerning the ruse of the Givonites, now made more incomprehensible since surrender was a viable option from the start, Nahmanides goes on to explain:

> Realize that the duplicitous plan of the Givonites was precipitated by the fact that they were unfamiliar with the Israelite convention to offer peace. They dispatched their messengers even before the peace overture from Joshua had been received. Thus they said: "We were very afraid for our lives" [Josh. 9:24]. Alternatively, perhaps they first spurned the overtures of Joshua but then became afraid and therefore had to disguise themselves [in order to secure a peaceful surrender]. The text therefore says that

---

1. See also Sota 35b *Tosafot* s.v. *lerabbot,* as well as the critique of Rabbi Abraham ben David to Maimonides, *Mishneh Torah,* Laws of Kings, 6:5.

"the people of Givon heard of all that Joshua had done to Jericho and to the Ai, and they then acted craftily" [vv. 3–4]. Additionally, their ruse was effective in securing the Israelites as their allies bound by treaty rather than simply their overlords. This explains the ire of the people of Israel who would have killed them if not for the oath extended to them by the tribal elders. By rights, the Givonites should have become tributaries and servants. Instead, they became Israel's equals and allies, bound by a treaty of mutual assistance and peaceful relations.... Therefore, Joshua cursed them and imposed upon them to become "hewers of wood and drawers of water," both expressions of tribute and servitude. (Nahmanides on Deut. 20:11)

Nahmanides thus offers us three possible explanations for the conduct of the Givonites, who could have surrendered without a fight: (1) They were unaware that the policy of the Israelite forces was to accept surrender. (2) They initially rejected the Israelite offer but then reconsidered. While these first two explanations are mutually exclusive, the last explanation, (3) that they sought ally status, could accord with either of them. Nahmanides' first explanation seems unlikely in light of the abundant publicity that the text indicates attended the news of the Israelite conquest of Jericho and Ai. After all, the Givonites only launched their plan in the aftermath of the overthrow of those cities (Josh. 9:3), astonishing events that must have been widely (and wildly!) recounted. How could the proclamations of Joshua's messengers to those cities have been completely overlooked or disregarded by anxious Canaanites hoping for a reprieve?

In light of our analysis last chapter, Nahmanides' second explanation is most plausible. Recall that we considered the broader context of the Givonite episode and discovered that it took place against the backdrop of widespread Canaanite antipathy to any consideration of a peaceful surrender. The Canaanite city-states were united in their resolve to repel the Israelite invaders and to prevent them from acquiring a foothold in the land and the Givonites stood with their brethren in initially embracing a belligerent posture. Thus, Nahmanides can claim with justification that the Givonites, like the rest of the seven nations, may have rejected Joshua's messengers and spurned their offer of surrender.

After a time though, especially in light of the fall of Jericho and the Ai, the people of Givon came to the sobering realization that they could not best the Israelites in battle, and would do better to sue for peace rather than perish. The Canaanite confederacy, however, could not be opposed openly, for to break ranks with it would be interpreted as an act of treachery and would invite immediate and overwhelming retribution. Thus, the Givonites were forced to adopt disingenuous methods to seal their treaty with Joshua and Israel. While the deceptive approach cost them Israel's goodwill and thus condemned them to lives of menial toil, it did provide them with a reliable pact that in the end was instrumental for securing their survival. The Givonites continued to dwell among the people of Israel during the entire biblical period, and their descendants were still tenuously aligned with the Jewish people during the time of the return from Babylon.[2] In the end, service of the glorious name of God that the Givonites insincerely espoused became their fate, for Joshua designated them as "hewers of wood and drawers of water *for the house of my God*" (Josh. 9:23)!

AN OATH IN GOD'S NAME

The commentaries may be in disagreement with respect to the questionable motives of the Givonites but perhaps the episode's most pertinent message concerns not the Givonites but rather the Israelites. The text emphasizes that although the Givonites secured the pledge through deception, nevertheless Joshua and the elders were not prepared to retract their commitment:

> Joshua made peace with them and concluded a pact to preserve them, and the elders of the congregation swore by oath. Three days after they had concluded the pact, they heard that the Givonites dwelt close to them and were in fact in their midst. The people of Israel traveled to their cities on the third day, these

---

2. Mishna Kiddushin 4:1 and Ezra 8:20.

being Givon, HaKefira, Be'erot, and Kiryat Ye'arim. The people
of Israel did not smite them because the elders of the congregation had sworn an oath to them by the name of the Lord, God
of Israel. (Josh. 9:15–18)

Here again, the narrative introduces a moral element that speaks worlds
about the revolution wrought by Israel's entry into Canaan. For all
intents and purposes the oath offered to the Givonites was legally non-
binding. It had been offered by Joshua based upon Canaanite pretenses
that were utterly false. But because it had been extended in the "name of
the Lord, God of Israel," Joshua and the elders insisted, against popular
opposition, that it had to be upheld, to indicate in no uncertain terms
that the God of Israel was a God of steadfast truth and trustworthiness.
Unlike the false gods of the Canaanite pantheon whose definitions of
right and wrong, good and evil, truth and falsehood were insubstantial
and capricious, the God of Israel insisted upon absolutes. If one had
offered one's word or pronounced an oath in His name then it had to be
fulfilled, because in failing to fulfill one cast doubt not only upon one's
own dependability but upon the constancy of God Himself. The Givonites thus become involuntary allies, punished for their fraudulence but
preserved nonetheless. Ironically, it was the novel idea of the Israelite
God, which they claimed had animated their "journey from afar," that
in the end secured their survival.

Joshua 10:1–14

Miracles and Men

S hortly after the Givonites sue for peace and secure an alliance with Israel, their Canaanite kin launch a devastating attack:

> Adoni-Tzedek king of Jerusalem heard that Joshua had captured and destroyed the Ai just as he had done to Jericho, and that the inhabitants of Givon had peacefully surrendered to Israel and were accepted into their midst. They became very fearful, because Givon was a great city, one of the cities of the realm, a city larger than the Ai with men who were all mighty. Adoni-Tzedek king of Jerusalem sent to Hoham King of Hebron, Piram King of Yarmut, Yafi'a King of Lakhish, and to Devir King of Eglon, saying: "Join me to smite Givon, for they have peacefully surrendered to Joshua and to the people of Israel!" (Josh. 10:1–4)

Besieged, the people of Givon send messengers to Joshua at Gilgal, some thirty kilometers distant in the Jordan valley, and request their immediate aid to defeat "all of the Amorite kings who dwell in the hill country" (Josh. 10:6). Not losing a moment, Joshua and the armed forces commence their uphill march at nightfall and continue their advance all night long. They surprise the Canaanite kings with their sudden arrival and "God discomfited them before Israel." The kings' forces flee but are pinned down by a sudden downfall of hailstones on the slopes of Beit Ḥoron, a miraculous intervention that inflicts heavy casualties.

What happens next is nothing short of remarkable, even in the context of the biblical books:

> Joshua addressed God on the day that God had given over the Amorites before the people of Israel, and he said in the presence of all Israel: "Oh sun, stand still in Givon, and moon in the valley of Ayalon!" The sun was still and the moon stood motionless, until the nation avenged its foes. Is it not written in *Sefer HaYashar*? The sun stood still in the middle of the heavens and did not hasten to set for a full day. There was never a day like that one, neither before nor after, that God should listen to the plea of a man, because God waged war for Israel. (Josh. 10:12–14)

As the day waned and the sun began to drop towards the horizon, Joshua realized that the enemy forces would soon escape under cover of darkness. Seeking to secure more daylight hours for the Israelites to rout their foes, Joshua called upon the sun and the moon to cease their inevitable course and to stand motionless, thus extending the radiance of the afternoon indefinitely. In a show of divine intervention never before witnessed in the history of the world, God acceded to his request and as a result, Israel inflicted a punishing blow on the Canaanite kings of the south.

The short passage raises many provocative questions. Did the celestial bodies, whose immutable motion is the paradigm for permanence and the basis of our Newtonian conception of conventional time as consistent and unchanging, truly stop their motion and stand still? What is the significance of the reference to the otherwise obscure *Sefer HaYashar* or Book of the Upright, a work mentioned in only one other biblical context (II Sam. 1:18)? Why did God choose to intervene in such a striking way in order to allow Israel the opportunity to vanquish its foes? Why was Joshua selected to be the recipient of such singular divine intercession?

Joshua's Campaign Against the Southern Kings

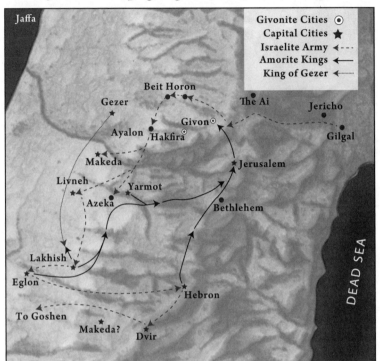

THE LITERALISTS

The first of our questions is the most pressing, and the commentaries are in disagreement on the matter. Most of them adopt the rabbinic tradition preserved in the Babylonian Talmud:

> The Torah states [concerning the offspring of Ephraim] that "His descendants will fill the nations" [Gen. 48:17]. When did the reputation of Ephraim become known worldwide? At the time that God caused the sun to stand still for Joshua [who was a descendant of the tribe of Ephraim]. For how long did the sun stand still? R. Yehoshua b. Levi says: for twenty-four hours…. R. Eliezer says: for thirty-six hours…. R. Shemuel b. Naḥmani says: for forty-eight hours. (Avoda Zara 25a)

Though the sages are in disagreement concerning the length of time that the sun stood still, they do concur that it *did* in fact stand still, just as the straightforward reading of the text indicates. If so, then the episode not only highlights God's resounding intervention in the Israelite triumph but also underscores a biblical axiom: God is a transcendent all-powerful being who bends nature to His will.

The ancients universally believed that the gods were powerful and mercurial beings, possessing in full measure the foibles of their human worshippers. In their heavenly abode, they were primarily engaged in banal and sensual pursuits or else bloody conflicts, in either case much resembling the goings-on down below on the terrestrial plane. The capriciousness of the gods derived in part from the fact that they too were subject to whims of fortune more powerful than they. Held in sway by fates that were beyond their control, the gods were often too feeble to intervene or to save. The sun, and to a lesser degree the moon, were regarded as gods by all polytheistic societies, many of whom venerated them as primary deities. The cause for such singular devotion is not difficult to understand: the rhythms of daily life, the seasons of planting and harvest, the steady counting of days, months, and years are all dictated by the arc of the sun disk across the heavens, while the great and inexorable cycles of birth and death are mirrored by sunrise and sunset, spring and autumn. The cycles of the moon's renewal helped humans regulate their time while its mysterious disappearance and reappearance instilled a hope in resurrection. The new moon, reborn as an exquisite crescent, evoked the curving horns of the ox that pulled the plow, nurturing further associations of fertility and bounty.

Shemesh was the female Canaanite version of the sun fetish. Because climatic conditions in Canaan yielded cloudy or stormy weather half of the year, and because the success of the crops was completely dependent upon sun-obscuring rainfall rather than upon irrigation, Shemesh never achieved the prominence accorded to the storm god "Baal" or Baal's seductive cohort Ashtoret, the goddess of fertility and love. In Canaan, Baal was the head of the pantheon while Shemesh was a lesser god. In Egypt, by way of contrast, the male sun god Ra was fervently and universally adored, for his brilliant radiance in the perennially cloudless skies nurtured the crops brought forth by the black alluvial fields watered by the Nile. Ra was in fact regarded as the progenitor of Pharaoh himself!

But even in Canaan, Shemesh was a god to be respected and appeased, and scattered biblical references make it abundantly clear that sun worship was not at all foreign to the Canaanite landscape (see Deut. 4:19, 17:3, II Kings 23:5–11, and Ezek. 8:16). The lowland town of Beit Shemesh, for instance, was a center of sun worship in Canaanite times. The moon god "Yerah," whose name may be mirrored in the name of Jericho (in Hebrew, *Yeriho*), was the companion of Shemesh in the same way that Baal and Ashtoret constituted a mythical (and licentious) pair.

As the battle at Givon came to a close, the Israelite forces triumphant, Joshua called upon the sun and moon to stand still in their tracks so that the people might avenge their foes. Miraculously, the celestial spheres complied, proclaiming with an astounding display that nothing was beyond the ability of the God of the Hebrews. Completely incorporeal, absolutely powerful, of a perfect oneness defying description, Israel's God, the God of heaven and earth and all that they contain, demonstrated His utter mastery over the forces of nature that all other peoples, in Canaan and elsewhere, submissively worshipped and irrationally feared. Taken together with the sudden downpour of hailstones that initiated the rout, perhaps the text here seeks to emphasize God's utter mastery over the most popular Canaanite gods: Thus, Baal the storm god bent to the will of the transcendent Creator while Shemesh and Yerah showed their devotion to Him. How unlike their limited abilities was His omnipotence, His closeness and immediacy wholly distinct from their indifference and remoteness! Israel stood witness as the sun, moon, and whirlwind complied, like loyal servants obeying their master, ceasing their inexorable progress until released by the Creator to finally complete the course.

THE COMMENTARY OF GERSONIDES

At least one of the medieval commentaries was loath to adopt the simple reading of our text, for to do so would allow Joshua's deed to easily eclipse the miraculous exploits of his own mentor Moses. Rabbi Levi ben Gershom, who was active in fourteenth-century France and known as Gersonides or Ralbag, explains that the thrust of the passage does not concern supernatural celestial events, but rather, the victory of the Israelites: "until the nation avenged its foes," "because God waged war for Israel." Joshua's plea was that:

> Before the sun had set at Givon or the moon at the valley of Aya-lon, the people of Israel would complete the rout of their foes.... The people were able to miraculously avenge themselves... in such a short time... for God's abilities are not limited... and He heeded Joshua's prayer. (Gersonides on Josh. 10:12)

In other words, the miracle was not that the sun actually stood still, but rather that the people of Israel succeeded in thoroughly trouncing the southern kings in such a very short time, *before the sun completed its course and began to set.* The physical motion of the sun did not slow, but rather Israel was able to inflict a crushing defeat that should have taken a much longer period of time to accomplish. God acceded by granting them a swift and utter victory, "because God waged war for Israel."

Besides being an accomplished biblical commentator and philosopher, Gersonides was also an astronomer and a mathematician. He was the inventor of the "Jacob's Staff," a device that was used to measure the angular separation between celestial bodies and that was the forerunner of the astrolabe. Gersonides's interpretation is a function of his scientific empiricism and its downplay or dismissal of miracles. The natural laws are God's ultimate creation and the universe is governed in accordance with them. God did not formulate perfect laws in order to upset them without good cause. It is important to emphasize that Gersonides does not question God's *ability* to slow or stop the sun's progress, but rather His *willingness* to do so: "God, blessed be He, does not affect miracles except for some pressing need or in order to inculcate true opinions, and here neither of these conditions applied." Why, avers Gersonides, need God intervene to halt the motion of the sun if the point of the matter was for Israel to achieve victory? After all, they could well accomplish that aim without recourse to such an overt display of divine prowess. At the same time, the text makes no mention of a didactic or pedagogic aspect to the episode, and instead casts the matter in a purely utilitarian light: God interceded so that Israel might militarily prevail, not so that they may come to appreciate some abstract truth about His governance of the world. Gersonides would not accept our earlier reading that detected in the event a rebuttal of polytheistic beliefs concerning the divinity of the sun god, the moon god, and their minions.

SEFER HAYASHAR AND THE INTERPRETATION OF IBN EZRA

Concerning the mysterious *Sefer HaYashar*, traditional sources offer a number of intriguing but fanciful theories, understanding the appellation to refer to an existing volume of the Torah or Prophets – be it Genesis, Deuteronomy, or Judges (see Avoda Zara 25a). As pointed out earlier, the only other explicit biblical reference to the work is in the Book of Samuel, from David's moving elegy over the death in battle of King Saul and Jonathan – Saul's son and David's true friend:

> David composed this lament concerning Saul and Jonathan his son, to teach the people of Judah to draw the bow. Behold it is recorded in *Sefer HaYashar*: "Beautiful Israel, on your high places have they been killed. How have the mighty fallen!" (II Sam. 1:17–19)

This fleeting reference provides us with no additional information concerning the provenance of this work except to suggest that it perhaps related to warfare and was probably composed in poetic form rather than in prose. While our reference from Joshua is one of triumph and victory, the elegy of David recalls a shattering defeat: the slaying of Israel's first monarch at the hands of the Philistines.

It is Rabbi Abraham Ibn Ezra who offers a more realistic interpretation concerning references to otherwise obscure texts, and in the process he sheds much light on an important but under-appreciated aspect of the biblical canon. In context, Ibn Ezra addresses the equally cryptic "Book of the Wars of the Lord," mentioned only one time, in Numbers 21:14:

> This book was a self-contained work that recorded God's battles on behalf of those that revere Him. It would seem that it dated from the time of Abraham. After all, many works have been lost and are no longer extant among us, such as the "Words of

Natan" [I Chr. 29:29], the "Vision of Ido the Seer" [II Chr. 12:15], the "Chronicles of the Kings of Israel" [I Kings 14:19], as well as the songs and proverbs of Solomon [I Kings 5:12]. (Ibn Ezra on Num. 21:14)

Ibn Ezra posits that the Book of the Wars of the Lord is actually part of a much larger corpus of works that are mentioned in passing in various biblical books but now lost. *Sefer HaYashar* should be counted among these works. What is striking about Ibn Ezra's formulation is that it indicates a fact that we seldom consider: that the books of the Bible do not at all comprise the total literary output of the Jewish people during the fifteen centuries of the biblical period. There were many other worthwhile works that were composed by worthwhile people but were lost to posterity. For Ibn Ezra, the incorporation of texts into the biblical canon was neither arbitrary nor a function of a paucity of material. Rather, only those works that carried the imprimatur of divine authorship (the Torah) or genuine divine inspiration (all else) were preserved, providing that the thrust of their message was deemed sufficiently vital for future generations. That the biblical books were preserved intact is nothing short of extraordinary and highlights more than anything else the reverence that ancient Israel had for its sacred texts. This was because these books addressed what were regarded as life's most urgent concerns: How to live meaningfully in relationship with God, how to live meaningfully in relationship with other human beings, and how to successfully synthesize these dual concerns.

Whatever the exact nature of the divine intervention that took place at Givon on that day, it was momentous enough to be included in a separate work documenting God's righteous acts of salvation. Although that work may have been subsequently lost, the effects of the Israelite triumph – and God's astounding involvement – continued to live on in the collective memory of the people of Israel for eternity.

Joshua 10:15–11:23

Divine Design and Human Initiative

At the battle of Givon, the enemy army was comprised of at least five distinct forces, the respective militias of the five kings of the south. These monarchs controlled territories in the southern hill country of Canaan as well as in its foothills that extended to the fertile coastal plain. Their defeat at the hands of Joshua effectively ended any military opposition to the slow but steady Israelite expansion into this territory, the area later associated with the tribal lands of Judah and Benjamin. At the same time, by capturing the towns of Yarmut, Lakhish, and Eglon, all of them strategically sited at the western approaches to these hills, Joshua negated the possibility of any military involvement by the Canaanites who dwelt on the coast. As for the remaining Canaanites of the hill country, they would have to oppose Joshua's army alone.

Recall that Israel's first battle was against Jericho, the border city in the Jordan valley that guarded the entry into the central area of the hills. After its miraculous fall, Joshua went on to attack the towns of Ai and Beit El, both situated in the highlands to the west of Jericho. He then concluded a pact with the people of Givon, to the southwest of Ai.

Significantly, the ancient and important city of Shekhem (modern-day Nablus), also inhabited by the same Hivite stock as Givon (see Gen. 34), is completely absent from the account of the Israelite conquest of the area, but is mentioned as the site of the national assembly held by Joshua after the fall of the Ai (Josh. 8:30–35). This may very well indicate, as some modern scholars believe, that its people offered no resistance to the Israelite onslaught and perhaps even abetted Israel's entry into the land.

The geographic progression of Joshua's battles can therefore be reconstructed: After taking Jericho that protected the Jordan valley, he attacked and captured the cities of the central hill country. By defeating Ai and Beit El, he was able to drive a wedge between the southern and northern halves of this territory. The southern kings were no longer able to enlist the support of their northern neighbors in the campaign against the Israelites, and this made Israel's task immeasurably easier. The northern kings now stood alone, led by the powerful king of Ḥatzor, who enlisted a huge fighting force that included chariots. But the Israelite victory over the kings of the south effectively precluded the formation of a broader and more menacing coalition, and the northern forces were defeated. In fact, the impressive ruins of the city of Ḥatzor, located north of Lake Kinneret, provide mute but unassailable testimony to the biblical account of Joshua's conquest and burning of the city.

THE THEMATIC PROGRESSION OF THE BATTLES

There is another progression embedded in the descriptions of Joshua's battles, and to recognize it is to appreciate one of the book's most enduring themes. Let us list the major battles of these first eleven chapters while noting any unusual indications of divine involvement:

1. Jericho – chapter six. The ramparts and walls of the city tumbled down at the sound of the people's outcry that followed the final, extended shofar blast.
2. Ai – chapter eight. At Joshua's signal of the raised spear, the ambush force seized the open city, while his remaining troops counterattacked and defeated the people of Ai and Beit El.

Joshua's Campaign Against the Northern Kings

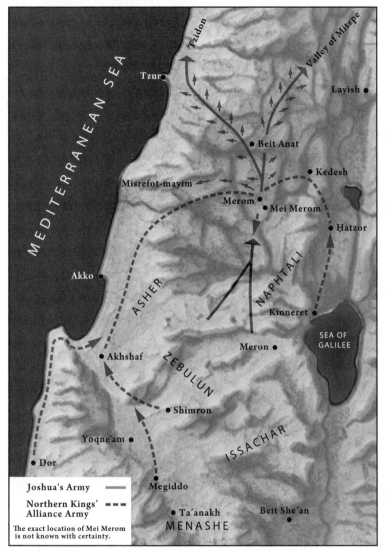

3. Southern kings – chapter ten. The fleeing Canaanite forces were struck down by a sudden storm of hailstones, and the sun stood still to allow Israel to complete the rout.
4. Northern kings – chapter eleven.

It will be immediately noted that no overt expressions of divine involvement at all seem to accompany the battles against the northern kings, although the text does state clearly that the victory was His: "God said to Joshua: 'Be not afraid of them, for tomorrow at this time I will give all of them as corpses before Israel. You shall cripple their horses and burn their chariots'" (Josh. 11:6). At Jericho, in glaring contrast, the narrative emphasized the role of the Ark of the Covenant (the physical manifestation of God's presence) while also highlighting the seven-day timeframe (the hallmark of God's involvement in human history). It was the shofar that waged war at Jericho, sonorous blasts that elsewhere in the Torah accompany the revelation of God's glory (Ex. 19:9–25, Lev. 23:23–25). The Israelites were mere followers in the procession around the walls, their only contribution to the victory consisting of an inspired shout let loose as the Ark completed its seventh circuit on the seventh day. If ever there was a clash that was convincingly won by troops who did not need to fire a single shot, it was at Jericho.

How different is the war against the northern kings! Here, it is Joshua who engages them in battle at Mei Merom, and, attacking suddenly, "falls upon them" (Josh. 11:7). The Israelites strike them and pursue them as far as Tzidon (Sidon on the Lebanese coast), leaving not a remnant of the enemy forces. They debilitate their battle horses and destroy their chariots. While the text mentions that "God gave them into Israel's hand" (v. 8), it offers no further elaboration on the nature of His involvement. In fact, the recurring emphasis of the text is not on God's role but rather on Joshua's role: "Joshua and all of the people of war arrived at Mei Merom suddenly" (v. 7); "Joshua did to them as God commanded" (v. 9); "Joshua returned at that time and captured Ḥatzor" (v. 10); "All of these king's cities as well as their kings, Joshua captured" (v. 12); "Joshua conquered all of this land" (v. 16); "For many days Joshua waged war against all of these kings" (v. 18); "At that time, Joshua came and cut down the giants" (v. 21); and finally, "Joshua captured the whole land, just as God had spoken to Moses, and Joshua apportioned it to Israel according to their divisions and tribes, and then the land was quiet from warfare" (v. 23).

The two intermediate battles, against the Ai and against the southern Kings, can now be more precisely located within the progression. At the battle of the Ai, it was God who provided both the battle plan as well as the pivotal signal. Joshua was bidden by Him to "place an ambush behind the city" (Josh. 8:2) which he dutifully did. After drawing out the town's defenders by feigning retreat, Joshua visually signaled to the ambush force to enter the open gates by raising his spear at God's behest. Therefore, while it was Joshua and the people who physically engaged the enemy in battle and defeated them, it was God who brought them victory by providing the strategic plan and the critical timing. The victory may therefore be described as a dynamic combination of divine intervention and inspired human deed.

Concerning the southern kings, they gathered their forces at Givon and prepared to attack their former comrades, in retaliation for the Givonites having concluded a non-aggression pact with the Israelites. Joshua mustered his forces and, marching all night from Gilgal, mounted a sudden counterattack. The enemy forces were discomfited and began to flee as their lines crumbled. It was only at that moment that God overtly intervened by raining down hailstones upon them and then delaying the setting of the sun, thus allowing Israel to completely rout and utterly destroy the enemy forces. Here, God's intrusion into the human arena to ensure an Israelite victory was only *after* His people had engaged the enemy in battle and roundly defeated them. His intervention was limited to the aftermath of their victory. God provided Joshua with the opportunity to wipe out the enemy forces so that they could not regroup for another battle, but the initial triumph was entirely a function of human initiative.

DECLINE OF OVERT DIVINE INTERVENTION

Considering these "chapters of conquest" in broad terms thus yields a remarkable evolution. As the narratives unfold, God's overt intervention declines, matched by a corresponding increase in the people of Israel's active participation in securing their own victory. However, the book is exceedingly careful to make clear that decreased overt divine intervention does not mean God's absence. God is just as aware, just as immediate, and just as instrumental in guiding events according to His will. The only thing that changes during the course of the chapters is the transparency and prominence of that involvement, in order to afford human beings the opportunity to take an active part in shaping their destiny, to choose the trajectory if not the outcome, and to spiritually grow and mature as a result.

Put differently, these chapters of the book argue forcefully for a transformation of the wilderness existence in which the tribes of Israel were miraculously nourished by bread from the sky, sustained by water from the rock, and shielded from harm by God's ever-present clouds of glory. In the dimension of wilderness living that characterized Israelite experience from the time of the Exodus until the entry into the land of Canaan, God was constantly manifest, His saving power and stern correction only a heartbeat away. Human autonomy may have been a real quantity even in the wilderness, but its impact was limited, inevitably overawed and overruled by divine transcendence.

On the other side of the Jordan, God invites the people to live more normal lives, sheltered from the constant and overwhelming glare of His radiance. As a result, the struggle of faith is made more acute, for God's intentional concealment behind the artifice of human initiative allows for an alternative interpretation of events that downplays or denies divine involvement while encouraging human pride. But there is inestimable value to God's self-imposed concealment, for it impels human beings to take an active role in their own lives, to experience the pain of their bad choices and the joy of the good, to learn from their failures and to overcome.

In short, during the course of these pivotal chapters, the people of Israel are slowly made to realize that to forge their own place in the world as God's nation they will need to exercise strength of will and employ ingenuity and ambition. If they can remain true to His teachings, He will not let them down. He will be quietly by their side as they build their state.

Joshua 12:1–24

War Against the Canaanites

hapter twelve of the Book of Joshua effectively completes the story of the land's conquest. It begins by recalling the impressive Israelite victories over the Amorite kings Siḥon and Og, the Transjordanian tyrants defeated by Moses on the eve of the people's entry into the land. The chapter then goes on to tersely enumerate the thirty-one potentates deposed by Joshua, as the people captured first the central hill country, then the southern ridge and its foothills, and finally the menacing kings of the north. Linking Joshua's victories to Moses' earlier triumphs indicates that Joshua admirably succeeded in his quest to fill the leadership void left by the demise of the lawgiver:

> These are the kings of the land that Joshua and the people of Israel struck down, on the western side of the Jordan River. [Their territories extended] from Baal Gad in the Lebanon valley until the cleft hills that ascend to Se'ir; Joshua gave it to the tribes of Israel as a possession in accordance with their divisions. [These lands included] the hills, the lowlands, the plain, the streambeds, the wilderness, and the dry southern lands, the territories of the Hittite, Amorite, Canaanite, Perizite, Hivite, and Jebusite. (Josh. 12:7–8)

THE SONG OF DOWNFALL

While written in the form of a biblical song, the list of the thirty-one kings follows a formal structure that nevertheless sets it apart from most other passages of biblical song:

> R. Ḥanina b. Papa said: R. Sheila of Kefar Timrata expounded that all of the passages of biblical song are written as "half bricks arranged upon whole bricks" and "whole bricks arranged upon half bricks." The exceptions to the rule are the list of the rogue Haman's ten sons (Est. 9:6–9) and the list of the kings of Canaan, for they are composed as half bricks arranged upon half bricks, and whole bricks upon whole bricks. What is the reason for the distinction? So that they should have no resurgence from their downfall. (Megilla 16b)

Each line of the song, devoted to the mention of a single one of the kings, is divided into a short stitch of text ("half brick") that is separated by a longer blank space ("whole brick") from the concluding stitch of text, like this:

The king of Jericho	one;
The king of the Ai by Beit El	one;
The king of Jerusalem	one;
The king of Hebron	one…
All of the kings thirty	and one. (Josh. 12:9–24)

The reason advanced by the Talmud to explain this atypical graphic form is quite compelling. Up until the modern period and the advent of steel-reinforced concrete and curtain wall construction, a building's maximum height could not exceed six to eight stories. Greater height could only be achieved by widening the base of the structure so that the load could be more widely distributed. Maintaining a uniform floor area over the course of a building's rise would produce an inherently less stable structure. The Talmud is therefore suggesting that the graphic form of these songs is an integral part of their interpretation. The tall and slender columns of text that preserve the names of wicked

Haman's ten sons, comprising eleven lines or "stories," are therefore not only a list of infamy but also an expression of the instability of evil and an unspoken prayer that having been toppled and deposed, their acts of villainy not recur. The list of Canaan's conquered kings, of even greater height, expresses the silent hope that Israel's triumph over their evil not be undone. But let it be noted that this "song" does not contain a single note of triumphalism; neither smug gloating over the enemies' downfall nor bloodthirsty glorifications of warfare. It is an austere, impassive list of victories that speaks worlds about biblical Israel's attitudes towards the need to defeat the enemy while not debasing him.[1]

Seventeen of the thirty-one kings on the list are mentioned explicitly in the battles that comprise chapters six through eleven of the book, while fourteen kings are mentioned only here. Overall, the thirty-one towns and cities mentioned cover the length and breadth of the land, from the Negev in the south until the Hermon in the north, and from the coastal plain in the west until the Jordan River in the east. The fact, however, that fourteen of the conquered towns are mentioned here for the first time and were not recounted earlier indicates that these earlier chapters, though they provide a broad overview of the conflict, do not

---

1. It is instructive to compare the tone of our book with the roughly contemporary Ugaritic myth of Baal, unearthed at Ras Shamra in northern Syria in 1929. In the following passage, Anat the consort of Baal does battle against her foes:

    Anat went to battle in the valley; she fought between the two cities. She killed the people of the coast, she annihilated the men of the east. Heads rolled under her like balls, hands flew over her like locusts, the warriors' hands like swarms of grasshoppers. She fastened the heads to her back, she tied the hands to her belt. She plunged knee-deep into the soldiers' blood, up to her thighs in the warriors' gore; with a staff she drove off her enemies, with the string of her bow her opponents.... She battled violently, and looked, Anat fought, and saw: her soul swelled with laughter, her heart was filled with joy, Anat's soul was exuberant, as she plunged knee-deep into the soldiers' blood, up to her thighs in the warriors' gore, until she was satisfied. (Michael D. Coogan, *Stories from Ancient Canaan*, Louisville: Westminster John Knox Press, 1978, p. 117)

    While biblical poetry is not entirely bereft of violent imagery – see for example, Isaiah 63:1–6 or Psalms 18:38–43 – there is no lusty reveling in the shedding of enemy blood.

intend to furnish a comprehensive description of every single battle and skirmish. Rather, the essence of those narratives is to suggest that the land as a whole had been secured and the main military alliances of the Canaanites had been smashed, even though many local battles remained to be fought.

THE MORAL DILEMMA

Before completing this second section of the book, the story of the land's conquest, we must consider its most troubling moral aspect, the seemingly indiscriminate slaughter of Canaan's indigenous inhabitants. It may be possible to make a case for the utter destruction of Jericho, the first town encountered by the Israelites that was razed to the ground never to be rebuilt. The denizens of Jericho, thanks to the untimely discovery of Joshua's spies in their midst, had ample time to sue for peace; their subsequent capture and decimation served as a powerful deterrent to the other Canaanite cities, thus averting even more bloodshed. Nevertheless, one cannot overlook the fact that nearly every encounter with the enemy Canaanite forces resulted not only in their unqualified defeat, but in the annihilation of their civilian populations as well. The recurring expression that runs as a refrain through the chapters of conquest is "He [Joshua] struck it by the edge of the sword, all of the souls that were in its midst, leaving not a remnant." (See Josh. 8:24–25; 10:28, 30, 32, 35, 37, 39; 11:11, 14.)

We may be tempted to dismiss the moral quandary by suggesting that the conquest unfolded in consonance with the ancient rules of warfare that were unforgiving and brutal as well as hopelessly out of touch with our more "refined" conventions that demand protection for the lives of non-combatants. The timelessness that tradition ascribes to the books of Tanakh, however, negates this superficial approach, that in other contexts as well charges the biblical text with being hopelessly out of touch with modernity and rejects its message as obsolete.

In order to provide a broader perspective on the matter, we must examine the other biblical evidence at our disposal. Bear in mind that although there is much archeological evidence to support the account of warfare presented in the Book of Joshua, there are no contemporaneous non-biblical textual sources that have been unearthed to substantiate its battle narratives. The burning of Ḥatzor, for example, described in 11:10–13, has been well corroborated by the excavations at the site that are still ongoing, but no textual sources besides the book itself attest to its chilling claim that "they smote all of the living souls that were there by the edge of the sword, destroying completely, so that none that breathed remained" (Josh. 11:11).

If the only extant texts that describe the annihilation of the Canaanites are those scattered verses in the Book of Joshua, and we are prepared to accept the vicious veracity of those verses, we must be equally prepared to trust the rest of the material concerning the war against the Canaanites preserved in the biblical books that *precede* Joshua – namely the Ḥumash. One cannot read the Book of Joshua in splendid isolation and expect to comprehend its message while remaining oblivious to the larger framework that is provided by the Ḥumash. Like the other books of the Hebrew Bible, Joshua is not only an independent book but also part of a larger literary framework that informs it. We have already seen evidence of this in the story of the crossing of the Jordan River and the entry into the land. While this material can certainly be understood in its own right, it is understood much better against the backdrop of the Exodus narratives that it so consciously draws upon.

On the topic of Canaan there is no dearth of information in the Ḥumash concerning its topographical features and the way of life of its inhabitants. Since the eve of the Exodus in the early chapters of the Book of Exodus, the land has been described to the people of Israel as their destination and as the reward for their exertions of faith. Israel's associations with the land, however, go back even further, for the patriarchs were many times vouchsafed by God that their descendants would one day possess it.

CONSIDERING THE SOURCES

The earliest source that supposes a concrete state of peoplehood (in contrast to the theoretical construct associated with the patriarchs or with Joseph) occurs in God's first words to Moses, as the latter stands transfixed by the spectacle of the burning bush and is about to be designated as Israel's leader who will free them from Pharaoh's iron grip:

> God said: I have surely seen the oppression of My people in
> Egypt, and I have heard their cries on account of their taskmasters,
> for I am aware of their anguish. I will descend to save them from
> the hands of the Egyptians and to bring them out of that land,
> to a good and expansive land, to a land flowing with milk and
> honey, to the place of the Canaanite, Hittite, Amorite, Perizite,
> Hivite, and Jebusite. (Ex. 3:7–8)

This hopeful passage, full of praise for the new land and promise for a
better future, indicates from the outset that Canaan is not a desolate
and empty tract of land but is inhabited by a whole series of tribes that
enjoy its bounty. There is nothing else that the verses tell us about the
Canaanites, except perhaps that they are sectarian and splintered, tribal
and tendentious, in contrast to the much more consolidated Egyptians.

A more telling reference occurs after the revelation at Sinai when
God proclaims His laws to the people encamped at its base. After setting out a detailed series of civil and ritual laws, the narrative turns to
a description of the land in which those laws are to be lived:

> Behold I send an angel before you, to guard you on the way and
> to bring you to the place that I have prepared. Be mindful of him
> and hearken to his voice not to be contentious, for he will not
> pardon your transgressions, for My name is in him. Rather, surely
> listen to his words and do all that I shall command, for then I
> will vanquish your enemies and defeat your foes. My angel shall
> go before you and bring you to the place of the Amorite, Hittite,
> Perizite, Canaanite, Hivite, and Jebusite, and I shall destroy them.
> *Do not bow down to their gods nor serve them and do not follow their*
> *practices.* Completely destroy [their idols] and break down their
> sacred pillars. Serve the Lord your God, for He shall bless your
> bread and water, and I shall remove sickness from your midst....
> I shall drive them out slowly, until you multiply and inherit the
> land.... Do not make a pact with them nor with their gods. Do
> not let them dwell in your land lest they cause you to sin against
> Me, for you shall then serve their gods and they shall be a source
> of ensnarement for you. (Ex. 23:20–33)

The tone of this section is much more circumspect. Apparently, there is much more than milk and honey that awaits the people of Israel in the Promised Land of Canaan. According to this passage, the inhabitants of the land represent a very real threat, but it is not their military prowess that the people of Israel must fear. Rather, it is their culture, their polytheistic outlook and its associated practices. These practices are not precisely spelled out in this text. Whatever rituals and forms of worship the Canaanites championed, they are presented as a grave threat to the future wellbeing of the people of Israel. It is that menace that serves as the impetus for the harsh directives to destroy, break down, and annihilate.

It is after the debacle of the Golden Calf that the Canaanites are next discussed. Having succumbed during that episode to idolatry, or at least to incarnation, the people of Israel secure God's forgiveness due to Moses' impassioned intercession. God's pledge of assistance is restored as He spells out to them anew the promise of the land:

> Observe carefully all that I command you this day. Behold I will drive out from before you the Amorite, Canaanite, Hittite, Perizite, Hivite, and Jebusite. Guard yourselves from concluding a covenant with the inhabitants of the land that you will enter, lest they be a snare in your midst. Rather, you shall break down their altars, smash their idolatrous pillars, and cut down their shrine trees. You shall not bow down to another god, because God is zealous, He is a zealous God. For if you conclude a covenant with the inhabitants of the land, then they shall stray after their gods and sacrifice to them, and they shall invite you to partake of their sacrifices. Then you will take their daughters for your sons, and their daughters shall stray after their gods and cause your sons to stray after their gods. You shall not make any molten images. Observe the festival of unleavened bread. (Ex. 34:11–18)

Here again, the directive to make no treaties and to destroy all indigenous expressions of idolatry is predicated upon the apprehension that the people of Israel will otherwise yield to the seductions of polytheism and become adherents of idolatrous rites. Intermarriage with members of the dominant culture will spell the end of Israel's unique mission. The progression is quite plainly spelled out: military or economic treaties will cement cultural ties which will invariably foster stronger social bonds and eventually intermarriage. Having married with the Canaanites, it will not be possible to refuse the worship of their gods and the adoption of their practices. In contrast to the prevailing polytheistic worldview that could easily accommodate the introduction of foreign or new gods into the pantheon, the "jealous" God of Israel demanded exclusivity and therefore rejected the adoption of any Canaanite practices.

While the text again avoids explicit mention of what those idolatrous rites may be, it does make clear that the insidious process of acculturation cannot be arrested midway. Political or commercial ties cannot but breed social intercourse and the adoption of the dominant value system. Therefore, a budding nation that proclaims the novel idea of monotheism and its corollary of absolute morality, but then culturally compromises with the Canaanites, seals its fate for its own extinction.

THE HOLINESS CODES OF LEVITICUS

It is in the holiness codes of Leviticus (chapters eighteen and twenty) that the Torah finally spells out some of the salient features of Canaanite worship and practice:

> God spoke to Moses saying: "Speak to the people of Israel and say to them that I am the Lord your God. Do not follow the practices of the land of Egypt where you dwelt, or those of the land of Canaan to where I bring you, and do not follow their statutes. Observe My laws and statutes and follow them, I am the Lord your God. Observe My statutes and laws, for a person who does them shall live, I am God. Let no man approach his kin to uncover nakedness, I am God." (Lev. 18:1–6)

The text goes on to enumerate no less than twenty examples of prohibited sexual partners, including one's mother, step mother, sister, daughter, daughter-in-law, aunt, and the menstruant. It outlaws promiscuity, adultery, homosexuality, and bestiality. Towards the end of the list, the worshipper of Molokh is singled out: "Do not give your children to be passed for the Molokh, do not desecrate the name of your God, for I am the Lord" (Lev. 18:21).

Here we have a fairly exhaustive catalog of Egyptian and Canaanite sexual practices, all of them pointing to a complete disregard of any absolute parameters to delineate conduct. Incest and adultery trample upon the sacred trusts that ought to govern human intimacy, while homosexuality and bestiality are conscious rejections of the demand to reign in the sexual drive or to inspire it with sanctity. The mysterious Molokh worship, here only mentioned for excoriation, is more fully spelled out in Deuteronomy:

> When the Lord your God dispossesses from before you the nations that you go in to inherit, so that you dispossess them and inherit their land, then you shall be careful not to be ensnared by them after they have been destroyed from before you. Do not inquire after their gods saying: "How did these nations serve their gods? I will do likewise!" Do not do likewise to the Lord your God, for all of the abominations that God abhors they did for their gods, and they even burned their sons and daughters in fire for their gods! Rather, do all that I command you and observe it, do not add to it nor subtract from it. (Deut. 12:29–13:1)

The worship of Molokh, a Semitic god popular in the region, was celebrated by the burning of children. Although the talmudic traditions (Sanhedrin 64b) dispute whether the offered children were in fact consumed by the flames or only made to pass or jump through them, the biblical evidence seems to indicate quite clearly that in at least some of the variations of Molokh worship, the children were actually sacrificed and killed.[2]

NUMBERS AND DEUTERONOMY

Another mention of the Canaanite menace occurs towards the end of the Book of Numbers (33:50–56), as the borders of the Promised Land are spelled out. Once again, the people of Israel are commanded to drive

---

2. See, for example, Psalms 106:34–39.

out the inhabitants of the land and to destroy their idolatrous shrines. The brief passage concludes with an unveiled threat:

> But if you do not drive out the inhabitants of the land from before you, then those that you allow to remain will be as thorns in your eyes and as thistles in your sides, and they will aggrieve you upon the land in which you dwell. What I had considered to do to them I shall instead do to you. (Num. 33:55–56)

Here, the Torah suggests that for Israel to suffer the Canaanites to remain is to risk being beguiled by their corrupt ways, which will eventually lead to Israel's own exile and doom.

The harshest polemic against the Canaanites occurs in the Book of Deuteronomy. In this book Moses addresses the new generation poised to enter the land. In measured words, he encourages them to remain strong in their faith and steadfast in their performance of God's laws. He recalls the trials of the wilderness, the scarcity and want, and God's ever-present concern and love. He reviews the laws and rituals, as well as introducing new legislation that will be needed when the people cross over the Jordan into the new land. While Moses paints the picture of the new land with vibrant colors, often contrasting its verdant promise with his own profound sadness at being denied entry, he also sounds notes of caution. Again and again, he indicates to the people that their success in the land will depend upon their dedication to not only settling its expanse, but to expunging the Canaanites and their culture of idolatry from their midst:

> Be very careful lest you corrupt your ways and fashion idolatrous images of anything.... Lest you lift your eyes skywards to look upon the sun, the moon, and the stars, all of heaven's host, and you shall stray and bow down to them and worship them. For God apportioned them to all of the nations beneath the heavens, but God took you and extricated you from the iron furnace that was Egypt to be His special nation this day. (Deut. 4:16–20)

When the Lord your God brings you into the land that you are
to inherit and drives out great nations from before you.... Utterly
destroy them, do not conclude a pact with them nor be compas-
sionate. Do not intermarry with them, giving your daughter to his
son or taking his daughter for your son. For then your son will
be led astray to serve other gods and God's anger will be kindled
to quickly destroy you. Rather, you shall do thus to them: break
down their altars, smash their sacred pillars, cut down their tree
shrines, and burn their images with fire. For you are a holy nation
unto the Lord your God, and the Lord your God chose you to
be His treasured nation from all of the peoples that are upon the
face of the earth. (Deut. 7:1–6)

The Lord your God will drive out these peoples from before you
slowly.... Burn by fire the images of their gods. Do not covet the
silver and gold upon them and take it, lest you be led astray by
it, for it is an abomination to the Lord your God. Do not bring
such an abomination into your house for then you will become
banned like it, rather shun it completely and consider it offensive,
for it is to be banned. (Deut. 7:22–26)

When the Lord your God drives them out from before you, do not
say in your heart: "It is because of my righteousness that God brings
me in to inherit this land!" Rather, it is because of the wickedness of
these nations that God drives them out from before you. (Deut. 9:4)

If your blood brother, son, daughter, loving wife, or dearest friend
secretly attempts to lead you astray, saying: "Let us go and serve
other gods" that neither you nor your ancestors knew, the gods of
the nations that are around you, near or far, from one end of the
earth to the other. Do not desire his words, do not hearken to him,
do not have compassion upon him, and do not conceal his deed.
Rather, you shall surely put him to death.... For he attempted to
drive you away from the Lord your God who brought you out
of the land of Egypt from the house of bondage. (Deut. 13:7–11)

> For you are about to enter the land that the Lord your God gives you, do not learn the abominable practices of these peoples. There must not be found among you one who causes his son or daughter to pass through the fire, one who practices divination, predicts auspicious times, augers, or does witchcraft. Also, not one who uses incantations, inquires of mediums and oracles, or consults the dead. All those who practice these things are abominable before God, and it is because of these abominations that God drives them out from before you. Instead, you shall be of perfect faith with the Lord your God. (Deut. 18:9–13)

XENOPHOBIA VERSUS SELF-PRESERVATION

It seems, therefore, that the consistent condemnation of Canaanite culture that underlies almost every mention of them in the text of the Torah is not a hysterical outburst of xenophobia or a calculated demonization paving the way for their future extirpation at the hands of the Israelites, but rather a somber assessment of their morally decadent civilization and its ethical failings. To adopt the ways of Canaan is to fall prey to superstition and magic, to become engrossed in immoral cults and rituals, to display insensitivity and numbness towards human life's sanctity and worth, and to perform every imaginable abomination under the heavens – all in the name of the gods. To be God's "chosen," in contrast, means not inherent superiority or unwarranted elitism, but rather the burden and responsibility of adhering to a life of ethical self-restraint and spiritual growth. The God of Israel is not appeased by burnt offerings of precious children, or placated by mysterious rites and strange incantations:

> With what shall I present myself before the Lord and bow low before the most-high God? Shall I come before Him with burnt offerings or year-old calves? Will the Lord desire thousands of rams or tens of thousands of rivers of oil? Shall I offer my firstborn to atone for my transgression, the fruit of my womb to absolve the sin of my soul? Man may have told you what is good, but what the Lord desires of you is nothing more than the doing of justice, love of kindness, and to walk humbly with your God. (Mic. 6:6–8)

In this connection, it is critical to bear in mind that the great chasm separating monotheism from polytheism is not solely mathematical, as if adopting the worship of a single deity differs from the worship of many only as an abstract numerical notion. Rather, the revolution wrought by Israel's monotheism fundamentally affects two complementary realms that together comprise the sum total of human interactions: those that take place with God and those that transpire between us and our fellow men. First of all, only if God is one can He be absolute and incorporeal. If there are many gods, then not one of them can exercise complete mastery over nature or his peers. If there are many gods, then they must be in confrontation, just like the capricious forces of nature that are in a perpetual state of conflict. If there are many gods, then they must possess materiality and be limited by it to become nothing more than grotesque reflections of human shortcomings. If there are many gods, then they cannot be depended upon to hear our prayers, to take an interest in our fate or to intervene in order to save. No wonder that the tribes that inhabited Canaan, though they were more technically advanced, culturally informed, and aesthetically accomplished in the plastic arts than their Israelite counterparts, have nevertheless bequeathed to us precious few texts that could stir the human soul and inspire it to nobility.

At the same time, and for our purposes this is decisive, any moral system that develops under conditions of polytheism cannot but be relativistic and hence non-binding and ultimately irrelevant. This is quite simply because the existence of many gods implies many standards of conduct, many acceptable codes of behavior, and therefore endless opportunities for the voices of self-gratification and self-gain to overwhelm the gods' feeble requests to act with altruism and magnanimity. Gods that are themselves limited cannot bequeath to their devotees a moral system that is categorical and therefore binding upon monarch and masses alike. Only an absolute God, all-powerful, all-knowing, and all-present, can demand fealty to an absolute morality that is often at odds with our personal wants and special interests. To put the matter into perspective, there are no other codes that have come down to us from antiquity that resemble anything like the Ten Utterances. No other ancient people save for the Hebrews ever presented humanity with anything remotely resembling the Torah's unequivocal demands for justice, righteousness, compassion, kindness, and holiness. But then again, how could they? If, by definition, multiples of contentious gods could not possibly come to a consensus in order to craft, impose, or even take more than a passing interest in a binding moral system, then certainly their human adherents would be unable and unwilling to do so.

As long as Israel dwelt in Egypt or wandered in the wilderness, the rampant heathenism and idolatry of their surroundings could be brooked. However, finally ready to assume their rightful place among the nations, by entering the land of Canaan and fashioning their own state, Israel now had to adopt a different and less tolerant stance. If it was to survive as a unique entity in the world, God's own "treasure" among the nations, the sole champions in all of antiquity of ethical monotheism – the only creed that provided for an island of moral absolutes in a sea of nasty relativism – then Israel had to categorically reject all indigenous expressions of idolatry and eradicate them from their midst.

MORAL CONFLICT VERSUS RACIAL HOSTILITY

So far, our investigation of the sources in the Torah that obligated Israel to wipe out all expressions of indigenous idolatrous worship clearly demonstrates that the underlying impetus for the campaign of eradication was moral rather than racial or ethnic. Almost without exception, every source in the Torah that commanded the conquest of Canaan also noted the moral degradation of its inhabitants. With Israel poised to settle the land and found their state, the peril represented by polytheistic relativism became acute. In our own day, we recognize only too well the inherent danger of granting clemency to dictators or to regimes that refuse to abide by any ethical principles. In the end, such individuals and societies destroy not only themselves but those around them as well.

A careful reading of one of the indicated sources highlights the moral rather than the racial nature of the conflict:

> God spoke to Moses saying: Speak to the people of Israel and say to them that I am the Lord your God. Do not follow the practices of the land of Egypt where you dwelt, or those of the land

of Canaan to where I bring you, and do not follow their statutes. Observe My laws and statutes and follow them, I am the Lord your God. Observe My statutes and laws, for a person who does them shall live, I am God. Let no man approach his kin to uncover nakedness, I am God. (Lev. 18:1–6)

As we have seen, the text goes on to list more than twenty prohibited sexual liaisons and to single out Molokh worship towards the end. But it is the conclusion of that source that proves to be decisive for our purposes:

> Do not defile yourselves by all of these practices, for all of the nations that I drive out from before you became defiled through them. The land became defiled and I punished it for its transgression, and the land spewed out its inhabitants. Rather, you shall observe My statutes and laws and not do any of these abominations, both the citizen as well as the sojourner that dwells among you. The people who dwelt in the land before you performed all of these abominations, and the land became defiled. *Let not the land spew you out for defiling it just as it spewed out the nation before you.* For whoever does any of these abominable things shall be cut off from among their people. Keep my observances and do not adopt any of these abominable statutes that were performed before you, and do not become defiled by them, for I am the Lord your God. (Lev. 18:24–30)

The above passage is proleptic, for although it is addressed to the people of Israel before their entry into the land, it describes the demise of the Canaanites as if it had already taken place. In the end, the people's entry into the land was delayed for forty years due to the debacle of the spies. But the implication of the past tense is clear: though the Canaanites had yet to be been driven out of the land, they had already forfeited their deed to it. The Torah indicates that their loss of possession was due to their moral failure. This theme of moral degradation, expressed in the passage as "defilement," is stated no less than five times. Remarkably, though, the point of the text is not to triumphantly enumerate the downfall of the

Canaanites and to highlight the superiority of Israel. Quite the contrary, the main thrust of the passage is to solemnly declare that *Israel will suffer a similar fate if they adopt the practices of their predecessors.* Just as the land "spewed out" the Canaanites because of their abominable practices, so too will it spew out the Israelites if they follow their example.

The critical issue, therefore, is not Canaanite versus Israelite, but rather immorality in contradistinction to morality. Israel's deed to the land is no more secure than that of the Canaanites and, practically speaking, is a function of one thing only: their fidelity to God's laws and to the moral absolutes that those laws proclaim. Though God may have extended His oath to the people's progenitors that their descendants would one day inherit and settle the land, their continuing presence in its midst will depend upon their moral choices and cannot be guaranteed by the merit of their forefathers:

> When the Lord your God drives them out from before you, do not say in your heart: "It is because of my righteousness that God brings me in to inherit this land!" Rather, it is because of the wickedness of these nations that God drives them out from before you. It is not because of your righteousness or the uprightness of your heart that you enter to inherit the land. Rather, it is because of the wickedness of these peoples that the Lord your God drives them out from before you and in order to fulfill the words that God pledged to your ancestors, to Abraham, Isaac, and Jacob. (Deut. 9:4–5)

It is instructive to note that in the end, the deep-seated fears of the Torah were realized. Israel entered the land, conquered and settled it, but eventually succumbed to the wiles of idolatry and became corrupted. The First Temple prophets railed against the people's ritual infractions and decried their moral failures, but to no avail. The three cardinal transgressions of idolatry, murder, and sexual immorality, the unholy trinity of Canaanite polytheism, were routinely committed. Finally, the Temple was destroyed and the people of Israel were driven into exile by the Babylonians. The very fate that had overcome the Canaanites some eight centuries earlier now befell the state of the Jews, thus indicating beyond a shadow of a doubt that possession of the land was a function of moral and ethical conduct and nothing else.[3]

HALAKHIC CONSIDERATIONS OF THE WAR

The above analysis is informed by a striking disagreement among the early authorities concerning the halakhic status of the Canaanites. Recall that in accordance with Torah law, Canaanite cities were to be completely destroyed if terms of surrender were not met:

> When you draw near to a city to wage war against it, then you shall first proclaim peace. If they respond in kind and open the gates for you, then all of the people that are in the city will pay tribute and serve you. If they do not surrender peacefully but rather fight against you…. But from the cities of these people that the Lord your God gives you as an inheritance, you shall not spare any soul. Rather, you shall completely destroy them, the Hittite, the Amorite, the Canaanite, the Perizite, the Hivite, and the Jebusite, just as the Lord your God commands you. This is in order that they not teach you to perform all of the abominations that they do in the service of their gods, for then you shall transgress against the Lord your God. (Deut. 20:10–18)

As we saw in an earlier chapter, there is an ambiguity in the above passage concerning the treatment of Canaanite cities. Must the peace overture extended to non-Canaanites also be proclaimed to Canaanite cities or

---

3. The commentaries speak at length concerning the uniqueness of the land of Israel that in accordance with its very nature cannot tolerate the presence of immorality or evil, since it is associated with God's presence. As Nahmanides explains in his commentary on Leviticus 18:25: "The land that is great God's possession spews out all those who defile it and will not tolerate those who practice idol worship or engage in sexual immorality." Canaan is unlike any other land. All other lands experience less of God's providence and may therefore be settled by nations that perform immoral acts with impunity. Canaan, on the other hand, is uniquely imbued with the manifestation of God's presence. Therefore, the person or nation that dwells in Canaan, whatever their race or ethnicity, must respect the sanctity of the land by exercising moral restraint.

are the Canaanites not to be offered any possibility of surrender? Rashi, it will be recalled, argued for the complete obliteration of the Canaanites while Nahmanides insisted that they too were to be offered at the outset the possibility of surrender.

Significantly, there is a further disagreement between Rashi and Nahmanides, and it concerns the contents of the said peace overture. Nahmanides maintains, based upon the conclusion of the above passage ("This is in order that they not teach you to perform all of the abominations that they do in the service of their gods, for then you shall transgress against the Lord your God") that the harsh decree of obliteration only applies when the Canaanites persist in their corrupt practices, for then the danger exists that Israel will learn from their ways. However, in accordance with the rabbinic tradition preserved in the halakhic Midrash of the *Sifrei* (Judges 20:2), that "if they repent, then they are not to be killed," Nahmanides maintains that if they "abandon their gods" and adopt the other Noahide principles, then they may be permitted to continue dwelling in the land of Canaan in the very midst of the Jewish state.

Rashi, in contrast, insists in his comments to the talmudic passage in Sota 35b that such grace is only to be extended to non-Canaanite cities, but concerning the Canaanites, "Even if they repent, we do not accept them, for they do so out of fear." Since, according to Rashi, when Canaanite repentance takes place it is insincere and only motivated by dread, the presumption remains that they will return to their depraved ways when the imminent danger of conquest subsides, and then the people of Israel will become corrupted by following their example.

There are therefore two points of disagreement between Rashi and Nahmanides. Rashi explains that Canaanite cities are not to be offered any terms of peace, whereas besieged cities beyond Canaan's borders must accept the seven Noahide principles or else perish. Nahmanides, on the other hand, insists that even Canaanite cities can sue for peace as long as they agree to abide by the Noahide laws, but distant cities that surrender and accept tribute can be spared even when they persist to practice idolatry.

The straightforward reading of the relevant scriptural and rabbinic texts (including the passage from Sota 35b) is in accordance with Nahmanides, and such appears to be the view of Maimonides as well

(Laws of Kings and Warfare 6:4). What emerges from the discussion then, is that Canaanite towns that abandon idolatry and its associated moral deficiencies and instead adopt the seven Noahide principles can continue to dwell in the land unmolested. These principles contain the basic tenets of civilized behavior and can be succinctly listed as follows: (1) Not to worship idols, (2) Not to blaspheme God, (3) Not to murder, (4) Not to commit adultery, (5) Not to steal, (6) Not to eat a limb torn from a living creature, (7) To establish a judiciary (see Sanhedrin 56a). *We must therefore conclude from this line of evidence that the war against the Canaanites was not a war against a race or a people but rather a war against a noxious moral system that refused to embrace even the most elementary expressions of humane conduct and civilized behavior.* After all, what functioning society could object to at least the final five of those seven ideas? As for the first two commands that pertain to our relationship with God, they are the necessary basis for the other five. Otherwise even these five would be observed only tentatively and jettisoned when convenient. Put simply, if there is no absolute God then there cannot be an absolute and binding moral system.

Concluding our discussion of the war of conquest, we realize that sensationalist readings of the matter are gratuitous and unwarranted. Those that perfunctorily read the first half of Joshua in isolation, as a bloodthirsty account of wanton Israelite conduct, do a disservice to the text and to the ancient traditions behind it. No one can deny the tragedy of war or its cruelty but that must not blind us to the awful truth that some wars are nevertheless justified and even obligatory.

The nation of Israel was the only people of antiquity to proclaim the existence of an absolute moral code, a revolutionary idea that was the direct consequence of their championing the existence of an absolute, single, and incorporeal deity. These were ideas that transformed history and that continue to guide humanity towards the good. But they are ideas that could not have survived this long had they not first been firmly planted in Canaan's fertile earth, to be nurtured by the nascent nation that first proclaimed God's name. Though Israel abrogated its mandate and was eventually exiled from that land, the ideas that it stood for as a nation could not be nullified. Like the people of Israel, they will endure forever to be eventually accepted by all of humanity.

Unconquered Territories

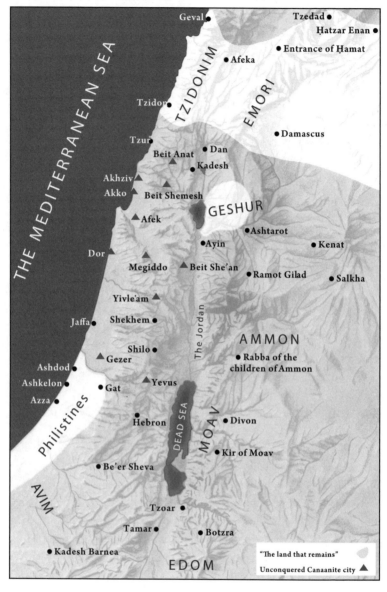

THE MEDITERRANEAN SEA

Geval
Tzedad
Ḥatzar Enan
TZIDONIM
Entrance of Ḥamat
Afeka
EMORI
Tzidon
Damascus
Tzur
Beit Anat
Dan
Kadesh
Akhziv
Akko
Beit Shemesh
GESHUR
Afek
Ashtarot
Kenat
Ayin
Dor
Megiddo
Beit She'an
Ramot Gilad
Salkha
Yivle'am
Shekhem
Jaffa
The Jordan
AMMON
Shilo
Gezer
Rabba of the
children of Ammon
Ashdod
Yevus
Ashkelon
Gat
Azza
Philistines
Hebron
DEAD SEA
Divon
MOAV
Kir of Moav
Be'er Sheva
AVIM
Tzoar
Tamar
Botzra
Kadesh Barnea
EDOM

"The land that remains"
Unconquered Canaanite city ▲

Joshua 13:1–14:15

Settling the Land of Canaan

Joshua was old, advanced in years, and God said to him: "You have become old, advanced in years, but so much of the land remains unsettled. This is the land that remains: All of the Philistine regions and that of the Geshuri. From the Shiḥor which is near Egypt until the border of Ekron northwards, which is the territory of the Canaanites. The five Philistine city-states of Azza, Ashdod, Ashkelon, Gat, Ekron, as well as the Avim. From the south, all of Canaan until the cave of the Tzidonites at Aphek, until the border of the Amorites. The land of the Givli and all of Lebanon eastwards from Baal Gad at the foot of Mount Hermon until the approach of Hammat. All of the inhabitants of the hills, from Lebanon until Misrefot Mayim, and all of the Tzidonim. I will drive them out before the people of Israel. Only assign it to Israel according to lot, as I have commanded you. Now then, divide this land by inheritance among the nine tribes, and the half tribe of Menashe. With the other [half of Menashe], the tribes of Reuben and Gad took their possession that Moses had given them on the eastern side of the Jordan River, as Moses the servant of God gave them." (Josh. 13:1–8)

Thus begins the second half of the Book of Joshua – the story of the distribution of the land of Canaan among the tribes of Israel. It describes Joshua as now advanced in age, and much of the land as yet unconquered. The regions demarcated by the verses above are found along the entire length of the Mediterranean coastline and among the hills and valleys of Lebanon. The areas of Israelite conquest and settlement were concentrated in the Canaanite hill country, the sparsely populated ridge that runs the length of the land from the arid Negev in the south until the fertile Jezreel Valley towards the sea of Kinneret northwards. The coastal plane and the fertile valleys southwest of the Kinneret, which were inhabited by the Canaanites, could not be conquered militarily.

While a superficial reading of the first half of the book may leave the impression that Israel under the leadership of Joshua succeeded in conquering the entire Canaanite population in short order, a more careful study indicates that this was not the case. Though Israel achieved impressive victories over the Canaanite military alliances and even took many of their towns in battle, the results were tenuous. Only by following up their victories with settlement of the land, a drawn-out process that was scarcely unfolding even after the smoke of the battles had long since cleared, could the people hope to possess it.

This, in fact, was the core of God's message to the aging leader, as the cycle of wars was coming to an end while Israel's hold on the land was far from firm:

> You have become old, advanced in years, but much of the land remains unsettled. This is the land that remains…. I will drive them out before the people of Israel. Only assign it to Israel according to lot, as I have commanded you. (Josh. 13:1–6)

God indicated to Joshua and to the people what every victorious general realizes and what had become apparent to the Israelite forces by virtue of their own experience: Conquest of territory does not equal its possession. While the former is a function of more advanced weaponry or superior strategy, the latter depends upon establishing a permanent presence of one's population. The former is quick and decisive, while the latter is protracted and often plagued by setbacks. While Joshua was singularly successful at the first task, God informs him that the second task, settlement of the land, will not be completed during his lifetime. God therefore bids Joshua while he yet lives, to formally assign the territory of Canaan to the tribes by lot, though the land will not be populated by Israelites until much later when they finally achieve hegemony.

FALLACIOUS READINGS

Modern archeologists and biblical critics have questioned the veracity of the book's description of a lightening victory over the Canaanites and, in its aftermath, an immediate settlement of the land, claiming instead that the tribes' entry and colonization was more akin to a gradual infiltration. It should be pointed out, though, that the material evidence for the swift military conquest of many of the sites mentioned in the account is beyond dispute. The excavations at Ḥatzor, for instance, the chief city in the alliance of the northern kings (Josh. 11:1–13) located to the northwest of the sea of Kinneret, have corroborated the book's claims that it was captured by Israel and then burned by fire:

> Joshua returned at that time and captured Ḥatzor, killing its king by the sword, for Ḥatzor had been the chief of all of these city-states. They killed by the sword all of the people that were in it leaving not a breathing soul, and he burned Ḥatzor with fire…. All of the towns that were on their mounds were not burned by Israel. Only Ḥatzor alone did Joshua burn. (Josh. 11:10–13)[1]

Some scholars contend that the Book of Joshua paints Israel's possession of the land as sudden, swift, and decisive, a reading that is then derided as an intolerable myth. But such an analysis is selective in the extreme and overlooks the text's own indications to the contrary. It is

---

1. Prof. Amnon Ben-Tor of the Hebrew University of Jerusalem, has directed the excavations at Ḥatzor since 1990. In the course of his work he has revisited many of the conclusions drawn by Yigael Yadin concerning the conquest of the city. See his latest summary in "Who Destroyed Canaanite Hazor?" *Biblical Archaeological Review* 39:04 (July/August 2013).

easy to misread statements such as: "Joshua captured all of the land, just as God had spoken to Moses, and Joshua gave it to Israel as their possession according to their tribal divisions. The land thus became quiet from warfare" (Josh. 11:23). But only by clearly distinguishing between *warfare* and *possession* can the matter be correctly understood. The time interval of the battles against the Canaanite confederacies may have been relatively brief, their noisy effects fairly short-lived, but the course of settling the land was long and drawn-out.

An appreciation of the broader context is helpful. The narratives of the Torah already made clear that the process of conquest and settlement would be slow, methodical, and incremental. Years earlier, as the people gathered at Sinai's foothills to hear God's word, He proclaimed to them not only His ten principles, but their future destiny as well:

> I will send My dread before you and discomfit all of the nations whom you shall encounter, and I shall cause all of your enemies to turn their backs towards you [in flight]. I shall send the hornet before you and it shall drive out the Hivite, Canaanite, and Hittite from before you. *I will not, however, drive them out from before you in one year, lest the land become desolate and the wild animals multiply. Rather, I will drive them out very slowly, until you increase and inherit the land...* I will set your borders from the Sea of Reeds until the sea of the Philistines and from the wilderness until the river [Euphrates] and I will give the inhabitants of the land into your hand and drive them out from before you. Do not conclude a pact with them or with their gods. Let them not dwell in your land lest they cause you to transgress against Me, for if you serve their gods then you will become ensnared. (Ex. 23:27–33)

Here, God indicated to the people that settling Canaan would take time, that lightening victories would sow desolation and therefore be counterproductive to the settlement endeavor. We must therefore conclude that the first half of Joshua, the epic battles against the kings of the south and the kings of the north, the lengthy list of thirty-one defeated monarchs, is in actuality a description of only the beginning of the conquest and settlement. During this first phase, the organized resistance of the large

Canaanite city-states was crushed by the decimation of their major military alliances in battle, but that was not the end of the matter. Though kings fell and cities were captured, the land could not be immediately settled. Practically speaking, most of it still remained in Canaanite hands, and the Israelite forces and population were in the main still encamped at their temporary lodgings at Gilgal. (See Josh. 9:6; 10:7, 15, 43.) Many more years would pass before the people would succeed in settling the territory and making it their own. Many regions, such as those outlined above in the opening verses of chapter thirteen, would remain outside of their control long after Joshua had passed on. It would be hundreds of years, in fact, until the dawn of the monarchy and the ascent of David to the throne, that the entire land of Canaan would truly be the uncontested possession of the Jewish people.

PARALLELS

The opening verses of the chapter draw an important parallel between the military campaign of Joshua and that of his mentor Moses:

> Now then, divide this land by inheritance among the nine tribes, and the half tribe of Menashe. With the other [half of Menashe], the tribes of Reuben and Gad took their possession that Moses had given them on the eastern side of the Jordan River, as Moses the servant of God gave them. (Josh. 13:7–8)

Moses fought the Amorite kings Siḥon and Og who ruled over the fertile Transjordanian territories, and on the eve of his own death he devastated them. He then assigned their lands to the tribes of Reuben and Gad who, on account of their great flocks, had looked desirously upon those lands and were reluctant to cross the Jordan River into Canaan with their brethren. As Moses had done earlier, Joshua does now by distributing the conquered land to the tribes by lot. Once again, the narrative emphasizes the bond between Moses and Joshua, between the lawgiver and his successor, between the generation of the wilderness and that of the entry into the land. The events associated with the settlement of the land are thus understood to constitute a continuum. The plodding process that commenced with the conquest of Transjordan and proceeded with the fall of the Canaanite military alliances, still awaits completion as Joshua grows old.

CALEB AND THE JOURNEY TO HEBRON

After outlining the tribal territories of Reuben, Gad, and half Menashe that had been assigned by Moses on the eastern side of the Jordan River, the text now turns its attention to the divisions of Canaan proper. The account begins with the general observation that the lands were distributed by Elazar the Kohen, Joshua son of Nun, and the tribal leaders of the people, all of whom had been appointed to the august task by God Himself while Moses yet lived (see Num. 34:16–29). It goes on to provide two critical details concerning the division, namely that the tribe of Levi received no formal tribal portion but rather only scattered cities, and also that the tribe of Joseph, composed of the distinct sub-tribes of Menashe and Ephraim, was counted as two separate tribes. Thus, in the end, twelve tribes inherit the land.

Unexpectedly, the border delineations that take up the majority of the upcoming eight chapters are introduced by a passage that again returns us to the debacle of the spies:

> The people of Judah approached Joshua at Gilgal, and Caleb son of Yefuneh the Kenizite said to him: "You remember that which God spoke at Kadesh Barnea to Moses the man of God concerning myself and yourself. I was forty years old when Moses the man of God sent me from Kadesh Barnea to spy out the land, and I returned with a sincere report. My comrades who went with me melted the heart of the people, but I followed the Lord my God. Moses swore on that day saying, 'Surely the very land upon which your foot trod shall be yours and your descendants' inheritance forever, for you followed the Lord my God.'" (Josh. 14:6–9)

The narratives of the tribal borders are here prefaced by the account of Caleb and his role in the mission of the spies. It will be recalled that of the twelve men whom Moses had sent to spy out the land, ten returned with a frightening report of a harsh land populated by invincible inhabitants, while only two had the audacity to claim that with God's help the "very good land" could be conquered. These two were none other than Joshua son of Nun of the tribe of Ephraim, and Caleb son of Yefuneh of the tribe of Judah.

While the other ten members of the spy mission perished by divinely initiated plague, and all of the adult Israelites were condemned to die in the wilderness, Joshua and Caleb were given a pledge that they would survive to one day enter the land:

> God said: "... As surely as I live, the glory of God will fill the world. All of the men who saw My glory and My signs that I performed in Egypt and in the wilderness – who nevertheless tested Me these ten times and did not listen to My words – they will not see the land that I swore to their ancestors. All of those that blasphemed Me will not see it. But My servant Caleb who was of a different spirit and followed after Me, him I will bring to the land to which he arrived, and his descendants will inherit it." (Num. 14:20–24)

THE REAPPEARANCE OF CALEB

While Joshua continued to occupy a prominent role in the account of the wilderness (Num. 27:15–23; 32:28; 34:17) and eventually succeeded Moses as leader of Israel, Caleb passed from the Torah's narratives until this episode in the Book of Joshua. Although there are two intervening mentions of him in Numbers (26:65; 32:12), both are references to the earlier incident of the spies. How astonishing then to hear from him again, more than four decades after our last encounter!

To be exact, it had been forty-five years since he had embarked on that fateful mission, as he himself relates: "I was forty years old when Moses sent me.... And now, behold I am today eighty-five years old" (Josh. 14:7, 10).[2]

---

2. Parenthetically, it is on account of Caleb's oblique reference to his age that we can derive the length of the initial period of conquest: the spies were sent in the second year after the Exodus (Num. 10:11; 13:20), and the people finally entered Canaan thirty-eight years later (see Deut. 2:14). Thus, when Israel crossed the Jordan and

Caleb now asks Joshua for a very particular plot of land:

> "And now, give me this ridge concerning which God spoke on that day, for you heard on that day that there are giants there, and great, fortified cities. Perhaps God will continue to be with me so that I will drive them out, as God has spoken." Joshua blessed him, and gave Hebron to Caleb son of Yefuneh as an inheritance. (Josh. 14:12–13)

The ancient city of Hebron, located at the southern end of the range of hills that runs the length of Canaan, is familiar to us as the burial site of Abraham and Sara, Isaac and Rebecca, Jacob and Leah – the patriarchs and matriarchs of the people of Israel. In our passage, Caleb maintains that Hebron was pledged to him by Moses himself: "Moses swore on that day saying, 'Surely the very land upon which your foot trod shall be yours and your descendants' inheritance forever, for you followed the Lord my God.'" When Moses recounts the incident of the spies in Deuteronomy, he makes clear that the pledge came from God: "Caleb son of Yefuneh will surely see it [the land] and I will give to him and to his descendants the land upon which he trod, for he followed God" (Deut. 1:36). This is also indicated by the original passage from the Book of Numbers, in which God is the speaker: "But My servant Caleb who was of a different spirit and followed after Me, him I will bring to the land to which he arrived, and his descendants will inherit it" (Num. 14:24).

Mysteriously, however, the travels of Caleb to Hebron that are here understood to be an unassailable fact and the basis of his claim to that territory are never mentioned explicitly in the original account of the episode of the spies. There, we are informed concerning the spies only that:

---

entered the land, Caleb was seventy-eight years old (40 + 38 = 78). Now, as the land stood to be formally divided, he indicated that he was eighty-five years old. In other words, seven years had elapsed since the time that the people entered the new land, until the tribe of Judah with Caleb at its head now stood ready to press their claim. The rabbinic tradition on this matter is quite emphatic: "They [Israel] conquered the land for seven years" (Arakhin 13a).

They went up [*VaYa'alu*] from the Negev and he arrived [*vayavo*] at Hebron, and there were to be found Aḥiman, Sheishai, and Talmai the sons of the giant. Now Hebron had been built seven years before Tzo'an [Tanis] in Egypt. They arrived [*vayavo'u*] at the wadi of Eshkol and there cut a vine with a cluster of grapes that two of them carried on a staff, and took also from the pomegranates and figs. That place they called Naḥal Eshkol because of the cluster [*eshkol*] that the people of Israel cut. (Num. 13:22–24)

In contrast to the other travels that the spies undertook, the arrival at Hebron is phrased in the singular. While this indicates that only one member of the expedition visited the site, nowhere does the text explicitly state that it was Caleb who traveled to Hebron. The matter is left unstated, obscured by the use of the indefinite pronoun. It is only in our passage in Joshua that the necessary clarification is provided: God and His servant Moses pledged to Caleb that he would receive the very land upon which he trod. That was none other than the place of Hebron, for it was none other than Caleb who arrived at Hebron!

Why would the text of the Book of Numbers leave that critical detail unmentioned? Conversely, why does the account of the tribal territories in the Book of Joshua begin with that very detail? It is the midrash mentioned by Rashi (Num. 13:22) and drawn from the Talmud that alerts us to a possible solution:

"He arrived at Hebron" – This refers to Caleb who went there alone and threw himself down at the graves of his ancestors, imploring God to preserve him from the seductive counsel of his cohorts. Thus it says, "I will give him the land upon which he trod" [Deut. 1:36], and it later states that "they gave Hebron to Caleb" [Judges 1:20]. (Sota 34b)

This midrash links the visit of Caleb to Hebron, a city inhabited by a race of giants, with critical data mentioned earlier in the Torah: Hebron is the burial place of the ancestors of Israel. Abraham and Sara spent many years as semi-nomadic shepherds in the environs of Hebron, and it was in the aftermath of her death that Abraham first established a more permanent presence there by purchasing the cave of Makhpela as a family sepulcher. The relevant passages in Genesis (23:1–20, 25:9–10, 35:27–29, 49:29–32, 50:13) leave no doubt that in the collective consciousness of the people of Israel, Hebron and its cave of Makhpela not only mark the final resting place of our ancestors, but also signify their intense connection to Canaan. Their desire to be buried in Makhpela's dark recesses was the final expression of their lifelong trust that God would one day give Canaan to their descendants, who would possess it as a nation and there realize their unique destiny. Caleb's visit to that place, in spite of the danger suggested by the presence of the "giants," was thus understood by the midrash to indicate more than a reconnaissance mission. Alone among the spies, he went to Hebron and to the cave of Makhpela, seeking to draw from there the spiritual strength that he would need in order to oppose their fatalistic report. But from that pilgrimage Caleb also hoped to draw inspiration for the people of Israel to remain steadfast in their faith that God's pledge to bring them into the land would be realized.

In our mind's eye, we can see him part from his tense brethren and set his sights for Hebron, even as they try to dissuade him with dire warnings of massive ramparts manned by giants. But he will not be discouraged. Drawing close to the city he frantically searches for an ancient marker on its hilly outskirts, but there is nothing. Were the coordinates from Moses, handed down faithfully for generations, erroneous? Suddenly, he sees a rocky outcropping covered by dense vegetation. Clearing away the overgrowth, his heartbeat quickening, he discovers an entrance to a cave. Entering its chill, his eyes still squinting from the bright sunlight, all is dark. Impatiently, he waits until he can make out its features: a low-ceilinged square space, each of its three walls arrayed with two niches, the top of each niche neatly incised with ancient but familiar letters. Falling to the ground, he cries, the hot tears running off his cheeks to mingle with the cool red dust.

THE VISIT TO HEBRON RECONSIDERED

If Hebron is the encounter with Israel's deepest roots in Canaan, if the progenitors there entombed signify an everlasting love for the land and the absolute trust in God's as-yet unfulfilled promise of nationhood, then the rest of the matter is clear. The tragedy of the spies preserved in the Book of Numbers is for the most part an exploration of the limits of trust. On the one hand, God indicated to the people that the land of Canaan was beautiful, bountiful, and within reach. On the other hand, the spies surveyed a land that was dotted by highly fortified cities populated by powerful and hostile tribes. How could Israel, scarcely freed from the grip of a prolonged Egyptian bondage that had enslaved the body and crushed the soul, persevere against them, except by believing in God's promise? The account of the spies, their crisis of confidence precipitated by a lack of trust, is no place to highlight the heroism of Caleb, who was so obviously filled with a "different spirit." Theirs was a tale of downfall and failure, while his was the story of conviction and triumph. They betrayed the traditions of their forefathers who believed God's word in spite of all, while he knew in his innermost heart that His pledge to them would be upheld. Their counsel won the day, that generation was plunged into the abyss, and Caleb's visit to Hebron was therefore concealed by the text.

Our passage in the Book of Joshua is Numbers' textual antithesis and the redemptive reversal of its calamity. The people of Israel weathered those forty years of infamy, and traversed the barren wilderness to successfully enter the land and to conquer its powerful Canaanite alliances. They finally stand at the threshold of God's promise being fulfilled. With the main battles over, they prepare to formally divide up the land among the tribes. What more fitting way to introduce this great undertaking than by emphasizing its necessary underpinnings of an unshakable faith? The section therefore begins with a moving recollection of Caleb's visit to Hebron some forty-five years earlier, an expedition that not only offers dazzling proof of his own mettle but also provided the people of Israel with a paradigm for the nurture of their own spiritual fortitude. Caleb is still alive to recount those ancient events, standing before them with his vigor undiminished and his trust in God undimmed, while his erstwhile comrades and their fearful followers have perished long, long ago.

This theme is reinforced by the tradition that pins the chronology of the conquest on Caleb's passing remark concerning his age. The calculation of the seven years of conquest, which is to say the successful entry of the people of Israel into the land of Canaan, is predicated upon his oblique mention of presently being eighty-five years old. In essence, the rabbinic tradition that saw in his age the key to calculating the duration of the conquest alludes to more than mere mathematics. It implies that Israel's success in the land will ultimately be a function of adopting not only Caleb's lifespan as the chronological anchor of their history, but also his lifelong trust as the foundation of their own, in order to complete the awesome task of settlement that God now places before them: "Therefore was Hebron given to Caleb the son of Yefuneh the Kenizite as an inheritance until this very day, for he followed after the Lord, God of Israel" (Josh. 14:14).

The Tribal Boundary of Judah

C hapter fifteen finally introduces the tribal divisions of territory. We should begin by noting, with no small measure of astonishment, that the tribal territories enumerated in the book faithfully preserved the memory of specific place names and landscapes for millennia, in spite of Israel's long exile from the land and the typical reader's utter lack of familiarity with Canaan's geography. This is testament to Israel's reverence for its biblical books and the great efforts that Jews expended in order to transmit an accurate text to later generations.

As our chapter opens, the alliances of enemy armies have long ago been smashed, the Canaanites are reconciled to the inevitable settlement of Israel in the land, and Joshua has become old. The account of courageous Caleb is now followed by the story of his kin, the tribe of Judah, always the foremost among the tribes of Israel. Recall that in the organization of the wilderness encampment, the tribe of Judah was assigned the coveted eastern quadrant (Num. 2:3), opposite the families of Moses, Aaron, and their children (3:38), and guarding the axis of approach to the Tabernacle itself (Ex. 27:13–16). Recall also that in the two censuses undertaken in the Torah, the first soon after the Exodus from Egypt and the second on the eve of the entry into the land, the tribe of Judah was the largest single entity. According to the former, the tribe of Judah numbered 74,600 adult males of military age (Num. 1:27), while according to the latter, it contained 76,500 (26:22). In both cases, Judah outranked its closest rival tribe by about ten thousand men.

It is therefore only natural that in the descriptions of the tribal boundaries the tribe of Judah should be mentioned first, and that of all the tribal boundaries outlined in the Book of Joshua, that of Judah is the most detailed. With the Dead Sea serving as a convenient reference point, Judah's borders are traced from their southeastern extremity. The tribe's territory began at the so-called "lisan," a triangular peninsula that in the pre-modern period jutted out from the eastern shore of the sea near its southern end, and effectively reduced its width at that point to only four kilometers of shallow and traversable salt flats. From here, the southern border continued along a southwestern line, eventually terminating on the Mediterranean coast at "Naḥal Mitzrayim" or present-day Wadi El-Arish. The eastern boundary of the tribe extended northwards along the shores of the Dead Sea and the Jordan River, terminating at a point on the river's banks roughly corresponding to the latitude of Jerusalem. The northern boundary then proceeded westward in a somewhat jagged line, until terminating at the Mediterranean Sea. Broadly speaking, then, the tribal border of Judah comprised the substantial area bounded by the Dead Sea to the east and the Mediterranean Sea to the west, with the addition of a band of more territory in the arid south.

The territorial lands of Judah included a representative selection of the major climatic zones of Canaan, arranged as a series of narrow strips from west to east. These were the flat and fertile coastal plain, the gently sloping foothills, the rocky central highlands, and the foreboding and barren wilderness overlooking the Dead Sea. Additionally, there was a fifth topographic zone: the parched southern expanse beyond Be'er Sheva known as the Negev. Perhaps the territory of Judah ought to be regarded as a sort of microcosm of the land of Canaan itself, much as the tribe of Judah was to become the pivotal tribe in Israel and, later in the biblical period during the ascendancy of Assyria in the eighth century BCE, the only remaining tribe of importance. Eventually, by the period of the Persian Empire that rose to prominence in the sixth century BCE, the people of Israel would be identified solely by their association with this one extant tribe, becoming known as "Jews" or "*Yehudim*" after its name.

Our text already alludes to this eventuality, as some modern commentaries note. Later in the chapter, verses twenty to sixty-three, the Judean towns and cities are grouped according to the topographical key described above. The Negev towns number twenty-nine, those of the foothills comprise thirty-nine, the mountain settlements are thirty-eight, and the sparsely populated Judean desert has but six. All together, the text spells out 112 cities and towns (29 + 39 + 38 + 6 = 112), excluding the coastal towns of Ekron, Ashdod, and Azza and their surrounding regions that are not counted because they remained outside of Judean hegemony. Significantly, the numbered cities of all of the remaining seven tribes that received their territorial borders at Shilo (Josh. chapters eighteen and nineteen) also equal 112: Benjamin – 26; Simeon – 17; Zebulun – 12; Issachar – 16; Asher – 22; Naphtali – 19 (the cities of Dan are mentioned but not numbered). The implication is that the tribe of Judah, here featured prominently as the first and most powerful in Israel, would one day remain alone as the surviving core.

There are other premonitions as well. While the text describes the borders of Judah with a fair amount of detail, it pays particular attention to the northern boundary, and singles out the topography in the environs of Jerusalem for special mention. This, too, is an allusion to the central role that Jerusalem would one day play in the national fortunes of the people of Israel, though at this time the citadel of the town was inhabited by the powerful Canaanite tribe of the Jebusites and beyond the reach of Israelite control: "As for the Jebusites that dwelt in Jerusalem, the people of Judah were unable to dispossess them. The Jebusites dwelt in Jerusalem among the people of Judah until this very day" (Josh. 15:63).

The borders and boundaries of the tribe of Judah, the obscure place names and tedious descriptions of topography, highlight a critical fact that we will revisit often during the course of the upcoming chapters: geographic information in the Book of Joshua is not inert data. The manner in which specific material is catalogued provides the reader not only with facts concerning the immediate context but also with pointed allusions to future developments.

CALEB, OTNIEL, AND AKHSA

Following the account of Judah's boundaries, the text indicates that Caleb son of Yefuneh was assigned "in accordance with God's word to Joshua, the city of Kiryat Arba, the father of the giants, that is Hebron" (Josh. 15:13). Though advanced in age, Caleb's warrior spirit is undiminished, and he succeeds in dislodging the descendants of the giant and in possessing the region. Continuing to Devir that is also known as Kiryat Sefer, Caleb offers his daughter in marriage to the one who will succeed in conquering the town. Otniel son of Kenaz, the younger kinsman of Caleb, is victorious, and takes Akhsa the daughter of Caleb as his wife. She in turn prevails upon her new husband to request additional territory from her father, springs of water to irrigate the otherwise "dry lands" that comprise the region, and Caleb readily agrees to her entreaties that she delivers as she forcefully alights from her donkey!

This curious passage contains a number of intriguing points. First of all, we must take note of Caleb's challenge. Much later, Saul, the first king of Israel, would make a similar offer under similar circumstances. 1 Samuel 17 records that during Saul's reign, the coastal-dwelling Philistines exercised harsh control over the tribes of Israel, buoyed by their superior armed forces and especially by their champion Goliath, a seasoned warrior of giant proportions. The fighting men of Saul were deathly afraid to engage Goliath or his hordes in battle, and the new king attempted to rally the people by making them an irresistible offer: "The man who strikes him down will be given great wealth by the king, will receive his daughter in marriage, and his household will be exempted from taxes in Israel!" (1 Sam. 17:25). In both instances the offer of the daughter serves as a grand incentive to battle with giants, highlighting the enormity of the task placed before the potential suitor and emphasizing the high esteem in which the one who makes the offer is held.

Otniel son of Kenaz conquers Devir and takes Akhsa as his wife. Significantly, this Otniel is later named as the first of the judges in the Book of Judges (1:8–15), who succeeds Joshua as leader during the twilight period before the people fell prey to Canaanite idolatry. The rabbinic sources indicate that Otniel was a scholar of unusual stature, rivaling even Joshua in his brilliance:

"Caleb said: Whosoever strikes Kiryat Sefer and captures it" [Josh. 15:16] – We learned: 1,700 doubts concerning parallel phrases [*gezerot shavot*], minor to major syllogisms [*kalim vehamorim*], and scribal nuances [*dikdukei sofrim*] were forgotten during the period of mourning over the death of Moses. R. Abahu said: Even so, Otniel son of Kenaz restored them through his acumen. (Temura 16a)

While the impetus for this rabbinic comment may have been the suggestive name of "Kiryat Sefer" or "Booktown," implying some sort of scholarly association, the talmudic source preserves an important tradition concerning the prominence of Otniel. As successor to Joshua, we would expect him to demonstrate exceptional leadership qualities, and here his military prowess is paired in the rabbinic sources with his erudition, just as it was for Joshua. The biblical texts tell us much less concerning Otniel than they did about Joshua, but his membership in the clan of Caleb, by blood as well as by marriage, his success as a strategist in defeating Kiryat Sefer, and the rabbinic traditions concerning his intellectual gifts all converge to destine him for greatness.

It will be recalled that Joshua's career was introduced by a very similar rabbinic comment, quoted by Rashi on Joshua 1:1 and drawn from the same talmudic source:

During the period of mourning over Moses' death, over three thousand *halakhot* that had been communicated by him were forgotten by the people. Joshua enquired of God how to resolve them. God responded: "Moses My servant has died, and the Torah is called by his name. To tell you is impossible. Rather, go and preoccupy the people with warfare." (Temura 16a)

Like Joshua, Otniel steps in to fill the breach, but unlike Joshua, he succeeds in restoring the "lost traditions." What we have here is an insightful reading of the people's post-bellum needs. Joshua succeeded in his transition role admirably, bringing Israel into Canaan and beginning the process of their settlement, but many new contingencies arose in the meantime, questions, doubts, and issues that required resolution. The "parallel phrases, syllogisms, and scribal nuances" are among the mainstays of traditional halakhic analysis and provide the keys for addressing new and unforeseen realities by delving deeply into the primary texts in search of guidance. At the same time, however, by their very text-based nature, these tools of interpretation highlight the eternity that the biblical words embody, the never-exhausted wellspring of divine inspiration and teaching that they contain.

By restoring them, Otniel therefore becomes not only the fitting successor to Moses and Joshua, but the inspired innovator as well, the next link in the unfolding chain that connects the teachings of Sinai to the future destiny of the people of Israel in their new land. The period of warfare stands to one day pass, but settlement and statehood must not become spiritual stagnation. The teachings of Moses, the laws of the Torah, must continue to provide the people of Israel with direction, even as they confront new circumstances that their parents could scarcely have anticipated.

AKHSA'S SPIRITED EXAMPLE

Finally, we have Akhsa, Caleb's forceful daughter who makes her point with such dynamic assurance. How are we to understand her remarkable conduct? In effect, her behavior recalls her own father Caleb's steadfast conviction even as it stands in critical contrast to her husband's successes on the battlefield. Confronted with the prospect of "dry lands" that appear barren and inhospitable, Akhsa does not lose her faith and throw up her hands in dejection. Rather, she is absolutely determined to make the best of her difficult situation, to improve upon it and to transform it into triumph. The commentaries understood that her forceful alighting from the donkey was calculated to attract her father's attention and perhaps represented a show of entreaty. There may be an additional dimension as well: The donkey is the beast of choice for the nomadic shepherd who covers short distances. The great caravan routes that crisscrossed the region were typically covered by camel, an animal built for transporting heavy loads over long distances through inhospitable terrain, but the nomadic shepherd who did not range quite so far covered territory on foot or by his sturdy donkey. Perhaps Akhsa's forceful dismounting is meant to indicate to her startled father that she is determined to leave nomadic existence behind in order embrace the overwhelming task of homesteading, of farming, and of putting down roots even in difficult territory.

With the national project of settling the land looming large on the horizon, her inspired conduct serves as an important example for her people. How will they confront the disappointment and disillusionment bound to arise when the wilderness "myth" of a land flowing with milk and honey is shattered by the more sobering reality of desolate and uncultivated expanses covered by scrub and forest and sometimes strewn with rock and ruin? Will the people of Israel lose heart because of the magnitude of the task placed before them and, like the spineless spies, surrender to despair? Or will they rather take up their mission enthusiastically, cognizant of the fact that the settlement of the land will be a slow and laborious process that will not be completed by them, nor by their children, nor even by their grandchildren? While Otniel secures a military victory over the enemy army, it is Akhsa who will win the day by settling the land. Her determined attitude serves as a profound paradigm to her people: if they can internalize her tenacity then they will achieve success in the new land, in spite of the great challenges that lie before them.

Joshua 16:1–17:18

Judah and Joseph

After the delineation of Judah's territory, chapters sixteen and seventeen of the Book of Joshua spell out the tribal boundaries of Joseph. These two tribes, Judah and Joseph, were the most important in ancient Israel. Their pivotal roles were already indicated by the arrangement of the camp of Israel, during the peregrinations in the wilderness. During that period, as we have mentioned, Judah and its associated tribes of Issachar and Zebulun were arrayed on the prestigious eastern flank, along the axis of approach to the Tabernacle and next to the leadership clans of Moses and Aaron (see Num. 2:1–9, 3:38). The Joseph encampment, in contrast, composed of the tribes of Ephraim, Menashe, and Benjamin, was positioned on the western side of the Tabernacle (2:18–24), opposite the sacred enclosure of the Holy of Holies and next to the priestly family of Gershon (3:23–26).

In effect, the Tabernacle was bracketed by these two tribes of Judah and Joseph, highlighting not only their importance relative to the other tribes, but also underscoring the tension concerning their conflicting claims to control over the sacred precinct and, by extension, to the exercise of authority and leadership over the nation. In fact, much was suggested in this array that presaged the future destiny of the people of Israel. Israel's first king, Saul, hailed from Benjamin – a member of the

Joseph camp. While Saul laid the groundwork for a secure state by defeating Israel's enemies, he did not achieve national unity. David, his nemesis and successor, was from Judah. Living some four hundred years after the Exodus, he forged a nation out of the disparate tribes of Israel, but his achievement was short-lived. Soon after the demise of his son Solomon, the ancient tribal rivalries resurfaced. The united kingdom of Israel dissolved, pitting Judah in the south against the kingdom of Ephraim or Israel in the north. And so, the people remained divided until the bitter end: the conquest and exile of the northern kingdom by the Assyrians in the eighth century BCE, followed by the destruction of Jerusalem and the kingdom of Judah some 150 years later by the Babylonians.

We may, in fact, trace the ancient conflict even further back in biblical history. Consider the saga of the sons of Jacob who were the progenitors of the tribes (Gen. 37–46). In that lengthy story the two most prominent brothers among the twelve were none other than Joseph and Judah. Joseph was his aged father's favorite, aware of his precocious talents early on and groomed for greatness by Jacob with the gift of the coat of many colors. Though his other brothers resented his pretensions mightily, they also knew in their hearts that Joseph's conceited dreams foretold his future rise to prominence. When Joseph unexpectedly fell into their clutches while far from the protective gaze of their father Jacob, the brothers seized upon the opportunity to plan his death. Though Reuben, the firstborn, won a brief reprieve for his brother, having him cast into the pit rather than killed, it was Judah who succeeded in preserving Joseph's life by initiating his sale to the Ishmaelites. Later still, it was Judah who won his father's confidence and took charge of Benjamin as the brothers descended to Egypt to secure more grain. After Benjamin's unjust arrest, it was Judah who argued the case so poignantly to the viceroy (none other than Joseph in disguise), in order to secure his release. This resulted in Joseph's revelation of his true identity and his tearful reunion with his brothers. When Jacob's household subsequently descended to Egypt during the famine then blanketing Canaan, it was Judah who served as the vanguard for the migration, arriving ahead of the family to prepare the way.

Both Joseph and Judah embodied dynamic leadership and ambition. Both brothers exemplified spiritual development and maturation, overcoming setbacks to triumph in the end. Both remained true to their ideals and loyal to their calling. In other words, while the Book of Joshua presents the centrality of the tribes of Judah and Joseph as a geographic phenomenon, the critical role of those two tribes is intimated much earlier, with the riveting account of Joseph and his brothers. In the Book of Joshua, the prominence of the two is awarded with expansive territories that are delineated ahead of any of the other tribes. But the fundamentals are to be found in the narratives of the Book of Genesis, where Judah is designated for leadership and Joseph for success. Initially, Joseph and Judah are pitted against each other as rivals, but in the end they are together responsible for reuniting the family of Israel and for ensuring its well-being in Egypt. It is therefore not only the perils of discord that are indicated by their tense relationship, but the promise of harmony and attainment as well.

If we search even earlier for the source of this primal conflict, as well as the hope of its eventual resolution, we come finally to the account of Jacob's strained marriage to the two sisters Leah and Rachel (Gen. 29–30). Recall that Jacob had fled eastward from the wrath of his brother Esau, who blamed him for the deceitful theft of the birthright and blessing. Jacob arrived empty-handed at the well on the outskirts of Haran, the ancestral home of his crafty uncle Laban, his mother Rebecca's brother. There Jacob first met the beautiful shepherdess Rachel, Laban's daughter, and immediately resolved to marry her. Laban set upon him a condition of seven years of tending sheep, and to this Jacob readily agreed. At the conclusion of the term, however, as the marriage canopy was festally arranged towards dusk, Laban deviously substituted Leah, the older sister. Jacob discovered the ruse too late, and while he eventually won Rachel's hand as well, the household was forever dominated by the bitter jealousy between the two sisters. How they each vied for Jacob's affection; how terribly the matter was exacerbated by Jacob's own natural preference for Rachel, whom he loved more. While the fertile Leah went on to mother six children, Rachel had only two, with the birth of each child raising the ugly specter of rivalry anew. What is significant for our purposes is to recognize that Leah's offspring included Judah, while Joseph and Benjamin were the only children of Rachel.

In essence, the competition that existed between the tribes of Judah and Joseph throughout the biblical period had as its source the fractious family of Jacob himself, the distressing dynamic that characterized the relationship between Leah and Rachel. Of course, we must wonder: Why did the Torah set up such a situation that was sure to produce friction? Why did the text in the Book of Genesis devote so much attention to the convoluted relationship of these two women? How do we explain the Torah's only recorded case of polygamy involving sisters, a practice later outlawed in Leviticus 18:18?

PERSONAL LIVES AND NATIONAL LIFE

The commentaries do not provide a comprehensive explanation for every episode in the pained story of Leah and Rachel. Although the local account strikes us as troubling, projecting the story to its national dimension makes it eminently intelligible. The story of Leah and Rachel and their children is much more than the account of their personal lives. It is a concise description of the awesome trials and challenges that their descendants will face, in their attempts to create a nation and then maintain its integrity in the face of the more natural tendency for narrow self-interest to win the day.

The children of Leah included a number of prominent players, but chief among them was Judah. In the course of the Joseph narratives, Judah emerged as the most significant of the brothers, and as biblical history unfolded, the tribe of Judah became the nation's most potent element. The Davidic line was descended from Judah and the capital of Jerusalem was established on its borders. Rachel's children were but two, Joseph and Benjamin. The entire last third of the Book of Genesis revolved around the saga of Joseph, and the tribe of Menashe and especially Ephraim that descended from Joseph's sons later constituted the counterweight to Judah's influence on the national polity throughout the biblical period. After all, the national shrine was housed at Shilo in Ephraim for a period of close to four hundred years, from the time that Israel entered Canaan under Joshua until the dawn of the monarchy. Joshua himself was a descendent of Ephraim while Israel's first king Saul hailed from the tribe of Benjamin. These two poles, Judah and Joseph, Leah and Rachel respectively, therefore represent two disparate elements that tended to be in a constant state of rivalry and conflict. As the larger biblical story played itself out over the course of a thousand years, Judah and Joseph, or Judah and Ephraim/Yisrael in the typical prophetic formulation, gradually draw apart, eventually becoming two separate kingdoms that were in the end exiled by greater powers.

Considering the matter from a more "cosmic" perspective suggests that the animosity and strife that colored the relationship of the two sisters foreshadowed the very difficult struggles that would unfold as the nation of Israel took form, and alluded to the conflicts that would rage until the termination of national independence, more than a millennium after Leah and Rachel had been laid to rest. The tribal territories recounted in the Book of Joshua are therefore much more than strings of arcane geographic data. The arrangement of the material, seemingly dry and tedious, intimates the great challenges facing the nascent nation of Israel: To enter Canaan not in order to follow the fractious example of the Canaanite city-states, but rather to become a cohesive people with common goals and shared aspirations. Joseph and Judah – brothers as well as tribes – each embodied different aptitudes and abilities but both were slated for greatness. Their different talents suggested variation and diversity, the critical characteristics for any people to possess if they are to fashion a rich and textured national life rather than a one-dimensional, shallow one. But how easily could different aptitudes spark friction and discord in the absence of an overwhelming sense of common destiny!

The biblical people of Israel never succeeded in overcoming sectarian and narrow interests to become a truly unified nation. Even while Joshua was still alive, but especially after his demise, the tribes often pulled in different directions as a function of their local needs and concerns. Their leaders frequently found it difficult to see beyond the limitations of tribalism and factionalism to address the broadest possible concerns of all of the people. First as tribal confederacies and later as independent kingdoms, Judah and Ephraim were often in competition with each other and occasionally even engaged in open warfare.

Nor did the destruction of the First Temple bring an end to the divisiveness. The strife of Leah and Rachel is sadly still with us awaiting its resolution. Fortunately, the prophets who lived through the destruction of the first Jewish state were granted a comforting vision of a messianic future, when Israel would be restored to its land and would finally succeed in transcending its internal divisions to become a single people:

> God said to me: "Mortal man, take a branch and inscribe upon it, 'For Judah and the children of Yisrael his compatriots,' and take another branch and inscribe upon it, 'For Joseph the tree of Ephraim and all of the House of Yisrael his compatriots.' Draw the branches together to become one in your hand.... For thus says the Lord God: Behold I will take the children of Yisrael from among the lands of their exile, and I will gather them from afar and bring them to their land. I will make them into a single nation in the land of the mountains of Yisrael and they will have one king. They will no longer be two nations and will no longer divide into two kingdoms....
>
> They will dwell in the land that I gave to My servant Jacob, the land in which their ancestors dwelt, and they will dwell upon it, they and their children and their children's children forever.... My presence will be upon them and I will be their God, and they will be My people. The nations will then know that I am God who sanctifies Yisrael, for My Temple shall stand in their midst forever." (Ezek. 37:15–28)[1]

---

1. The rivalry between Judah and Joseph, finally resolved in the Book of Ezekiel's vision of the end of days, did not escape the attention of the ancient rabbis. In describing the process of the final redemption of the people of Israel, they provocatively spoke of two messianic figures. The first, a political and military leader, would hail from Joseph. The second, a spiritual leader, would hail from Judah and the line of David. Both would be indispensable for the realization of God's redemptive plans for His people Israel. See Sukka 52a.

Joshua 16:1–17:18

The Territory of Joseph

L ast chapter, we considered Joseph's tribal assignment, detailed in chapters sixteen and seventeen of the Book of Joshua. We studied the special relationship between Joseph and the tribe of Judah, whose territory was spelled out in chapters fourteen and fifteen. From that study it emerged that the book did not arbitrarily single out these two for consecutive and lengthy mention, but rather because together they constituted the linchpins of ancient Israel. As the most important and powerful of the tribes, it was Joseph and Judah, eventually the northern kingdom and southern kingdom, who together charted the course of the people of Israel during the thousand-year period of biblical history.

We investigated the antecedents to that binary arrangement, focusing upon the sons of Jacob and especially upon Jacob's wives – the two sisters Rachel and Leah. What emerged from that analysis was a cautious conclusion that at once highlighted the great potential for diversity and cultural richness that the tribal arrangement yielded, but also the possibility for more harmful developments such as dissent, confrontation, and internecine warfare. In retrospect, biblical history was colored more by the latter than by the former, as the people of Israel struggled mightily but never fully succeeded in transcending narrow tribalism in order to embrace the true unity of purpose and collective resolve that characterizes the most developed expressions of nationhood. The realization of the ideal vision of concord, harmony, and shared mission, wistfully enunciated by Israel's ancient prophets, would be delayed interminably until the end of days.

When we carefully analyze the structure of our section, many other comparisons and contrasts to the Judah account of chapters fourteen and fifteen emerge, thus reinforcing the implied connection between the two tribes. First, both accounts preserve very lengthy and detailed descriptions of the respective tribal boundaries. For Joseph there are two separate lists, one each for its two constituent clans of Ephraim and Menashe, while for Judah there is but one. For Judah, a thorough listing of specific towns that are arranged according to their topographical regions follows the delineation of the tribal borders, but for the clans of Joseph there is only a demarcation of boundaries. In both cases, though, the narrative pays close attention to place names and landscapes, devoting more detailed attention to these two tribes than to any of the others.

In general terms, the tribal portion of Joseph mirrored that of Judah, for it too stretched from the Jordan River until the Mediterranean. Ephraim's lands were situated just northwest of the Dead Sea, separated from Judah by only a small strip of territory assigned to the tribe of Benjamin (whose portion is spelled out in chapter eighteen). The territory of Ephraim stretched along the Mediterranean coast to the west, and along the banks of the Jordan to the east. It continued northwards until the natural border provided by Wadi Kaneh, a tributary of the Yarkon stream that begins its descent from the hill country to the sea just south of Shekhem (modern-day Nablus). The clan of Menashe was positioned north of Ephraim, and their territory extended all the way to the fertile Jezreel Valley that is situated southeast of the Carmel range (modern-day Haifa) and the sea of Kinneret. Of course, Menashe also had lands on the Jordan River's eastern side that paralleled those on the west, for the Gilad and Bashan (modern-day Golan Heights and southwards) had earlier been assigned to part of the clan by Moses.

PROMINENT WOMEN

In addition to providing detailed border descriptions for Judah and Joseph, the text in both passages balances the dull and dry boundary descriptions with a colorful personal component, in which women are featured with unusual prominence. In the case of Judah, the text incorporated the bittersweet reminiscences of Caleb son of Yefuneh (14:6–15), and somewhat later mentioned the efforts of Akhsa his daughter to secure springs of water (15:18–19). Recall that Caleb had challenged any potential suitors for his daughter to first capture the fortified town of Kiryat Sefer. Otniel son of Kenaz, his kinsman, did so and was awarded not only headstrong Akhsa as his wife, but a portion of land as well, presumably in the environs of the captured Canaanite stronghold. But alas, the land was arid and infertile, prompting Akhsa to dramatically plead with her father for a deed to sources of water. Significantly, the text relates that Otniel himself, though admittedly a capable warrior, was reluctant to press their claim to the springs, and only did so after being urged along by his able and ambitious wife! The implication is clear: While the warrior men of Israel did not shirk their responsibility to wrest the land from the grip of the Canaanites, the task of settling it was embraced by Israel's industrious women, whose love for Canaan was no less ardent.

For Joseph, the warrior of note is a certain Makhir son of Menashe who wrested the extensive eastern lands of Gilad and Bashan from the mighty Amorite kings, as described in Numbers 32:39–41. His exploit, recalled in Joshua 17:1, therefore much resembled the triumph of Otniel over the giants of Kiryat Sefer. The analog to Akhsa is provided by the five daughters of Tzlofhad, spirited women all, who determinedly secure for themselves in perpetuity their deceased father's tribal portion in the land (17:3–4). The background to their story is related in Numbers 27, where the people of Israel, still stationed on the Jordan's eastern banks, underwent a census. At that time, the men of military age were counted in preparation for the war of conquest, and the mechanism for apportioning the land according to tribe and clan was introduced. Suddenly, the five daughters of Tzlofhad appeared before Moses, Elazar the High Priest, the elders, and the whole congregation of Israel, who had all solemnly assembled at the forecourt of the Tabernacle to ponder God's instructions. The women related:

> Our father died in the wilderness, but he was not a member of the group that rallied against God as part of Korah's gathering.

> Rather, he died by his own transgression, but had no sons. Why should our father's name disappear from among his kin because he had no son? Instead, give us a portion of land among our father's brothers! (Num. 27:3–4)

Moses presented the women's claim before God for His adjudication, and He did not disappoint:

> The daughters of Tzlofhad speak fittingly! Assign them an inheritance of land among their father's brothers, and transfer their father's portion to them. Further, tell the people of Israel that if a man dies without a son, then his portion is to be assigned to his daughter.... This shall be a statute of law to the people of Israel. (Num. 27:7–11)

In both narratives, that of Judah as well as that of Joseph, the text pointedly indicates that the women demonstrated a sincere attachment to the land and a willingness to overcome obstacles in order to secure their place in it. In both stories these women were singled out by name, a fact that may come to emphasize the glaring difference between military triumphs on the one hand and settlement on the other, the twin pillars of the Book of Joshua as a whole. While the former is secured by anonymous masses of fighting men that triumph precisely because of the suppression and sacrifice of their individuality for the common good, the latter can only be achieved by specific personalities brave enough to clear and work their particular plot of land in order to build their own homes and raise their own families upon it. In the biblical world, the woman or mother figure takes responsibility for the care of the house and the nurturing of the children, while warfare is undertaken by the man. In the end, the contribution of both is essential for the overall success of the endeavor, and the accounts of Judah and Joseph therefore mention both.

OVERCOMING CANAANITE RESISTANCE

Lastly, in both sections, the verses tell us that there were portions of the assigned territories that had an entrenched Canaanite presence that could not be dislodged. In the case of Judah, the stronghold of the Jebusite tribe who dwelt in the environs of Jerusalem remained beyond Judah's reach (Josh. 15:63). In the case of Joseph, the territories that remained in Canaanite control were more extensive: the town of Gezer in the coastal plain (16:10) in a region assigned to Ephraim, as well as the fertile area of the Jezreel valley encompassing the towns of Beit She'an, Yivle'am, Dor, Ein Dor, Ta'anakh, and Megiddo, all in the lands of Menashe (17:11–13). These facts indicate once again that the conquest and settlement of the land of Canaan was a lengthy process that unfolded slowly.

The account of Joseph's tribal boundaries concludes with a discussion that ensues between its leaders and Joshua concerning the assignment of its territory:

> The people of Joseph said to Joshua: "Why did you give me one portion, a single allotment and only one territory? See that I am numerous, for so much has God blessed me!" Joshua said to them: "If indeed you are numerous, then go up to the forested land and clear territory for yourself in the land of the Perizite and the Refaim, if the hill country of Ephraim is too small." But the people of Joseph said: "The hill country is insufficient, and the Canaanites who dwell in the valleys have chariots of iron, those that are in Beit She'an and its towns as well as those in the Jezreel Valley." But Joshua said to the house of Joseph, to Ephraim and to Menashe: "You are a numerous people and have great power, you shall not have only one allotment. You shall also have the hill country, for though it is forested you will cut it down and possess its limits. You shall also drive out the mighty Canaanites in spite of their chariots of iron." (Josh. 17:14–18)

In their opening remarks, the people of Joseph express surprise at having received so little land. Though they are numerous, the portion of their assigned territory in the hill country that is both cultivable as well as unsettled by the threatening Canaanites is relatively small. Most of their allotted tribal lands are either forested slopes and hence unsuitable for immediate settlement, or else already inhabited by the technologically superior Canaanites, who farm the fertile valleys and possess chariots of iron. How then are they to succeed in the new land if they have insufficient tracts for their needs?

Joshua listens attentively, but his response is unsympathetic. There is no choice but to clear the forested hills *and* to dispossess the Canaanites. Both tasks represent, of course, very different challenges. The one involves the back-breaking labor of felling trees, clearing brush, collecting the ubiquitous limestone that everywhere dots the soil, erecting terraces on steep slopes, and only then engaging in subsistence farming until bounty can be wrung from the earth. The other is no less daunting, for it is to confront the iron chariots and horses of the Canaanites who dwell in the verdant valleys, while only armed with light weapons of inferior bronze. But, says Joshua, Joseph is capable of doing so. After all, wasn't the entire success of their conquest up to this point just as unlikely, considering the overwhelming military confederacies that they faced? The conversation between Joshua and his tribe Joseph provides us with our final parallel to the earlier account of Judah. Who could fail to hear in Joshua's encouraging words to Joseph the echo of his colleague Caleb's earlier challenge to his own tribe of Judah, to fight the giants of Kiryat Sefer and to prevail?

Joshua 18:1–10

The Tabernacle at Shilo

With the completion of the border descriptions of Judah and Joseph, the text now turns its attention to the territories of the remaining tribes. That discussion is introduced by an oblique reference concerning the national sanctuary, the Tabernacle:

> The entire congregation of Israel gathered at Shilo and there they set up the Tent of Meeting, for the land was conquered before them. There remained seven tribes from among the people of Israel who had not apportioned their territories…. Joshua cast lots for them in Shilo before God, and there Joshua divided the land for the people of Israel according to their tribal divisions. (Josh. 18:1–10)

Recall that until this point, the assembly point for the people, the site of the Tabernacle and the locus for their encounter with God, was Gilgal. That place, just west of the Jordan River and opposite the city of Jericho, was where they had first encamped after they had crossed the swollen waters of the Jordan River on a radiant spring day some fourteen years earlier. At Gilgal, the people of Israel had renewed the rite of circumcision. There, they had celebrated their first Passover in the new land, and during the course of the wars of conquest they had always returned to Gilgal to regroup. Now, with the territories of Judah and Joseph apportioned and with the rest of the territories soon to be allotted, an important transition took place with the relocation of the Tabernacle to Shilo.

The town of Shilo, located some thirty kilometers northeast of Jerusalem, is within the borders of Ephraim. Its exact location is spelled out with unusual precision in a biblical verse from the Book of Judges: "They said: Behold there is a festival to God in Shilo every year. It is north of Beit El, east of the trail that goes up from Beit El to Shekhem, and south of Levona" (Judges 21:19). Shilo is nestled in the highlands, among the rugged hills that form the backbone of the land of Canaan. Geographically speaking, Shilo is found in a scenic but otherwise unremarkable location; the town was nonetheless destined to play a fateful role in Israelite history because of the presence of the Tabernacle in its midst.

THE PROGRESSION IN THE MISHNA

The traditional sources see in the relocation of the Tabernacle to Shilo a crucial development, as this lengthy citation from the Mishna indicates:

> Before the Tabernacle was erected, sacrifice upon the high places was permitted, and the service was performed by the firstborn. After the establishment of the Tabernacle, however, the high places were forbidden and the service was performed by the priests. The most holy sacrifices could be eaten only within its perimeter curtains, while sacrifices of lesser sanctity could be consumed anywhere within the Israelite encampment.
>
> When the people came to Gilgal, the high places were again permitted. The most holy sacrifices could be eaten only within the perimeter curtains of the Tabernacle, while sacrifices of lesser sanctity could be consumed anywhere.
>
> When the people came to Shilo, the high places were forbidden. [At Shilo] the Tabernacle had no ceiling. It was provided with walls of stone below, while the covering above was made of curtains, and it constituted the "resting place" [*menuha*]. The most

holy sacrifices could be eaten only within its perimeter curtains, while sacrifices of lesser sanctity, as well as the second tithe, could be consumed anywhere within its field of vision.

When the people came to Nov and to Givon, sacrifice upon the high places was again permitted. The most holy sacrifices could be eaten only within the perimeter curtains, while sacrifices of lesser sanctity could be consumed among any of the cities of Israel.

When the people came to Jerusalem, the high places were again forbidden and were never permitted again, for it constituted the "possession" [*naḥala*]. The most holy sacrifices could be eaten only within the perimeter walls [of the Temple Mount], while sacrifices of lesser sanctity and second tithe could be consumed only within the city wall. (Mishna Zevaḥim 14:4–8)

The above *mishnayot* describe a number of issues that require elaboration. In pre-Tabernacle days, when there was no central sanctuary for the people of Israel, sacrifice could be offered to God at any location. These so-called "high places" were often makeshift altars located upon the summits of hills and the associated sacrificial service would entail little in the way of formal ritual. Any family could take an active part in the ceremony through the agency of their firstborn who would perform the requisite rites.

The situation changed dramatically with the completion of the Tabernacle about a year after the Exodus, during the beginning of the wilderness sojourn (early fourteenth century, BCE). This building and its appurtenances, described in exhaustive detail in the second half of the Book of Exodus, ushered in a new period of Israel's religious development. Henceforth, the sacrificial service was a centralized affair, to be carried out under the meticulous jurisdiction of the priests, who descended from Aaron. This reformation had the welcome result of putting an end to informal and unofficial sacrificial services that were more often than not devoted to idolatrous worship rather than to the homage of the one true God. (See Lev. 17:1–7.) In addition, the Tabernacle was important for the unification of the desert tribes, who now rallied around a single, central sanctuary.

After the people left the wilderness and crossed into Canaan (thirteenth century, BCE), the high places were again permitted, at least as long as the Tabernacle was sited at Gilgal and the wars of conquest were being waged. The centrality of the Tabernacle was nevertheless preserved by the stipulation that certain grades of sacrifices, the most sanctified, could only be offered and consumed within its boundaries.

Eventually, when the people established the Tabernacle at Shilo (thirteenth century, BCE), corresponding to the beginning of Joshua chapter eighteen, the high places were again forbidden. The Shilo sanctuary became the only acceptable venue for the sacrificial service. Also, as the people planted crops in the new land and harvested the produce of their fields, the practice of the "second tithe" began. This was a portion of the crop, separated every first, second, fourth, and fifth years of the seven year agricultural cycle, and consumed in the proximity of the Tabernacle.

In the end, the sanctuary at Shilo was destroyed by the Philistines (tenth century, BCE), a traumatic event described in the opening chapters of the Book of Samuel that ushered in a period of intense instability. Eventually, the sanctuary was tenuously reestablished, first at Nov and later at Givon, and during this time, the high places were again permitted.

Finally, the Temple was built in Jerusalem by Solomon (ninth century, BCE), and worship upon the high places was discontinued forever. It goes without saying that no limitations of location were ever placed upon the worship of God through prayer, for the yearnings of the human heart must not be limited by time or place.

The sweep of history concisely described by these *mishnayot*, from the Exodus until the building of the Temple, corresponds to a period of almost five hundred years and includes some of the most pivotal moments in biblical history: the Exodus from Egypt, the entry into Canaan, the conquest and beginning of settlement, the period of the judges, and the dawn of the monarchy. According to the traditional chronology, the Tabernacle stood at Gilgal for fourteen years, at Shilo for 369 years, and at Nov and Givon for fifty-seven years.[1] When taking into

---

1.   Maimonides, *Mishneh Torah*, Laws of the Temple 1:2.

account the forty years of the wanderings in the wilderness, a total of 480 years therefore elapsed from the Exodus until the building of the Temple at Jerusalem (40 + 14 + 369 + 57 = 480), just as recorded in 1 Kings 6:1.

THE ARCHITECTURAL ACCOUNT

Interestingly, the Mishna was not content to simply describe the ritual ramifications of the Tabernacle's peregrinations, but its architectural progression as well: "[At Shilo] the Tabernacle had no ceiling. It was provided with walls of stone below, while the covering above was made of curtains" (Mishna Zevahim 14:6).

Before Shilo, the Tabernacle was a temporary, tent-like structure, as the Book of Exodus describes. Its walls were made of gilded boards of acacia wood that would be disassembled and reassembled at every encampment in the wilderness, and its covering consisted of a series of curtains and animal hides that gave it a tent-like quality (Ex. 26). Hence, the Torah often refers to the building as the "Tent of Meeting" (Ex. 40:2). Once the Tabernacle was established at Shilo, however, the temporary prefabricated walls of acacia wood, previously fastened together by an ingenious combination of bars and rings, were stored away forever. The walls of the Tabernacle were built out of stone. The cover of textiles and skins, however, was retained. At Jerusalem, the Temple structure was provided with walls of stone as well as with a sturdy roof of cedars, extravagantly covered on the interior with pure gold (1 Kings 6:9, 22).

Considering the architectural narrative carefully, a startling observation emerges: the developments in the structure of the Tabernacle perfectly mirror the national story of the people of Israel as they experience the process of securing permanent settlement in the land. As long as the people of Israel were confined to the wilderness, the Tabernacle was an exclusively temporary affair that reflected that condition. Entering the land and embarking on the wars of conquest unleashed a transitional period of national flux, reflected in the life of the tent-like Tabernacle by the temporary suspension of the ban on sacrifices at the high places.

Eventually, after Joshua completed the initial wars of conquest, the Tabernacle was established at Shilo, but this time as a sanctuary taking on the trappings of *permanence*. Hence, while the tent-like, temporary cover was preserved, the walls were fashioned out of stone to indicate that the people of Israel had reached an important benchmark in their national development. They had succeeded in entering the land and had started to put down roots in its rocky slopes. Historically, the period of Shilo corresponds to the rule of the judges, a provisional era in which central authority was weak, external threats were myriad, and tribal unity was still an unrealized dream. But the unstoppable process of securing the land, though often plagued by setbacks, was nevertheless underway.

In the end, the Tabernacle at Shilo was destroyed by the Philistines, a culturally advanced coastal people who opposed the Israelite advance at every step. For a time, chaos reigned, until the prophet Samuel arose to guide the people and to lay the groundwork for the establishment of the monarchy. During this time, the Tabernacle was again temporary, now at Nov, then at Givon, as first King Saul and finally David ascended to the throne. In the meantime, the high places returned to vogue, as if to highlight the provisional character of the era as well as its dangerous instability.

It was David who finally succeeded in both unifying the tribes and neutralizing their enemies, eventually founding the national capital at Jerusalem and initiating the process of building the Temple. Solomon, his son, built that edifice, upon sacred Mount Moriah, as the prolonged odyssey of the people of Israel finally came to an end. The national stability, unity of purpose, security from external threats, and cultural ascendancy that Israel enjoyed during the brief period of his reign corresponded to the building of the Temple, a building that was structurally permanent in every sense of the term. Again, the fortunes of the people were perfectly mirrored by the architectural form of their holy place, for rising above Jerusalem, the Temple told the story of finally achieving permanence.

Insofar as the high places are concerned, the critical principle is this: Whenever there is prolonged physical separation between the Ark and the Tabernacle, the high places are permitted. Whenever there is acute national instability, then the Ark is in one geographic location while the rest of the Tabernacle is elsewhere. During the period of the wilderness, the Ark was always stationed with the Tabernacle and therefore sacrifice at other locations was forbidden. When the people of Israel entered the land and embarked on the wars of conquest, the

Ark would accompany them into battle while the Tabernacle remained at Gilgal. Hence, the high places were permitted. At Shilo, the Ark was deposited in the Tabernacle, rarely leaving its enclosure, and the high places were forbidden. After Shilo was destroyed, the Ark went into exile – first among the Philistines who seized it (1 Sam. 4–5) and then in Beit Shemesh and Kiryat Ye'arim. All the while, the Tabernacle had been reconstituted at Nov (21–22) and then at Givon (1 Kings 3:3–5) but the Ark was not stationed with it – therefore, the high places were permitted. Finally, David initiated the process of reunification by bringing the Ark to his new capital at Jerusalem (11 Sam. 6). The vessels of the Tabernacle were eventually restored to the Ark's embrace when Solomon built the Temple, and the high places were outlawed forever.

The connection between the Tabernacle, the Ark, and the process of settlement should not be surprising. As the expression of God's abode on earth among the people of Israel, the fortunes of the Ark and the Tabernacle ought to reflect the travails and triumphs of the Jewish nation. As surely as God's presence is among them and His concern is never far removed, the Tabernacle/Temple and its precious Ark mirror their destiny. Therefore, the architectural form of the Tabernacle or the Temple reflects the physical fortunes of the nation of Israel in their land; the location of the Ark in relation to that building delineates the limits of their spiritual stability and hence the acceptability of the high places. No wonder that in the Tanakh, the exile of the nation of Israel from their land and the promise of their eventual restoration are paired with the destruction of the Temple on the one hand, and the prophetic vision of its ultimate rebuilding on the other.[2]

---

2. Of course, there is also the political aspect to consider and we have already traced its contours in an earlier chapter. Shilo was located in the hill country of Ephraim, Jerusalem in the Judean hills. The transition from one to the other spoke of the two houses of Israel – Joseph and Judah – and how each one had a pivotal role to play in the unfolding drama of securing a place in the land. At Shilo, the Tabernacle stood for 369 years and at Jerusalem the First Temple stood for 410 years, so that biblical history could be roughly divided between the ascendancy of Joseph and that of Judah. The pivot point that marks the dividing line is the tragic end of Saul's kingship and the commencement of David's reign (see Ps. 78:54–72).

These epochs of Israel's biblical history closely follow the framework of the prophetic books of the Tanakh. The Book of Joshua is almost entirely transitional, and its narratives therefore correspond to the Tabernacle leaving the wilderness, arriving at Gilgal and, towards the end of the book, finally arriving at Shilo as the settlement drive begins in earnest. The events of the Book of Judges, full as they are of the painful struggle to found a nation and unite it around its mission, all take place while the Tabernacle stands at Shilo – more established and secure but vulnerable nonetheless.

The Book of Samuel opens with the Tabernacle's destruction, as the uncertain and perilous passage from the rule of the judges to the founding of the monarchy unfolds. Without exception, the events of the book transpire while the Tabernacle is temporarily located first at Nov and then at Givon, all the while as the rival high places enjoy a resurgence – a direct function of the uncertainty of the times.

Finally, the Book of Kings begins with the ascent of Solomon to the throne. Full of spiritual ambition, thoughtful enough to make good use of all of his father David's preparatory work, Solomon quickly consolidates his reign and then embarks upon the most memorable accomplishment of his illustrious reign: the building of the Temple at Jerusalem. The remainder of the Book of Kings, of course, is bound up with the physical fortunes of this edifice, and when the people of Israel are exiled to the rivers of Babylon at the book's conclusion, the Temple is razed to the ground.

In sum, it is not an exaggeration to say that Israel's biblical history can be read in its entirety in conjunction with the fate of the house of God that is in its midst.

A TELLING VERSE

The Shilo-Jerusalem nexus, representing two distinct but intertwined stages of national consolidation – the beginning of settlement and the securing of permanence – is suggested by an illuminating verse from the Book of Deuteronomy. As Moses prepares to take leave of the people forever, he exhorts them to follow God's commands and encourages them to remain steadfast in the new land:

> Do not do as all of us now do here today, everyone as he sees fit in his own eyes. For you have not yet arrived at the state of rest

[*menuha*] or possession [*nahala*] that the Lord your God gives to you. You shall traverse the Jordan River and dwell in the land that the Lord your God causes you to possess, and He will grant you rest from all of your enemies around and you shall dwell in security. Then, at the place that the Lord your God shall choose to cause His name to dwell there, you shall present all that I command you, your burnt offerings and sacrifices, your tithes and dues, and all of your best vow offerings that you shall promise to God. (Deut. 12:8–11)

Moses tells the people that although the process of settling the land will be drawn out and difficult, one day they shall enjoy national peace and tranquility, and at that time they will build a sanctuary to God and serve Him there. One day they will achieve the state of rest and possession that will be the foundation of a viable and permanent state, reflected in the establishment of an enduring edifice to God's glory, a Temple. The early sources identified the state of rest – *menuha* – with Shilo, and the state of possession – *nahala* – with Jerusalem (*Sifrei* Deuteronomy 66), as spelled out in the mishna:

> When the people came to Shilo, the high places were forbidden. [At Shilo] the Tabernacle had no ceiling. It was provided with walls of stone below, while the covering above was made of curtains, and it constituted the "resting place" [*menuha*]…. When the people came to Jerusalem, the high places were again forbidden and were never permitted again, for it constituted the possession [*nahala*]. (Mishna Zevahim 14:6)

Returning to our context, the oblique mention in Joshua chapter eighteen that the people repaired to Shilo and set up the Tabernacle in more permanent form, constitutes an important comment on the process of Israel's consolidation in Canaan. While much remained to be done, tribal territories still remained to be apportioned, Canaanite enclaves still remained to be absorbed and much land remained to be populated, the people of Israel had nevertheless achieved an important milestone. They had secured their place in the land and had put down roots. Building the Tabernacle at Shilo, Israel paused to "rest" before embarking on the next stage of their national mission: unifying the tribes around a central authority and capital and then building an enduring empire that would proclaim God's teachings to the world. With the Tabernacle founded at Shilo, the acute uncertainty about their national future in the new land began to dissipate, just as surely as the tenuous wooden walls of the wilderness Tabernacle were replaced with much more permanent stone.

Joshua 18:11–19:51

The Remaining Tribal Territories

W e now turn our attention to the distribution of the remaining tribal territories. Remember that Judah and Joseph, the two largest and most powerful tribes, received their allotment first (chapters fifteen to seventeen), thus anchoring the nascent state to the south and to the north. The next tribe to be introduced is the tribe of Benjamin, whose portion of land falls in between that of Joseph and Judah. The Joseph clan was composed of Ephraim and Menashe, the former assigned to the area northwest of the Dead Sea, the latter straddling both sides of the Jordan River to the south of the sea of Kinneret. More precisely, then, the ribbon of land assigned to the tribe of Benjamin was bordered on the south by Judah and to the north by Ephraim. The specific towns and landmarks enumerated in the description of Benjamin's borders correspond exactly to those spelled out earlier in the respective demarcations of Judah's northern and Ephraim's southern boundaries.

While Benjamin's territory may have been rather small in comparison with his other brothers, its true importance was not a function of its size or fertility, but of something else entirely: the city of Jerusalem – the future site of the Temple – was located in its midst. While the building of the Temple was far off in the future, dependent upon the securing of national peace and permanence as we described last chapter, the text nevertheless makes several pointed allusions to that hopeful vision:

> The territory assigned to the tribe of Benjamin, according to their families, was allotted next, and the borders of their allotment fell between the people of Judah and the people of Joseph. Their northern border ascended from the Jordan River to the *slopes* north of Jericho... and thence passed towards Luz, the *slopes* of Luz to the south, namely Beit El.... The southern boundary... descended to the mountain ridge opposite the valley of Ben-Hinnom... to the *slope* of the Jebusite towards the south.... [The line] passed to the region opposite Maale Adumim and then descended by the stone of Bohan son of Reuben. It passed by the *slope* opposite the Arava northwards and then descended to the plain. The border passed to the *slope* of Beit Hogla northwards... and extended to the northern edge of the Salt Sea at the south of the Jordan [River]. This is the southern border. (Josh. 18:11–20)

In contrast to the other tribes, the borders of Benjamin are very often demarcated by a "slope" or "*katef*" because their territory occupied hilly plateaus that were naturally separated from the surrounding landscape by inclines. The unusual topographic term, however, is familiar to us from another context. At the conclusion of Moses' farewell address at the end of the Book of Deuteronomy, he extends a prophetic blessing to each one of the tribes in turn: "To Benjamin he said: 'Beloved one of God, He will dwell securely beside him. He will protectively cover him all the day and between his slopes (*katefav*) He will dwell'" (Deut. 33:12). Describing the tribe of Benjamin as "beloved of God," the verse goes on to relate that God will dwell among them and protect them from harm. The recurring verb in the passage is "to dwell," or in Hebrew "*lishkon.*" This root, of course, is the basis of *Mishkan* ("dwelling place") and *Shekhina* (God's presence manifest). Taken together, the verse intimates that God's dwelling or Temple will be found among the slopes of Benjamin, who is His beloved. This reading is one that is preserved in early sources, for the talmudic tradition

The Territories of the Tribes

Thus, they completed distributing the land. (Josh. 19:49–51)

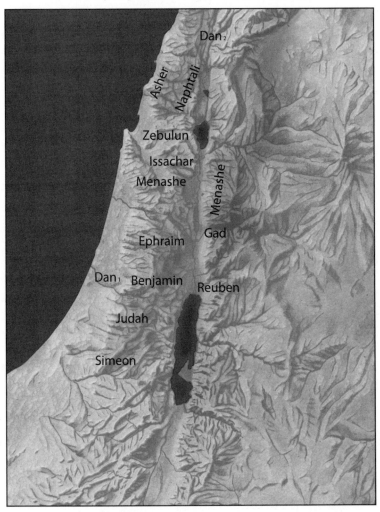

(Zevaḥim 54b) understands the phrase "between his slopes" to indicate that the Temple was to be protectively sited at a slightly lower elevation than the surrounding hills in order to emphasize God's safeguarding presence. It is instructive to note that the noun "*katef*," when used in an architectural sense as the sides of a portal, mainly occurs in the descriptions of the Tabernacle (Ex. 27:14–15) and the Temple (1 Kings 6:8, Ezek. 40:41).

Benjamin's central position between the Joseph clans to its north and Judah to its south, is indicative of the tribe's mediating role, to be achieved ultimately through the instrument of the Temple. Recall that the tense relationship between the tribes of Joseph and Judah was presaged by the struggles between Jacob's wives and their respective sons. But in that story of fraternal strife Benjamin served as the buffer between the brothers before becoming the source of their reconciliation. After all, didn't all of the other brothers accept Benjamin's special status, because he was the beloved youngest, possessed of none of Joseph's enraging hubris? Didn't Judah's valiant efforts to preserve Benjamin from the viceroy's clutches (none other than Joseph himself), by offering himself as a slave in his place, serve as the catalyst for the complete reunification of the family? Benjamin the brother was destined to play the role of reconciler, just as surely as the hallowed ground of the Temple Mount, located in the territory of that tribe, was slated to one day serve as the source of Israel's unity and of its ideal vision of a peaceful and harmonious world.

The implications of all of this are startling: embedded in the Book of Joshua's geographical data are critical textual cues concerning future events, just as we saw in the earlier chapters concerning the tribes of Judah and Joseph. By invariably describing Benjamin's boundaries as being demarcated by "slopes" the text tells us not only the story of that tribe's hilly topography but also provides us with an allusion concerning their future role: one day, the unifying Temple will be built in their territory!

THE REMAINING TRIBES

The frontiers of the remaining six tribes of Simeon, Zebulun, Issachar, Asher, Naphtali, and Dan are described in chapter nineteen. The text devotes approximately eight verses to each one of them, not nearly as much detail as that accorded to Judah, Joseph, and Benjamin. In contrast to those three, the borders of these six are generally not described in terms of lines and landmarks but rather are presented as listings of specific place names, the towns and villages that were inhabited by the respective tribe. In general, these tribal territories represent ideal geographic expanses that were only attained long after the close of the Book of Joshua.

The area assigned to the tribe of Simeon falls within the borders of the tribe of Judah (Josh. 19:1). Simeon did not receive an independent allotment but was federated with his much larger and more powerful brother. Simeon's portion consisted of a series of towns found within Judah's southern reaches, the arid and mostly barren Negev (literally "dry land"). Again, we are struck by the correspondence between our account and an ancient tradition. Last time, we considered the borders of the tribe of Benjamin in light of Moses' blessing. This time we must turn to patriarch Jacob's blessings that he bestowed upon his children as he lay on his deathbed, as recorded towards the end of the Book of Genesis. While each one of the sons merited his father's acclaim, Simeon and Levi were singled out for censure. Jacob recalled his sons' brutal attack on Shekhem (Gen. 34) and pronounced sentence upon them:

> Simeon and Levi are brothers; weapons of violence are their legacy. May my soul not be included in their plans, may my spirit not be counted in their gathering, because in their fury they killed men and in their passion they destroyed oxen. May their fury be cursed for it was overpowering, and their rage for it was harsh, *I will divide them in Jacob and I will scatter them in Israel.* (Gen. 49:5–7)

Jacob's ancient words now come to pass, for the tribe of Simeon never receives a clearly delineated portion of land in Canaan and instead is dispersed among the southern cities of the tribe of Judah, all as a result of ancestor Simeon's recklessness. For comparison, we may note that the tribe of Levi received an even more diffuse inheritance, for the population of that tribe was settled in assigned Levitical cities that were scattered throughout the length and breadth of the land.

The border descriptions of the Book of Joshua, while never stating the matter explicitly, provide us with a foundation principle in Tanakh: The moral choices made by the individual human being reverberate not only during his or her lifetime, but far into the future as well. Often the effects of our actions seem to us to become more muted and insignificant

with the passage of the years, certainly over the course of the generations, but the Tanakh intimates that this is not necessarily the case. The
seeds that we unwittingly plant during our ethical interactions with others sprout, take root, and flourish over an extended period of time and
often mature in a most unexpected fashion. While an appreciation of the
final outcome must escape us because our life spans are so brief, from
the perspective of the Eternal One, which the Tanakh aims to provide,
the connections are obvious.

The territories of the remaining tribes were in the north. Zebulun
was to settle the area west of the sea of Kinneret, which included the
prominent topographical marker known as Mount Tabor. Their territory
continued westwards until the coast of the Mediterranean near Akko just
north of the Carmel range, and their maritime connection was a confirmation of both Jacob's blessing as well as that of Moses. Jacob said that
"Zebulun will dwell next to the sea coast, where the ships land at the
coast, for his margins will be at Tzidon" (Gen. 49:13), and Moses had
blessed the tribe with "suckling the bounty of the sea and the treasures
of the sand" (Deut. 33:19).

Issachar's territory included the fertile Jezreel Valley, which arcs
southeast from the coastal Carmel range towards the sea of Kinneret
and to the Jordan River. The Jezreel Valley was not only an important
agricultural asset but a prime strategic one as well. This is because the
Via Maris, or "Way of the Sea," the most traveled route from Egypt to
Asia Minor and on to Mesopotamia, made its way along the Mediterranean coast until reaching the wadi of Kaneh at Jaffa. At that point, the
route detoured eastwards and then continued until Afek. From Afek
the route went northwards until reaching Megiddo, thus avoiding the
impassable Carmel Mountains. At Megiddo, a fortress town that guarded
the approaches to the Jezreel Valley, the route branched off northwest
towards the maritime trading towns of Phoenicia and northeast towards
Ḥatzor and then on to Damascus and Mesopotamia. To control the
Jezreel Valley was therefore to control the major trade routes of the
region, and throughout the biblical period the valley was a battleground.

The tribe of Asher possessed a huge swath of land along the coast
that included some of the most important Phoenician towns such as
Tzor and Tzidon. Most of these remained in the hands of the Canaanites

and were not successfully settled. Naphtali took the land east of the tribe of Asher, and their territory included what is known today as the Upper Galilee. In their possession was the fertile Ḥula Valley as well as some of the headwaters of the Jordan River that surge at the foothills of Mount Hermon.

Similar to its wilderness position as the rearguard of the tribes (Num. 10:25), the territory of Dan is enumerated last. Its portion was bordered by Benjamin to the east, Judah to the south, Ephraim to the north, and the Mediterranean at Jaffa to the west. It thus included what is today the most densely settled area of modern-day Israel, the so-called "Dan Region" that contains Tel Aviv and its suburbs. The tribe of Dan was not successful at settling its territory, as implied by the remark that "the borders of the children of Dan went out from them" (Josh. 19:47). Part of the tribe later journeyed far north of their territory and staked a claim at Leshem or Layish, on the eastern headwaters of the Jordan River (Judges 18). Dan's territory, identified in rabbinic sources with the Banias spring, borders the present day Golan Heights. Moses' prophetic remark that Dan would be "a young lion darting forth from the Bashan" (Deut. 33:22) was ultimately fulfilled, for it refers to the rushing headwaters of the Jordan River that shoot forth at Layish, a biblical synonym for a young lion (see Prov. 30:30, Is. 30:6). This northern colony of Dan would in time become identified with the extremity of the Israelite kingdom. With its southern limits at Be'er Sheva, the state would be described by the biblical proverb "from Dan to Be'er Sheva" (1 Sam. 3:20).

Having completed the account of the tribal territories, the text turns its attention to one final, and most appropriate, distribution of land:

> They completed giving out the land according to its borders, and the people of Israel gave a possession of land to Joshua son of Nun in their midst. By God's word, they gave him the town that he had requested, Timnat Seraḥ in Mount Ephraim, and he built the city and dwelt in it. These then are the territories that were distributed by Elazar the Priest, Joshua son of Nun, and the tribal leaders of Israel, in accordance with the lots cast at Shilo in God's presence at the entrance to the Tent of Meeting. Thus, they completed distributing the land. (Josh. 19:49–51)

Cities of Refuge and Levitical Cities

T he remaining five chapters of the Book of Joshua contain a variety of topics: the cities of refuge and those of the Levites that together complete the account of the tribal territories, the return of the Transjordanian militias to their homes east of the Jordan, and Joshua's concluding exhortations to the people. While the content of the chapters appears disparate, there is a common thread that draws the material together. Successful settlement of the land introduces its own challenges: How do we remain loyal to God and to His Torah even after hardship is overcome and difficulty is defeated? Once we have achieved success, how do we maintain our fidelity?

FULFILLING A COMMAND

> God spoke to Joshua saying: "Speak to the people of Israel and say, set aside the cities of refuge of which I told you by Moses. This is in order that a killer who took a life through negligence and without premeditation may find refuge from the avenger of the blood." (Josh. 20:1–3)

The Cities of Refuge

God spoke to Joshua saying: "Speak to the people of Israel and say,
set aside the cities of refuge of which I told you by Moses." (Josh. 20:1-2)

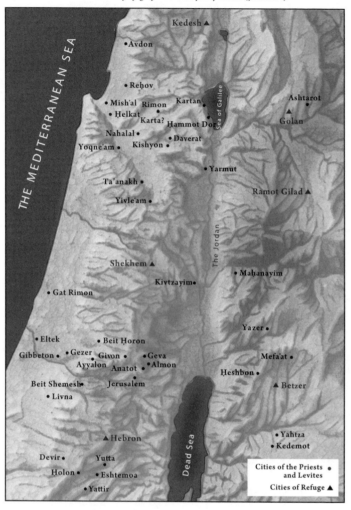

The commandment concerning the designation of special cities of refuge was comprehensively presented in the Torah at the very end of the Book of Numbers, as the people of Israel expectantly encamped east of the Jordan River, at the plains of Moav opposite Jericho (Num. 35:9–34). At that time, God told Moses to command the people concerning these six cities, so that they might fulfill the injunction after they had secured their place in Canaan. The cities were to be located roughly equidistant from each other along the length of the land, three in Canaan proper and three in Transjordan. The mention of the matter in the Book of Joshua now, towards the very end of the book, emphasizes that Israel achieved God's promise of possessing the land, and Joshua accomplished the daunting task of taking Moses' place.

Concerning the cities themselves, their function was clear. While the case of intentional homicide on the one hand and accidental manslaughter on the other typically presented the courts with straightforward evidence either way, the situation of gross criminal negligence causing death was potentially more complex. Such a case provided no express evidence of premeditation but the circumstances could be suspicious enough to warrant a more thorough investigation. In the meantime, the family of the victim might be distraught enough to take matters into their own hands, without awaiting the judicial exercise of due process.

Like a lethal game of cat-and-mouse, the "avenger of the blood" could execute vengeance upon the killer as long as he had not entered the confines of a city of refuge. But having entered one of the enclaves, he was assured of its protection until such time as he would stand trial in the town or city in which the crime had taken place. If the judges subsequently found him guilty of murder, then he would be sentenced to death. If he was acquitted of all wrongdoing, then he was free to return to his home and the courts would hold all who attempted to harm him accountable. If, however, the killer was convicted of criminal negligence causing death, then he would be returned to the city of refuge where he would live his life in exile until the death of the High Priest. If he willfully chose to leave the city's protective custody before the death of the High Priest, then the avenger of the blood could kill him with impunity. (See Josh. 20:1–6, Deut. 19:1–13, and Ex. 21:12–14.)

There is no question that the Torah's legislation, while acknowledging existing cultural norms, at the same time attempted to moderate and to eventually replace them with more advanced models of morality and justice. It is instructive to note that "avenging the blood," by taking the life of the killer (innocent though he may have been of intent to murder) before law enforcement authorities can intervene, happens in many Middle Eastern societies today. Blood feuds, honor killings, and clan infighting are not uncommon in tribal societies; the cities of refuge are the Torah's response to these phenomena, a demand over three thousand years ago to replace cruel frontier justice with a functioning and impartial judiciary.

These cities of refuge were associated with the Levites, whose own forty-eight designated cities included these six. The exile of the killer to the city of refuge was therefore not simply an act of justice and compassion, but one of absolution as well. The killer had to not only experience the anguish of banishment from his own town but also make the acquaintance of the Levites, whose special role was to provide spiritual instruction and guidance in ancient Israel. In this way, the killer could achieve pardon by serving his "sentence" of expulsion until the death of the High Priest, for that landmark event would usher in a new era of religious leadership.

In cases of premeditated homicide, however, the Torah makes it very clear that there can be no sanctuary from justice. In the bold language of *Parashat Mishpatim*: "If a man schemes against his fellow and kills him intentionally, then even from My altar you shall take him to die!" (Ex. 21:14). The institution of the cities of refuge was a sensible middle ground, preserving from harm those undeserving of death while at the same time brooking no compromise with murderers.

LINKING THE LEVITES

Chapter twenty-one naturally follows the account of the six cities of refuge, for they were counted among the forty-eight Levitical cities. According to the Book of Numbers, Moses was commanded to tell the people of Israel to:

> Give cities to the Levites from their landed inheritance for dwelling, as well as open areas outside of those cities. The cities will be for the Levites to live, while the open areas will be for their animals and for their possessions.... The cities that you shall give to the Levites shall be comprised of the six cities of refuge for the escape of killers, as well as forty-two additional cities. (Num. 35:2–6)

As moderns, only too familiar with urban sprawl and environmental degradation, we note with satisfaction that the Levitical cities were to be ringed by a "green lung" that could not be developed. The tribe of Levi was scattered among all of the other tribes and effectively rendered landless; the rise of a rapacious priesthood controlling vast tracts of real estate while amassing political power was thus inhibited. At the same time, the arrangement effectively freed the Levites from servitude to the land, from the all-consuming toil of the farmer who devoted his time and efforts to the cultivation of the earth. Instead, the Levites could be dedicated to other pursuits, to the service of God and to the teaching of His laws. As the passage in *Parashat Korah* relates concerning the priests: "In their land you shall not inherit, neither shall you have a portion among them. I am your portion and your inheritance in the midst of the people of Israel" (Num. 18:20).

Aaron the priest and his descendants, denied the gift of land like the tribe of Levi their kin, were instead charged with the dual responsibility of serving God at the Tabernacle as well as serving the people of Israel as teachers, judges, and guides. But it is this latter role which is their primary one. They therefore often appear in Tanakh as mentor figures and inspired religious leaders, and when the prophets criticize the priests or Levites, it is for their failure to teach and to exhort rather than for their disregard of ceremonial obligations (see Jer. 2:8; Mal. 2). In his farewell blessing of the people of Israel, Moses spells out the dual responsibility of the Levites, while placing special emphasis on their need to demonstrate loyalty to God and impartiality towards the people:

> Concerning Levi he said: Your perfect lights belong to Your pious ones, those whom You tested at Massah and with whom You contended at Mei Meriva. He [the tribe of Levi] said of his father and mother, "I do not see them," of his brothers, "I recognize them not," and of his children, "I do not know them," for they instead observed Your words and safeguarded Your covenant. *They shall teach Your laws to Jacob and Your instruction to Israel; they will place incense before You and wholly burnt offerings upon Your altar.* May God bless his efforts and favor the work

of his hands, may He crush his foes so that his enemies rise no more. (Deut. 33:8–11)

The landlessness of the Levites and priests did necessitate other arrangements: both were supported by public funds. The priest was the recipient of the *teruma* or priestly due (Num. 18:11–13), consisting of a small percentage of the produce. The Levite received the tithe (vv. 21–24), and was himself duty-bound to extend one-tenth of it in turn to the priest (vv. 25–32). The priests and the Levites that ministered at any given time at the Tabernacle partook of certain elements of the various sacrifices (Lev. 7:6–10, 32–36; Num. 18:8–10, 14–19; Deut. 18:1–8) and were thus provided with a steady source of immediate sustenance. Nevertheless, in light of the Torah's recurring association of the Levites with society's more vulnerable members such as the widow, orphan, and convert (Deut. 12:12–19; 14:27, 29; 16:11; 26:11), it would seem that the Torah never intended for the tribe to wax fat from the people's offerings. Rather, they were to maintain their focus on their more exalted calling and therefore were denied access to landed property and to the wealth that it typically conferred.

Maimonides best expressed the special responsibilities of these clans, as well as the implications for us, in his famous conclusion to the codification of the agricultural laws at the end of *Sefer Zera'im*:

> Why did the tribe of Levi not merit a portion in the land of Israel and in its spoils with his brethren? This is because they were designated to serve God and to minister before Him, to teach His righteous ways and upright laws to the masses, as the verse states: "They shall teach Your law to Jacob and Your Torah to Israel." Therefore, they are separated from the ways of the world. They do not wage war like the rest of Israel nor do they inherit land or secure sustenance by their own efforts. Rather, they are God's army, as the verse states: "May God bless his efforts" [literally "his forces"]; and He, blessed be He, provides for them, as it states "I am your portion and your inheritance."
>
> The above is not only true of the tribe of Levi, but of any human being at all whose spirit moves him and whose wisdom

inspires him to be separated to stand before God, to minister and serve in order to know Him. If such a one walks in sincerity just as God made him, and he casts off from upon himself the heavy yoke of vain pursuits that consume the masses, such a one has become as sanctified as the Holy of Holies. God will be his portion and his inheritance forever, and will provide for him in this world with sufficiency, just as He provided for the priests and Levites. David himself exclaimed [Ps. 16:5]: "God is my measured portion and share, You shall sustain my destiny." (Maimonides, *Mishneh Torah*, Laws of *Shemitta* and *Yovel* 13:12–13)

THE POTENTIAL OF POWERLESSNESS

While we tend to focus upon the pomp and privilege of the tribe of Levy, one cannot but be struck by the contrasting formulation of Maimonides. For him, man's highest calling is not the service of the earth or the pursuit of its bounty; these are only the means to an end. Fortunate is the man who is able to transcend them, casting off the petty concerns that consume the majority of our lives and distract us from our true calling: to serve God and to comprehend His ways. According to Maimonides's reading, the Levites represent an ideal that ought to inspire every man in every place at every time, in spite of the fact that the practice of the Levitical cities has been dormant for thousands of years.

But the life of a biblical Levite is often a life of subsistence, for though God never fails to provide, He rarely enriches. The Levite's goal, however, and by extension the goal of every thoughtful person, ought not to be material excess that breeds spiritual torpor, but rather sufficiency, contentment, and the ultimate meaning that only awareness of God can bestow. The designation of the Levitical cities was the first attempt in human history to foster not the rejection of the world or its debasement, but rather a more profound understanding of what ought to be our ideal relationship towards it.

The prophet Malachi expressed the matter best:

My covenant was with him, the life and the peace, and I gave them to him to revere Me, for before My name he shows deference.

True teaching was in his mouth and there was no iniquity upon his lips; he walked with Me in peace and honesty and turned many away from transgression. For the lips of the priest preserve knowledge, and guidance shall be sought from him, for he is like an angel of the Lord of hosts. (Mal. 2:5–7)

Joshua 22:1–34

Settling the Lands East of the Jordan

T he major battles for the conquest of Canaan are now over and the process of Israel's settlement in the new land is well underway. The territories of the tribes have been painstakingly mapped out and the Levitical cities have been designated. Joshua himself will soon complete his term as leader of the people and they in turn will be called upon to remain loyal to God's Torah. With the end of the fighting, Joshua now prepares to release the tribes of Reuben, Gad, and Menashe from their vow that they had undertaken on the eve of Moses' death, when the people of Israel were still encamped on the Jordan's eastern banks. There, they solemnly pledged to cross the river with their brethren in order to serve as the vanguard of their armies until the conquest of Canaan would be completed:

> At that time, Joshua summoned the tribes of Reuben, Gad, and half Menashe. He said to them: "You have observed all that Moses, God's servant, commanded you and have hearkened to me in accordance with all that I commanded you. You have not abandoned your brethren for many days until now, and you have

carefully observed the Lord your God's command. Now, the Lord your God has granted rest to your brethren just as He spoke, therefore turn now and go to your tents in the land of your possession that Moses, God's servant, granted you on the Jordan's other side. But be very careful to fulfill the commands and the teaching that Moses, God's servant, commanded you – to love the Lord your God and to follow His ways, to keep his commands and to cleave to Him, to serve him with all of your heart and with all of your soul." Thus, Joshua blessed them and sent them on their way, and they returned to their tents. (Josh. 22:1–6)

The background events to the discharge of these tribes from active service were described towards the end of the Book of Numbers (21:21–35 and chapter 32). At that time, the people of Israel had just defeated the Amorite kings Siḥon and Og, who ruled over the fertile Transjordan from the Wadi Arnon that empties into the Dead Sea midway along its eastern shore, all the way up to the foothills of snow-capped Mount Hermon in the Lebanon Mountains. In the aftermath of that battle, two of the tribes diffidently approached Moses to broach the subject of settling the recently conquered territory as their own:

> The people of Reuben and Gad had immense flocks. They saw that the land of Y'azer and Gilad was pastureland. The people of Gad and Reuben said to Moses, Elazar the Priest, and the princes of the congregation: "Atarot, Divon, Y'azer, Nimra, Ḥeshbon El'aley, Sevam, Nevo, and Be'on – the land that God struck down before the congregation of Israel – is grazing land, and your servants have flocks."
>
> They said: "If we have found favor in your eyes, then let this land be given to your servants as an inheritance, and do not cause us to pass over the Jordan River." (Num. 32:1–5)

The two tribes of Reuben and Gad, blessed with large numbers of herds, began to wonder whether the vast tracts of fertile grazing land that they then occupied might not better meet their material needs than the rocky Canaanite highlands. Perceptively, the fifteenth-century Spanish commentator Rabbi Isaac Abarbanel detected in the phrasing of their request a wavering note of hesitation:

> Initially, these tribes voiced their appeal in allusive terms for they were ashamed to state it explicitly.... Therefore, the text of the Torah introduced a paragraph division after their first statement. Moses understood their intent but chose not to reprove them immediately. Rather he remained silent to allow them to openly divulge their request. When they saw that Moses remained silent and did not respond to their intimation, they were forced to ask again with greater directness. Hence, the text states that "they said" a second time. (Abarbanel on Num. 32:1–5)

We can certainly imagine these tribes' reluctance to be more direct as they stood before Moses and the tribal leaders. After all, hadn't thirty-eight years been dissipated in purposeless wandering in the wilderness because of an earlier generation's reluctance to enter the new land? Understandably, Moses was incensed:

> Shall your brethren go to fight while you remain here?! Why do you break the people's resolve to cross over into the land that God gave to them? Just so did your fathers behave when I sent them from Kadesh Barnea to spy out the land.... Now you have arisen in their place as a brood of sinful folk, only to increase God's anger against Israel. By turning away from Him you will cause Him to leave them in the wilderness even longer, and you shall thereby destroy this people! (Num. 32:6–15)

The striking contrast between Moses and these tribes was mirrored perfectly by the two disconnected territories of Canaan and the Trans-jordan. On the one side stood the aged lawgiver, flanked by Joshua and Elazar the Priest, the new leaders of the people. Moses remembered the debacle of the spies only too well. That mission ended so tragically because the people had lacked the steadfastness to trust in God's assistance. Perhaps the troubling thought of his own more recent exclusion from entering the land also occupied his thoughts, for he wished nothing more than to lead the people to their promised destination. Couldn't these tribes recognize the folly of their ways in rejecting the very future that he so desired?

On the other side, separated from Moses by only a few paces, stood the tribes of Reuben and Gad. Certainly, they had fully shared in the people's fate up until this point and had experienced the communal calamity imposed by God's decree. Had they not sufficiently "paid the price"? Besides, why did God grant them victory over those vast tracts if not to settle them? Wasn't the natural division imposed by the meandering Jordan River rather inconsequential, in light of their cohesive connection to the other tribes and to the shared destiny of the people of Israel?

> They approached him and said: "We shall build sheep pens for our flocks and towns for our children. We shall quickly proceed at the vanguard of Israel until we have brought them to their place, while our children remain in the fortified towns because of this land's inhabitants. We will not return to our own homes until the people of Israel have received their possession. But we will not possess with them on the other side of the Jordan River because our possession is rather to be on its eastern side." (Num. 32:16–19)

With a curious mixture of compromise tinged with defiance, the two tribes spelled out their plan: they *would* fight with their brethren and help them to secure their land, but in the end they *would not* settle it with them. After the territories in Canaan would be secured, they would return to their own homes east of the Jordan. Resigned, Moses acquiesced and placed an oath upon them in the presence of Joshua, Elazar, and the tribal leaders.

RETURNING FROM CANAAN

In the end, Reuben, Gad, and half of Menashe fulfilled their oath and dutifully accompanied the people over the Jordan River to fight on their behalf, as recorded in the early chapters of the Book of Joshua (4:12–13). Canaan was eventually conquered, and after a good many years the battles for the land subsided. As recounted in our book, Reuben, Gad, and half of Menashe now returned home with Joshua's blessing, but when they reached the shores of the Jordan River they left their mark:

> They reached the region of the Jordan River in the land of Canaan, and there Reuben, Gad, and half of Menashe built a massive altar next to the Jordan River. When the people of Israel heard of their deed...they gathered against them with arms. (Josh. 22:9–12)

Interpreting their act as an invitation to idolatry, as an attempt to set up an alternate center of worship to rival the national shrine recently constructed at Shilo, the people sent the fiery Pinḥas son of Elazar (see Num. 25 for more on his career), accompanied by ten tribal elders, to dissuade them. Again, just as they had almost two decades earlier, Reuben and Gad explained their true motives and calmed Israel's fears:

> Mighty Lord God, Mighty Lord God, He knows and Israel will know that if [we did this] in rebellion or as a trespass against the Lord, He will not save us this day. We did not build this altar to rebel against the Lord, we did not erect it to offer sacrifice.... We were rather concerned that in the future, your children would say to ours: "What do you have with the Lord, God of Israel? Did the Lord not place a boundary between us, Reuben and Gad, the Jordan River! You have no share with the Lord!"... We therefore decided to build this altar...as a witness between us and you for generations to come...that we will serve the Lord...so that your children will not say tomorrow to our children, "You have no share with the Lord!"... Pinḥas the priest, the congregation's princes, and the leaders that were with him heard the explanation offered by Reuben, Gad, and Menashe, and they received it favorably. (Josh. 22:22–30)

The elements of this episode parallel those of the Book of Numbers. As before, the tribes of Reuben and Gad now decided on a striking unilateral move, the ire of Israel was aroused when their motives were justifiably misinterpreted; Reuben and Gad mollified the people and explained that their true intent was above reproach and only then was the matter finally resolved to everyone's satisfaction. Unlike the earlier situation though, in which Reuben and Gad feared Moses' reaction but never doubted their decision, here their misgivings were openly expressed. By consciously choosing to remain on the eastern bank of the Jordan, Reuben, Gad, and Menashe realize that they have driven a wedge between themselves and the rest of Israel. Though they may have fought on Israel's behalf when the people entered Canaan, though they may wish to participate in the national service of God centered at Shilo, they know that their future role in shaping Israel's destiny will be smaller. The fears that earlier had worried Moses, now worry them. Israel may come to resent their non-involvement in the daily trials and triumphs of national life in Canaan, and may eventually reject their claim to be part of the people.

UNDERSTANDING MOSES' MOTIVES

All of the above explains with greater clarity the role of Menashe in the settlement of the Transjordanian territories. The initial petition presented to Moses in the Book of Numbers was offered by Reuben and Gad only. After the matter was resolved by their swearing an oath, Moses assigned some of the territories to Menashe:

> Moses gave to them, to the children of Gad, and to the children of Reuben, and to half the tribe of Menashe son of Joseph, the kingdom of Sihon king of the Amorites, and the kingdom of Og king of Bashan, the land, with its cities and their borders, the cities of the land round about. (Num. 32:33)

> The sons of Makhir, son of Menashe, captured the Gilad and drove out the Amorites who were there. Moses gave the Gilad to Makhir son of Menashe, and he dwelt there. Yair son of Menashe went and captured their farms, and called them Ḥavot Yair. Novaḥ went and captured Kenat and its villages, and called it Novaḥ after his own name. (Num. 32:39–42)

Moses' conduct is puzzling in light of his earlier reluctance to entertain the appeal of Reuben and Gad at all. Why would he in the end strengthen a claim that he had regarded as potentially ruinous, by assigning yet another tribe or part thereof to the lands east of the Jordan? Nahmanides explains:

> At the outset, the tribe of Menashe did not approach Moses. But after Moses apportioned the land to the two tribes, he realized that the territory was too large for their needs. He therefore requested volunteers to settle it with them. Some of the members of Menashe agreed, perhaps because they also possessed flocks, and he therefore gave them their appropriate portion. (Nahmanides on Num. 32:33)

We may go one step further than Nahmanides and posit that Moses *intentionally* selected Menashe, with due deliberation and care. Recall that Moses feared that Reuben and Gad had abandoned the national destiny by casting their lot with the territory of Sihon and Og. Recall also from our context that in hindsight Reuben and Gad themselves had serious misgivings about the consequences of their decision. Perhaps the rest of the people of Israel would one day reject them and come to regard them as a selfish and irrelevant diaspora.

Moses considered the matter carefully and acted to limit the danger. By actively assigning part of Menashe to the lands east of the Jordan while the bulk of this important tribe would settle on the west, Moses introduced a mechanism intended to preserve a cohesive connection between all of the tribes on both sides. The bulk of Menashe's descendants would remain within Canaan proper but the powerful tribal bonds that are a function of shared culture, language, and history would ensure that a strong link was maintained with the families to the east. In this way, the other tribes to the east would also not be cut off from the national enterprise and would have an interest in maintaining their connection to their compatriots in Canaan proper.

This effect was enhanced by the fact that not only Menashe's descendants settled east of the Jordan River. As Rabbi Abraham Ibn Ezra demonstrates from the lineage lists preserved in 1 Chronicles 2:21–22, "Yair son of Menashe" was actually a member of the tribe of Judah who was descended from Menashe on his mother's side only: "Hetzron [of Judah] took the daughter of Makhir father of Gilad as his wife.... She bore him Seguv, whose son was Yair, who possessed twenty-three towns in the land of Gilad." Thus, not only were the eastern tribes joined to their western brethren by the tribe of Menashe, they were also connected by an important family from the tribe of Judah.

For hundreds of years, during the period of the judges and the kings, the eastern tribes remained involved in the life of the people of Israel. But in the end, the bonds between Reuben and Gad and the other tribes could not be preserved. Though regarded as part of the people and often active in the issues of the day, Reuben and Gad eventually suffered an ignoble fate that mirrored their own conscious choice generations earlier – exile to distant lands by the Assyrians, never to be heard of again:

> They trespassed against the God of their ancestors and strayed after the gods of the land that God had destroyed from before them. The God of Israel inspired Pul king of Assyria and Tilgat Pileser, and they exiled the tribes of Reuben, Gad, and half Menashe. He brought them to Ḥalaḥ, Ḥavor, Hara and the river of Gozan until this very day. (1 Chron. 5:25–26)

The Midrash puts it most acerbically, in attempting to pinpoint the cause of their downfall:

> The tribes of Gad and Reuben were wealthy and had many flocks. Because of their love of their possessions, they decided to dwell outside of the land of Israel. Therefore, they were exiled before any of the other tribes.... What brought this fate upon them? The fact that they separated themselves from their brethren because of their wealth, as the verse states: "The tribes of Reuben and Gad had immense flocks." (Numbers Rabba 22:7)

The most sincere oaths of allegiance, the most moving of monuments and memorials, even taking an active part in fighting the people's wars, cannot create a shared destiny with those that dwell in the land. As Reuben, Gad, and half Menashe painfully realized as they prepared to cross the Jordan, spatial separation does matter and distance from the land is decisive. The destiny of Israel would be decided in Canaan without them, and only by settling in that land with the tribes of Israel could they hope to share in that destiny in the most comprehensive and meaningful way.

While our episode ultimately ends tragically, it nevertheless presents us with a hopeful paradigm. Disagreements between the tribes of Israel have a long history in the Bible – rarely are they solved without bloodshed. But here, both versions of the dispute – the earlier one concerning the eastern lands and the later one concerning the altar – are resolved amicably. The lesson for us is clear: There is much to be said for dialogue. By allowing the two-and-a-half tribes to explain their motivations, even while justifiably suspecting the worst, Moses, and later Joshua, introduce the tribes of Israel to a new dynamic, in which words replace warfare and compromise is the goal. Gersonides expresses the matter well:

> The eighth lesson concerns Israel's sending of a delegation consisting of Pinḥas and the tribal elders to the Transjordanian tribes. This was in order to investigate the truth of the matter before attacking them. Even concerning things that require an urgent response, it is critical that one reflect and investigate the matter. Look what would have happened had such an investigation not taken place: great harm would have ensued had the people of Israel attacked their brethren. (Concluding comments to the Book of Joshua)[1]

---

1. Gersonides completes his comments to each section of the biblical text by offering the reader a lengthy series of life lessons that can be derived from the story. These meaningful gems address all aspects of living, from the mundane to the profound.

Joshua Addresses the People

It came to pass long after God had granted Israel respite from all of their enemies around, and Joshua was old and had lived many days. Joshua summoned all of Israel – their elders, leaders, judges, and officers – and he said to them: "I am now old, I have lived many days. See what the Lord your God has done on your behalf to all of these peoples, because the Lord your God wages war for you." (Josh. 23:1–3)

The final two chapters of the Book of Joshua constitute Joshua's parting words to the people of Israel. There are two discrete addresses contained in these chapters, the last offered at a great assembly of the people at Shekhem, and ours communicated to the people at an unnamed location. In both, Joshua employs the oratorical conventions of encouragement and warning, inspiration and rebuke. God's providential care of the people is recalled, His unwillingness to brook their disloyalty evoked. Joshua's words recall those of his mentor Moses, who also assembled the people of Israel on the eve of his death, in order to impress upon them the great privilege and responsibility of having been chosen by God.

A NOTE OF CAUTION

While Joshua indicates the extent of their miraculous conquest ("from the Jordan River…until the Great Sea where the sun goes down"), he also reminds them that much of the land remains to be settled. It would in fact be many, many years until the entire land was inhabited and the Canaanite menace was wholly removed, for not until the ascent of David to the throne some four centuries later did Israel finally achieve rest. But Joshua is not bitter, as if all of his endeavors have failed to yield the promised outcome. Far from it, for he understands that though his own personal role has been limited, it has nevertheless been instrumental, and that the larger divinely-guided process will continue to unfold long after his own demise. In essence, the text casts Joshua in the mold of Israel's other great leaders, inspired people who could peer beyond their own fleeting lifetimes towards a future that they had helped set into motion, but would not merit to see fully realized.

But Joshua is cognizant of the dangers that lurk at Israel's door. He knows that so much remains to be done and he is keenly aware of the hostile forces that could insidiously undo all that he and the people have labored so mightily to achieve:

> Strengthen yourselves greatly, to observe and to fulfill all that is written in the book of Moses' teaching, not to turn aside to the right or to the left. Do not mingle with these nations that remain with you, do not mention the names of their gods nor swear by them, do not serve them nor to bow down to them. (Josh. 23:6–7)

Joshua correctly posits, as Moses had before him, that Israel's success will depend upon their ability to resist the siren call of Canaan's loutish pantheon, the seductive gods of grain and wine, passion and death, sun and storm, fertility and flocks, whose shameless shrines and profligate cults were to be found "on every mountain top and hill, and under every leafy tree" (Deut. 12:2). The military threat posed by Canaan's confederacies had long passed, but the more serious cultural and moral threats posed by their beliefs continued to live on and to claim new adherents. In order to fully appreciate Joshua's fears, one must put the matter into perspective: Of all of the people in the ancient world, only the Israelites proclaimed the principle of a single and transcendent God, only they declared its corollary of an absolute moral code, only their teachers were consumed with a vision of a united humanity striving for the realization of a higher purpose. All around them, in Canaan and beyond its borders, the shrill flutes captivated while the lyres entranced, and pagan humanity's greatest achievements were gauged in terms of bloodshed, debauchery, and deceit:

> Rather, cleave to the Lord your God as you have done until this very day. God drove out great and powerful nations, while no one has withstood you until this very day. One of your men will pursue a thousand, for the Lord your God fights on your behalf, as He has spoken to you. (Josh. 23:8–10)

Like Moses before him, Joshua juxtaposes conquest with caution, never allowing the elation over their remarkable victories in the land to overshadow the enormity of the task that remains. Much of the language of this chapter, impassioned words of reassurance underscored with intimations of doom, resembles Moses' final addresses preserved in the Book of Deuteronomy. But while Moses could only dream of the future and its challenges, Joshua can already see it clearly taking shape:

> Be very careful concerning your lives, to love the Lord your God. For if you turn back and cleave to these nations that remain with you, to marry them and to be part of them and them of you, then you must surely understand that the Lord your God will not continue to drive out these nations from before you. They shall be for you a trap and a snare, thorns in your sides and barbs in your eyes, until you are lost from upon this good earth that the Lord your God has given you. (Josh. 23:11–13)

The people's response to Joshua's address is not recorded in the text. How did they react to his message of sobriety? How did they relate to his solemn warnings? Were they moved by his earnest tones or were their minds elsewhere, perhaps lost in thoughts of building their homes or planting their fields? It must surely have been difficult for the people of Israel to mark their well-earned achievements with a speech such as this one. But Joshua is unrelenting. His words reverberate across the assembly place, his warnings carried far by the winds. Completing his exhortation, he exclaims:

> Just as all of the good things have come upon you as the Lord your God spoke to you, so too the Lord your God will bring all of the evil things upon you, until He destroys you from this good earth that the Lord your God has given you. If you abrogate the covenant of the Lord your God that He commanded you by worshipping other gods and bowing down to them, then God's anger will be kindled against you, and you will be swiftly displaced from the good land that He has given you. (Josh. 23:15–16)

This remarkable conclusion celebrates the people's triumphs while simultaneously spelling utter doom for Israel should they fail to heed God's laws. It thus presents us with an extreme contrast that is perfectly matched by chapter twenty-eight of the Book of Deuteronomy, towards the end of the section known as the "Admonition" or *Tokheha*. In this passage, Moses graphically describes the destructive consequences should Israel abrogate their covenant with God and after briefly enunciating a series of blessings, he spells out fearsome curses, completing the description with the following:

> You shall remain but a few after you had been as numerous as the stars, for you did not hearken to the voice of the Lord your God. Just as God delighted over you to do good for you and to multiply you, just so God will delight over you to destroy you and to obliterate you, and you shall be swept off of the land that you enter to possess. (Deut. 28:62–63)

An even more disquieting parallel can be found in chapters eight and nine of the Book of Kings, which describe the completion and dedication of the Temple at Jerusalem by Solomon, king of Israel. For the people, the building of the Temple represented a critical watershed, for its completion signified that Israel, by embracing their mission as God's chosen nation, had finally achieved rest in their land. In fact, one could persuasively argue that the saga of the Book of Joshua came to its final conclusion with the building of the Temple more than four centuries later. After all, the challenges of our book – to overcome adversity and achieve a foothold in the land, to resist idolatry and mature into God's nation – were not overcome until the time of David and Solomon. David secured Israel's borders from external threat and united the tribes into a kingdom; Solomon ruled wisely, broadcasting Israel's message of ethical monotheism to a larger world for the first time. It was a brief era of peace and prosperity, justice and integrity, the ascendancy of cultural and religious ideas that had the power to transform the region; the period was auspiciously capped by the building of the Temple.

God was pleased with the work and responded favorably to Solomon's prayer that he offered before all of the assembled people of Israel. He later appeared to the sleeping monarch in a vision and expressed His satisfaction. But, most strikingly, His words of encouragement and love were soberly concluded with a dire warning:

> God said to him: I have heard your prayer and entreaty that you have offered before Me. I have sanctified this house that you have built to place My name upon it forever, for My eyes and heart will be upon it forevermore. As for you, if you walk before Me as David your father did with pureness of heart and uprightness, performing all that I have commanded you, observing My statutes and laws, then I will establish your throne upon Israel forever, just as I spoke concerning David your father that his descendants would never cease ruling over Israel. But if you and your descendants turn back from Me and fail to observe My commands and statutes that I have placed before you, if you instead go and serve other gods and bow down to them, then I will cut Israel off of the face of the earth that I have given them, and the house that I have sanctified I will send away from My presence, for then Israel will become a byword and source of mockery among all of the nations. All that will pass by this house, now supreme, will be filled with astonishment and will whistle derisively, for they will say: "Why did God do this to this land and to this house?" They

will then answer: "It is because they abandoned the Lord their God who had brought them and their ancestors out of the land of Egypt, and they grasped for other gods, bowed down to them and served them, therefore has the Lord brought upon them all of this evil." (I Kings 9:3–9)

Joshua's address is therefore part of a literary paradigm in which Israel's greatest moments of triumph are tempered with grave words of caution. It would be a mistake to understand Joshua's words, like those of Moses before him, as intimations of inevitable doom, as if Israel's fate was early on sealed for destruction. Rather, the technique of introducing dire warnings precisely at moments of great national success can be better understood as an emphatic statement about the precariousness of the human condition. Throughout history, nations that achieved shining glory were unable to sustain it for long. The pedestal was quickly vacated for others, while its former occupants faded into oblivion or ignominy. This is because in the life of nations, just as in the lives of individuals, equilibrium can only be maintained with great effort. Today's triumphs breed the indolence and apathy that spawn tomorrow's defeats. By employing the literary technique of always appending a note of caution to even the most exalted moments, the Tanakh makes it abundantly clear: Our success as individuals or as the nation of Israel can only be sustained as long as we steadfastly hold on to our principles even when it appears that the battle has been won. Attainment of any sort, and certainly of the spiritual variety, is always transitory – unless a constant effort is expended in order to sustain it. And while we are able to dream of a brighter future and to sacrifice mightily in order to realize it, we often become complacent once the noble goal has been achieved. The great challenge, then, is to prepare not only for the day of triumph, but for the day after as well.

Joshua 24:1–33

Joshua's Final Address

Finally, we have arrived at the closing chapter of the Book of Joshua. Patiently, we followed the trials of Israel's selfless leader as he labored mightily to remain faithful to the example of his exalted mentor Moses. We saw Joshua don the mantle of leadership and confidently proceed to prepare the people for entering the land, for battling the Canaanites, and for striking down roots in the new territory.

Simultaneous with the account of Joshua's personal progress, we also witnessed the spiritual maturing of the people of Israel. Slowly and sometimes reluctantly, they shed the passiveness of their former wilderness existence, a life that had been characterized by immediate and overt expressions of divine intervention and providential care. In its place, they acquired precious self-sufficiency and the intense satisfaction that comes with expending effort, even while remaining aware that success is just as much due to God's assistance: "Remember the Lord your God, for it is He who gives you the strength to achieve greatness, in order to fulfill this day His covenant that He swore to your ancestors" (Deut. 8:18).

Summoning the people for the last time, Joshua gathers them to ancient Shekhem. Radak explains the significance of the location in his comments to Joshua 24:1: At Shekhem, nestled picturesquely between Mount Gerizim and Mount Eival, their ancestor Abraham had first arrived. He and his wife Sara had answered God's summons to leave kith and kin behind at Ur upon the Euphrates, and to journey westwards to the land of Canaan:

> Abram took Sarai his wife and Lot his nephew, and all of their possessions that they had acquired, and the entire household that they had gathered at Ḥaran, and they departed to journey towards Canaan, and they arrived in the land of Canaan. Abram traversed the land, until the site of Shekhem, until Alon Moreh, and the Canaanite was then in the land. (Gen. 12:5–6)

Joshua carefully chooses the location of his last address to the people, for there they had gathered in a great assembly years earlier not long after they had entered the land – to hear the Torah's words of instruction and to inscribe them upon the stones (Josh. 8:30–35). To Shekhem, then, Israel now returns – to reflect upon their accomplishments and to be re-inspired with the tenets that underlie their mission. In consonance with Radak's above interpretation, Joshua also intends to recall for the people their ancestors' lives of devotion to God and deep connection to the land of Canaan:

> Joshua said to all of the people: Thus says the Lord, God of Israel, Beyond the river [Euphrates] your ancestors had always dwelt, Teraḥ the father of Abraham and the father of Naḥor, and they worshipped other gods. I took your ancestor Abraham from beyond the river and caused him to traverse throughout the land of Canaan, and I multiplied his descendants, and I gave him Isaac. To Isaac, I gave Jacob and Esau; to Esau, I gave Mount Se'ir to possess, but Jacob and his children went down to Egypt. (Josh. 24:2–4)

AN OUTLINE OF ISRAEL'S HISTORY

Schematically, Joshua traces the history of the people of Israel, focusing upon their most significant trial: Was it not about abandoning a comfortable but corrupt life of idol worship in order to embrace the demanding service of the absolute God? Briefly, Joshua recalls the oppression in Egypt and the Exodus, the parting of the Sea of Reeds and the conquest of the Transjordanian kings, the ineffectual curses of Balaam and

the conquest of Jericho, concluding his address with a ringing and rhetorical challenge:

> I have given you a land for which you toiled not, cities that you
> did not build but in which you now dwell, vineyards and olive
> groves that you did not plant but whose fruits you now consume.
> Now therefore, revere God and serve Him in sincerity and truth,
> and remove the gods that your ancestors from beyond the river
> served and the gods that they served in Egypt, and serve God!
> *If you regard it as repulsive to serve God, then choose for yourselves*
> *today whom you will serve:* Will it be the gods that your ancestors
> from beyond the river served, or else the gods of the Amorites
> in whose land you now dwell? As for me and my household, we
> will serve God! (Josh. 24:13–15)

What is most remarkable about Joshua's presentation is that he distills
the rich and full account of Israelite history – the storied lives of their
ancestors and their odyssey of trust, the degradation of Egypt and the
triumph of the Exodus, the securing of a place to call their own in the
Promised Land – all of it, into a single irreducible notion: Follow God
and faithfully fulfill His commands in order to succeed and prosper, or
else abandon Him, betray Israel's unique destiny, and perish.

While the people are quick to accept Joshua's challenge and
unequivocally proclaim their fealty to God and to His Torah, Joshua is
not convinced. Again, he impresses upon them the gravity of the choice
before them, for to choose God is also to choose the burden of fulfilling
His moral, ethical, and ritual obligations. Above his protests, the people
again proclaim their willingness to comply, and this time Joshua relents.

Some of the early commentaries understood that Joshua's offer
to the people to reject God and embrace idolatry if they so desire is
not to be taken literally. Rather, it is a rhetorical flourish that is calculated to exhort. Gersonides presents this view by drawing the strands
of our discussion together:

> He said to them that if service of God was not favorable to them
> then they should rather choose the gods of their ancestors who

dwelt beyond the river. But God had forcefully distanced them from all of that by taking Abraham from there and bringing him to the land of Canaan! If on the other hand, they desired to serve the gods of the Amorites whose lands they now inhabited by His grace, then they should bear in mind that the deceitful beliefs and coarse practices of the Amorites were the reason for their expulsion from the land…. All of this was therefore a technique for distancing Israel from serving their gods. With all of that, Joshua told them that even were they to choose to worship those other gods, he would not agree to it but rather he and his household would remain faithful to God. This was in order to distance them further from embracing idolatry. (Gersonides on Josh. 24:15)

For Gersonides, Joshua recalls the idolatry of our ancestors only in order to reiterate that God separated Abraham from its corrosive influence; Joshua invokes the idolatry of Canaan only to remind the people that the tribes that inhabited the land were expelled on its account. The message is therefore crystal clear: the worship of other gods and the embrace of their values is not a viable option if Israel is to survive in the new land!

THE POWER OF CHOICE

Rabbi Yosef Kara, an eleventh-century contemporary of Rashi, disagrees by offering a bold interpretation that is more in consonance with the straightforward reading:

"Choose for yourselves today whom you will serve" – up until this point, God had forced you to accept His authority for had you refused Him at Mt Sinai…then He would have buried you under the mountain!… But now, there is no coercion, so that later you will not be able to defend your conduct by saying, "We had no choice! We were forced to accept Him as our God!" Therefore choose for yourselves whom you shall serve. Will it be the gods that your ancestors from beyond the river worshipped? If so, there is no shame in that, since your ancestors from beyond the river served them. If you instead choose to worship the God of Abraham your father then it is an honor to choose your father's good path. But know that I and my household will choose nothing but the God of Abraham! (Commentary on 24:15)

In these remarkable comments, Rabbi Yosef Kara suggests that the people of Israel had not chosen God of their own volition when they stood at Sinai but only because they were overwhelmed by His revelation and threatened by His demands. How could they then be held accountable to a covenant that they did not freely accept? But now, Joshua offered them an out – to be relieved of their obligations and to choose other gods instead![1] This was absolutely necessary in order to hold the people of Israel responsible for the consequences of their choice.

Rabbi Yosef Kara thus reinforces our ongoing thesis even as the story nears its climactic conclusion: the Book of Joshua is not only a record of Israel's entry into the land; it is also the story of their spiritual coming of age. If enterprise was the order of the day, if God needed to subdue His overt intervention so that Israel might be able to take initiative, then reframing the covenant was critical. The people of Israel had to choose God for themselves as an independent and sincere exercise of their will. Accountability is the benchmark of mature behavior – to take responsibility for one's actions is the highest form of choosing.

Having secured their fealty, Joshua reminds them of the great and awesome covenant sealed by Moses on the eve of his death, as the people of Israel stood at the plains of Moav poised to enter the land (Deut. 29–30). Just as then, Joshua now calls the people as witness:

Joshua said to the people: "You are witnesses for yourselves that you have chosen God to serve Him," and they said: "We are witnesses." "Now" [he said,] remove the foreign gods from

---

1. The idea that Israel's acceptance of the Torah at Mt. Sinai was not the product of their free choice but rather a divine imposition was stated by the ancient rabbis in Shabbat 88a. Their solution, more astonishing than Rabbi Kara's but predicated upon the same fundamental premise, was that Israel re-accepted the Torah freely only at the time of the events of Purim, almost a thousand years after the revelation at Sinai! In the end, it seems, Israel must choose freely for their covenant with God to have eternal validity.

your midst and turn your hearts to the Lord, God of Israel." The people said to Joshua: "The Lord our God we will serve, and to His voice we will hearken." Joshua concluded a covenant for the people on that day, and he set for them a statute and law in Shekhem. Joshua recorded these things in a book of the Torah of God, and he took a great stone and set it up beneath the doorpost that was in the sanctuary of the Lord. Joshua said to all of the people: "Behold, this stone will serve as our witness, for it heard all of the Lord's words that He spoke with us. Therefore, it will serve as a testimony lest you deny your God." Joshua then sent the people forth, each man to his plot of land. (Josh. 24:22–28)

The above passage describes how Joshua recorded the terms in the form of a text. The ancient rabbis disagreed as to the identity of the text in question: "R. Judah and R. Nehemiah disagreed. One explained that it refers to the final eight verses of the Torah while the other explained that it refers to the section of the cities of refuge" (Makkot 11a). According to R. Judah, Joshua now completes the Torah scroll, inscribing the final eight verses that describe Moses' death. Joshua's crowning achievement is therefore the *completion* of the Torah, just as he had fulfilled his mission as Moses' successor. For R. Nehemiah, Joshua does not now complete the Torah scroll but rather records in his book the account of the cities of refuge, just as they had been spelled out earlier in the Torah. In this reading, it is *continuity* that is emphasized, for Joshua transcribes Moses' message in his own words for posterity. Both of these opinions understand that the text in question is somehow related to earlier material, but Radak disagrees:

> It seems to me that according to the straightforward reading, neither of these opinions is plausible. The true meaning is in accordance with Yonatan's translation, who explained that "Joshua wrote these things which he placed with the scroll of God's Torah." (Radak on Josh. 24:25)

For Radak, Joshua inscribes something entirely new, namely the terms of the covenant now concluded between God and Israel. The text containing these terms is placed in proximity to the master Torah scroll kept safely in the Ark of the Covenant, in order to highlight the seriousness of the agreement. The matter is reinforced by the placement of a physical marker to commemorate the covenant, a great stone that suggests the permanence of its provisions. Joshua's setting up of the stone recalls earlier events in the book, such as the stones placed in the Jordan River in chapter four, or the building of the altar at Mount Eival at the end of chapter eight. The stones in the book therefore create a powerful bracketing effect even as they suggest the immutability of God's word. But the closest parallel to our moment occurs in the aftermath of the revelation at Mount Sinai, where a text and towering stones are first brought together:

> Moses came and told the people all of God's words and all of the laws, and all of the people said in a single voice: "All of the things that God has spoken, we will do." *Moses wrote all of God's words* and arose in the morning to build an altar at the foot of the mountain, and he erected *twelve stone pillars* for the twelve tribes of Israel. (Ex. 24:3–4)

In all probability, Joshua intended to call to mind that moment, as the people stood before God and swore to fulfill His Torah. In the last public moment of his leadership, Joshua thus becomes Moses' worthy successor, for like his mentor before him, he secures the people's sincere pledge to serve God.

The next verse records Joshua's death at the ripe old age of 110, tellingly describing him as "Joshua the servant of God" (Josh. 24:29). Although this description was used of Moses innumerable times, particularly in the book's first chapter, it was *never* used to describe Joshua until this moment. The epitaph is fitting: As the people of Israel now don the mantle of responsibility, Joshua dies as God's loyal servant, having achieved in full his life's potential, and having succeeded in perpetuating Moses' legacy.

THE THEME OF TRANSITION

In a passage reminiscent of *Parashat Ḥukkat* (Num. 20) that saw the demise of Miriam and Aaron, as well as the sealing of Moses' fate to not enter the land, our final verses are also full of transition. With the death of Joshua, a new generation prepares to continue the process of settlement and to secure their place in the land, under God's watchful eye. With the death of Elazar the son of Aaron, the priesthood is transmitted to Pinḥas his own son, who will no doubt face new and different challenges than those addressed by his capable father. The leadership transitions noted in the final verses – Joshua to the elders and Elazar to Pinḥas – neatly bring the book to a close by recalling its earliest chapters. In its penultimate verse, the book notes a final event associated with those times:

> The bones of Joseph that the people of Israel had taken up from Egypt they buried in Shekhem, in the plot of field that Jacob had purchased for one hundred *kasita* from the sons of Ḥamor the father of Shekhem. It thus became part of the territory of the children of Joseph. (Josh. 24:32)

Joseph's burial completes our account, the same Joseph who had been sold by his brothers down to Egypt and there rose to prominence as Pharaoh's viceroy. Joseph's descent to Egypt was in the end the cause of his family's survival, for they too came down when famine blanketed the land of Canaan. There they were welcomed by Pharaoh and enjoyed his beneficence, but eventually the welcome turned to resentment, and a new Pharaoh arose to enslave them. But those events took place quite some time after Joseph's death. During the years spent in Egypt in loyal service to the Pharaoh, he enjoyed honor, respect, and wealth. Nevertheless, the Torah records that at the time of his death Joseph longed to return home: "Joseph placed an oath upon the children of Israel saying: 'God will surely remember and redeem you, and you will then take up my bones from here!'" (Gen. 50:25). Though Joseph achieved greatness in his adopted land, he never forgot the legacy of his ancestors and the special status of Canaan in their story. Though held hostage to Egyptian soil by his own success, Joseph was perceptive enough to realize that a nation cannot fulfill its mission without a land, and that Israel's land was Canaan, and Canaan only. The conclusion of the Book of Joshua with the story of Joseph's burial therefore closes a great circle. The saga that began with the children of Jacob in Canaan, was followed by their descent to Egypt and lengthy sojourn there as strangers, continued with their jubilant exodus and return to the land as a nation, now concludes with the burial of Joseph. While Joseph himself died in Egypt far from Canaan's hallowed earth, his descendants returned to the land, lovingly carrying his bones back home.

Conclusion

The Book of Joshua is the most optimistic book in the Hebrew Bible. In it, the people of Israel accomplish their objectives: to enter the new land and to begin the process of striking down roots in its fertile soil. Their leader Joshua achieves his objectives as well: to succeed his mentor Moses and to lead his people to triumph. While the book is not without its setbacks for the people and their leader, these are quickly overcome and the overall trajectory remains positive. One might say that the Book of Joshua is composed of two intertwined stories simultaneously told: the personal story of Joshua and the collective story of the people of Israel. The life of a true leader can never be entirely separated from the lives of his people. His challenges are theirs as are his failures and achievements.

When the people of Israel left the land of Egypt they dreamed God's dream of one day soon creating a new nation in their own land, the land of Canaan. Arriving at Mount Sinai, they received His guiding words and His covenant and sometime thereafter began their journey. But the journey was long and arduous and the trials too great. To tired serfs, physical liberation is a sustaining vision, but it is only after that freedom has been secured that the real work begins. How shall slaves oppressed for centuries transform themselves into autonomous and confident people prepared to take their destiny into their own hands?

The Book of Joshua began by reminding us of those formidable struggles as the defining events that surrounded the Exodus from Egypt were echoed over and over. The sending of the spies to Jericho, the crossing of the Jordan River, the mass circumcision, and the celebration of Passover in the new land all recalled earlier formative moments. But this time there was no hesitation, no panic, and no turning back – the forty-odd years of wilderness wandering during which God had patiently inculcated in Israel self-reliance and a spirit of gratitude had done their work.

The conquest of the land followed as first Jericho and then the Ai fell. The southern Canaanite kings and their northern counterparts all collapsed in short order before the Israelite onslaught, their self-serving vicious values no match for the words of the living God. With growing self-confidence, the Israelite tribes pressed forward, advancing tentatively into the hill country of Canaan. With each successive battle, God's overt intervention decreased so that by the end He lurked only in the shadows as Israel defeated their enemies. How else could He nurture initiative and enterprise if not by receding to encourage Israel's independence – which included extending to His people the freedom to fail? So while Akhan took from the spoils and Israel suffered setback at the ramparts of Ai, a precious lesson was borne home: while God wishes nothing more than for us to succeed and always stands ready to assist, we must make our own sometimes ruinous choices. To learn from one's failures and to do better next time is life's greatest gift.

Conquest of land does not create connection with it; only by setting down concrete roots is that bond forged. The military menace of the Canaanites was neutralized relatively quickly but the settlement of the land went on for centuries. In the process, the scrubby and rock-strewn hill country was cleared and terraced while the nomadic Israelite shepherd self-transformed into a farmer. The second half of the Book of Joshua described the beginnings of that progression as tribal territories were allotted and lands were secured. Memorable figures such as Caleb and Akhsa his daughter appeared in this section – to strengthen the resolve of the people by offering them a critical paradigm. One need not fear the giants or the most colossal of undertakings if one's trust in God is steadfast and one's belief in oneself is sure.

The final part of the book returned us to its beginning as aged Joshua now prepared to take his leave of the people as Moses had done before him. Calling them to assemble, he offered words of encouragement tinged with caution, for he knew that so much remained to be done. Forging the disparate tribes of Israel into a nation, completing successfully the process of settlement, building a God-centered ethical society in the midst of corrosive pagan surroundings would be near impossible tasks and Joshua would not be alive to bring them about. As the book closed, he could only hope, as Israel did with him, that success would one day be theirs. He took his leave of them with parting words that recalled those of his mentor: "You are witnesses for yourselves this day that you have chosen God to serve Him…now remove the alien gods from your midst and incline your hearts to the Lord, God of Israel!" (Josh. 24:22–23).

As students of the Tanakh, we know that the people of Israel did not succeed in securing permanence in the land. After the elders who succeeded Joshua had passed on, the people succumbed to the deadly intoxication of Canaan's polytheistic cults. Israel strayed from God and was eventually driven out, just as the aged leader had warned. More often than not, the people of Israel languished in the lands of their exile, suffering calamity, catastrophe, and death; the land that they yearned for was entirely beyond their reach. Sometimes, exile to distant lands brought them prosperity, permanence, and the balm of forgetfulness. But the land was never entirely forgotten from their hearts. With the preservation of that ancient memory, the way back to the Promised Land was secured, just as it was for us.

The fonts used in this book are from the Arno family.

Other books in the
Maggid Studies in Tanakh series:

1 Kings: Torn in Two
Alex Israel

Jeremiah: The Fate of a Prophet
Binyamin Lau

Ruth: From Alienation to Monarchy
Yael Ziegler

Maggid Books
The best of contemporary Jewish thought from
Koren Publishers Jerusalem Ltd.